BLACK PROPHETIC FIRE

CORNEL WEST

BLACK PROPHETIC FIRE

In Dialogue with and Edited by
CHRISTA BUSCHENDORF

BEACON PRESS
BOSTON

BEACON PRESS
Boston, Massachusetts
www.beacon.org

Beacon Press books
are published under the auspices of
the Unitarian Universalist Association of Congregations.

17 16 15 14   8 7 6 5 4 3 2 1

This book is printed on acid-free paper that meets the uncoated paper
ANSI/NISO specifications for permanence as revised in 1992.

Text design and composition by Kim Arney

Chapter 2, "The Black Flame—W. E. B. Du Bois," was published in an earlier form
as "'A Figure of Our Times': An Interview with Cornel West on W. E. B. Du Bois"
in the *Du Bois Review* 10, no. 1 (2013): 261–78. Chapter 3, "Moral Fire—Martin
Luther King Jr.," was published in an earlier form as "We Need Martin More Than
Ever" in *Amerikastudien/American Studies* 56, no. 3 (2011): 449–67; a shortened
version was published in the German political journal *Die Gazette* (Summer 2013).

Photography credits: *Frederick Douglass*, c. 1850–1860; *W. E. B. Du Bois*, 1918, by
Cornelius Marion (C. M.) Battey (1873–1927); *Martin Luther King Jr.*, 1964; *Ella
Baker*, 1964, by Danny Lyon (Magnum), reprinted here with permission; *Malcolm X*,
1964, by Marion S. Trikosko; *Ida B. Wells*, 1893, by Mary Garrity. Photographs are
from Wikimedia Commons/Library of Congress, unless otherwise noted.

Library of Congress Cataloging-in-Publication Data
West, Cornel.
   Cornel West on Black prophetic fire / in dialogue with and edited by Christa
Buschendorf.
      pages cm
   Includes bibliographical references and index.
   ISBN 978-0-8070-0352-7 (hardback : acid-free paper)
   ISBN 978-0-8070-0353-4 (ebook)
   1. Douglass, Frederick, 1818-1895—Political and social views. 2. Du Bois,
W. E. B. (William Edward Burghardt), 1868-1963—Political and social views.
3. King, Martin Luther, Jr., 1929-1968—Political and social views. 4. Baker, Ella,
1903-1986—Political and social views. 5. X, Malcolm, 1925-1965—Political and
social views. 6. Wells-Barnett, Ida B., 1862-1931—Political and social views.
7. African Americans—Biography. 8. Prophets—United States—Biography.
9. Revolutionaries—United States—Biography. 10. West, Cornel—Interviews.
I. Buschendorf, Christa. II. Title. III. Title: Black prophetic fire.
   E185.96.W47 2014
   920.009296073—dc23
   [B]

                                                              2014010359

To the memory of two spiritual giants
always full of Black prophetic fire:

David Walker and Harriet Tubman

That man has a truly noble nature
Who, without flinching, still can face
Our common plight, tell the truth
With an honest tongue,
Admit the evil lot we've been given
And the abject, impotent condition we're in;
Who shows himself great and full of grace
Under pressure. . . .

—GIACOMO LEOPARDI

winds of change are blowing
i know because of the revolutionaries and most of all the
people—
        the wretched of this earth
                will be free

—ERICKA HUGGINS

CONTENTS

Why We Need to Talk About Black Prophetic Fire

Are we witnessing the death of Black prophetic fire in our time? Are we experiencing the demise of the Black prophetic tradition in present-day America? Do the great prophetic figures and social movements no longer resonate in the depth of our souls? Have we forgotten how beautiful it is to be on fire for justice? These are some of the questions I wrestle with in this book.

Since the assassination of Martin Luther King Jr., it is clear that something has died in Black America. The last great efforts for Black collective triumph were inspired by the massive rebellions in response to Dr. King's murder. Yet these gallant actions were met with increasing repression and clever strategies of co-optation by the powers that be. The fundamental shift from a we-consciousness to an I-consciousness reflected not only a growing sense of Black collective defeat but also a Black embrace of the seductive myth of individualism in American culture. Black people once put a premium on serving the community, lifting others, and finding joy in empowering others. Today, most Black people have succumbed to individualistic projects in pursuit of wealth, health, and status. Black people once had a strong prophetic tradition of lifting every voice. Today, most Black people engage in the petty practice of chasing dollars. American society is ruled by big money, and American culture is a way of life obsessed with money. This is true for capitalist societies and cultures around the world. The Black prophetic tradition—along with the prophetic traditions of other groups—is a strong counter-force to these tendencies of our times. Integrity cannot be reduced to cupidity, decency cannot be reduced to chicanery, and justice cannot be reduced to market price. The fundamental motivation for this book is to resurrect Black prophetic fire in our day—especially among the younger generation. I want to reinvigorate the Black prophetic tradition and to keep alive the memory of Black prophetic figures and movements. I consider the Black prophetic tradition one of the greatest treasures in the modern world. It has been the leaven in the American democratic loaf. Without the Black prophetic tradition, much of the best of America would be lost and some of the best of the modern world would be forgotten.

All the great figures in this book courageously raised their voices in order to bear witness to people's suffering. These Black prophetic figures are connected to collective efforts to overcome injustice and make the world a better place for everyone. Even as distinct individuals, they are driven by a we-consciousness that is concerned with the needs of others. More importantly, they are willing to renounce petty pleasures and accept awesome burdens. Tremendous sacrifice and painful loneliness sit at the center of who they are and what they do. Yet we are deeply indebted to who they were and what they did.

Unfortunately, their mainstream reception is shaped according to the cultural icon of the self-made man or the individual charismatic leader. This is especially true for the male figures. This is not to say that they did not fulfill the function of leaders and speakers of their organizations. But I want to point out that any conception of the charismatic leader severed from social movements is false. I consider leaders and movements to be inseparable. There is no Frederick Douglass without the Abolitionist movement. There is no W. E. B. Du Bois without the Pan-Africanist, international workers', and Black freedom movements. There is no Martin Luther King Jr. without the anti-imperialist, workers', and civil rights movements. There is no Ella Baker without the anti-US-apartheid and Puerto Rican independence movements. There is no Malcolm X without the Black Nationalist and human rights movements. And there is no Ida B. Wells without the anti-US-terrorist and Black women's movements.

There is a gender difference in regard to men's and women's roles assigned in social movements. This shapes their reception in history books and in popular culture. Male figures are prominent on the basis of their highly visible positions. They often are chosen to represent the movement, usually due to their charismatic qualities. Yet despite the charisma of many women leaders, it is difficult for them to be chosen to represent the movement. They are often confined to untiring efforts in organizing the movement. As a consequence, even when women give speeches, even when they contribute to the political thinking of movements, their words are not taken as seriously as they ought to be. One of the aims of our dialogues about the Black prophetic tradition is to bear witness to the fiery prophetic spirit of Ida B. Wells by presenting examples of her fearless speech and action, and to bear witness to the deep democratic sensibilities of Ella Baker, who understood better than any of the others the fundamental role of movements in bringing about fundamental social change.

This book becomes even more important in the age of Obama, precisely because the presence of a Black president in the White House complicates our understanding of the Black prophetic tradition. If high status in American society and white points of reference are the measure of the Black freedom movement, then this moment in Black history is the ultimate success. But if the suffering of Black people— especially Black poor and working people—is the ultimate measure of the Black freedom movement, then this moment in Black history is catastrophic—sadly continuous with the past. With the Black middle class losing nearly 60 percent of its wealth, the Black working class devastated with stagnating wages and increasing prices, and the Black poor ravaged by massive unemployment, decrepit schools, indecent housing, and hyperincarceration in the new Jim Crow, the age of Obama looks bleak through the lens of the Black prophetic tradition. This prophetic viewpoint is not a personal attack on a Black president; rather it is a wholesale indictment of the system led by a complicitous Black president.

■ ■ ■

The Black prophetic tradition highlights the crucial role of social movements in the United States and abroad. The Occupy Wall Street movement was a global response to the thirty-year class war from above, which pushed the middle class into the ranks of the working class and poor, and even further exacerbated the sufferings of working-class and poor people. The 2008 financial crisis, primarily caused by the systemic greed of unregulated Wall Street oligarchs and their bailout by the Wall Street–dominated US government, revealed the degree to which American society is ruled by big money. And the fact that not one Wall Street bank executive—despite massive criminality on Wall Street—has gone to jail, while any poor and, especially, Black person caught with crack goes straight to prison, shows just how unjust our justice system is. The realities of the power of big banks and corporations are hidden and concealed by a corporate media that specializes in generating weapons of mass distraction. This systemic concealment also holds for the military-industrial complex, be it the Pentagon or the CIA. Rarely are the death-dealing activities of both institutions made public to the American citizenry. And courageous whistle-blowers—such as Chelsea Manning, Julian Assange, John Kiriakou, and Edward Snowden—who reveal to the public the corrupt activities of the US government are severely punished. Even the recent discussions about drones dropping bombs on innocent civilians remain confined to American citizens. The thousands of non-American civilian victims—including hundreds of children—receive little or no attention in the corporate media. The Black prophetic tradition claims that the life of a precious baby in Pakistan, Yemen, Somalia, Haiti, Gaza, Tel Aviv, Lagos, Bogotá, or anywhere else has the same value as a precious baby in the USA.

The Black prophetic tradition accents the fightback of poor and working people, be it in the United States against big money, be it in the Middle East against Arab autocratic rule or Israeli occupation, be it against African authoritarian governments abetted by US forces or Chinese money, be it in Latin America against oligarchic regimes in collaboration with big banks and corporations, or be it in Europe against austerity measures that benefit big creditors and punish everyday people. In short, the Black prophetic tradition is local in content and international in character.

The deep hope shot through this dialogue is that Black prophetic fire never dies, that the Black prophetic tradition forever flourishes, and that a new wave of young brothers and sisters of all colors see and feel that it is a beautiful thing to be on fire for justice and that there is no greater joy than inspiring and empowering others—especially the least of these, the precious and priceless wretched of the earth!

—CW

■ ■ ■

It was November 1999. On the occasion of the publication of *The Cornel West Reader*, Harvard's African American studies department honored the author for his outstanding academic achievements, and it was announced that Cornel West would give a talk in Emerson Hall, the home of Harvard's philosophy department, in Harvard Yard. I was on sabbatical doing research in the Harvard libraries, revising a book-length manuscript on the US reception of the German philosopher Arthur Schopenhauer. I decided to seize the opportunity to hear one of the stars of the widely praised "dream team" that Professor Henry Louis Gates Jr. had brought together. I had heard much about West, but I had read very little—and I was in for a great surprise.

In his talk, West directed the audience's attention to the life-size portraits of Harvard's Golden Age of Philosophy, which adorn the walls of the lecture hall. They include, among others, William James and Josiah Royce, who figure prominently in West's book about American pragmatism, *The Evasion of American Philosophy*. Then, to my amazement, West started to talk about Royce's lifelong struggle with Schopenhauer's profound pessimism. Royce, he explained, was convinced that one had to come to terms with this philosopher's dark yet realistic view of the omnipresent suffering and sorrow in human life. But, West claimed, as much as Royce wrestled with Schopenhauer, he would not give in to Schopenhauer's hopelessness but, rather, would resort to the only option to Schopenhauerian pessimism: a leap of faith. I couldn't believe my ears!

After the lecture I introduced myself to Cornel West and said that my work-in-progress was related to Schopenhauer (and to Royce, for that matter). He answered, "Well, I heard there is a woman in Germany who works on the reception of Schopenhauer in America." "Yes," I said, "that's me." "We have to talk," he said. And since then we have been in conversation.

By now I am, of course, aware of the fact that given Schopenhauer's focus on human suffering and his great compassion with all living beings, Cornel West's interest in his work does not come as a surprise. Nor does his attention to Royce because notwithstanding West's unflinching acknowledgment of the deep sense of the tragic in human lives, he has remained what he calls a "prisoner of hope." In fact, West's strong affinity to these philosophers derives from the fact that the questions they raised have been fundamental to his own thinking and, moreover, to his understanding of American democracy. After all, as West confesses in the lecture "Pragmatism and the Tragic," he believes, like Melville, that "a deep sense of evil in the tragic must inform the meaning and value of democracy."[1] If, as West expounds in the same text, "a sense of the tragic is an attempt to keep alive some sense of possibility. Some sense of hope. Some sense of agency. Some sense of resistance in a moment of defeat and disillusionment and a moment of discouragement,"[2] then who is better qualified to understand this than Black people? After all, as West reminds us, Malcolm X's definition of a "nigger" is "a victim of American democracy."[3]

But in contrast to Schopenhauer, Royce, and Melville, Cornel West is an activist not just of the word but also of the deed. This is why the twentieth-century Marxist thinker Antonio Gramsci and his concept of the organic intellectual is a key figure in these dialogues on the Black prophetic tradition. As West has professed repeatedly, his own thinking and activism have been inspired by the Gramscian notion that intellectuals should be rooted in or closely tied to cultural groups or social organizations. Again, this is not surprising, for the practical counterpart to Gramsci's theoretical concept is the long history of the Black struggle for freedom, in which the firm entrenchment of leaders in their group's organizations has been a vital practice.

My own contributions to our transatlantic dialogue have been very much shaped by the theory of the French sociologist Pierre Bourdieu. Black prophetic leaders are clear-sighted observers of the various kinds of violence Black people experience as a group and as individuals. Consequently, they tend to look at the evils of their day through a lens resembling a sociological view, which allows them to lay bare the power imbalances deeply ingrained in society. Yet they do so without ever losing sight of the concrete suffering of Black people. To understand their "logic of practice" (a term coined by Bourdieu that refers to the need to overcome the binary opposition of theory and practice) and, more generally, to reach a better understanding of the situation of Black people in America, I have found Bourdieu's concepts immensely helpful. Bourdieu assumes that there is a correlation between the structures of the social world and the mental structures of agents, so that divisions in society—divisions that, for example, establish and reproduce power relations between the dominant and the dominated—correspond to the principles of vision and division individuals apply to them. In addition to an insight into the thoroughly relational character of the social world, which implies a refutation of the myth of individualism, Bourdieu also offers precise analyses of mechanisms of power. One of the core concepts of Bourdieu's theory is the notion of symbolic violence. Being soft and inconspicuous, this type of symbolic force is an apt means to naturalize the social order and thus sustain its inherent inequalities. There is a striking passage in one of Bourdieu's major books, *Pascalian Meditations*, in which he draws on a passage from James Baldwin's essay "Down at the Cross" in *The Fire Next Time* in order to illustrate the subtle psychosocial mechanisms of symbolic violence and their function and consequences in the socialization of a Black child. According to Bourdieu, Baldwin's description shows how Black parents unconsciously pass on the dominant vision and division of the social world, as well as their intense fear of that dominant power and the

no-less-terrifying anxiety that their child will be harmed by trans-
gressing the invisible boundaries. Baldwin writes:

> Long before the Negro child perceives this difference, and even
> longer before he understands it, he has begun to react to it, he
> has begun to be controlled by it. Every effort made by the child's
> elders to prepare him for a fate from which they cannot pro-
> tect him causes him secretly, in terror, to begin to await, without
> knowing that he is doing so, his mysterious and inexorable pun-
> ishment. He must be "good" not only in order to please his par-
> ents and not only to avoid being punished by them; behind their
> authority stands another, nameless and impersonal, infinitely
> harder to please, and bottomlessly cruel. And this filters into the
> child's consciousness through his parents' tone of voice as he is
> being exhorted, punished, or loved; in the sudden, uncontrolla-
> ble note of fear heard in his mother's or his father's voice when
> he has strayed beyond some particular boundary. He does not
> know what the boundary is, and he can get no explanation of it,
> which is frightening enough, but the fear he hears in the voices
> of his elders is more frightening still.[4]

Baldwin, himself a powerful prophetic voice in the Black literary tradition, addresses both the structural power imbalances and injustices
of the social order, and the terror the dominant evoke in the dominated, who suffer from the violence exerted upon them be it physical
or symbolic.

And so do each of the great six prophetic figures we discuss in
our dialogues. Obviously, they are all prophets of the past who bat-
tled against very specific ills of their day. But though these particular
evils may have vanished—owing in part to the very battles the prophets fought and the sacrifices they made—the power differential and
resulting inequalities are still deeply ingrained in the social order,
although they exist under a different name. To give but one example,
the symbolic violence of signs reading "whites only," which once divided social space into privileged and unprivileged sites and erected
boundaries that served the functions of excluding, denigrating, and
controlling the dominated, today is exerted in the practice of racial

profiling called "stop and frisk." Thus, though we have to contextualize the historic figures we talk about so that we may appreciate their merits, as well as understand their shortcomings, we should also be aware of their exemplary natures, which enabled them to transcend the horizon of their times and become relevant to us today.

Given that we touch upon current political events in these talks, we decided to print the conversations in the order they were recorded rather than in the chronological order of the historical figures we discuss.

As outstanding intellectuals, all the Black prophetic figures in this book offer astute analyses of the mechanisms of power that help us discern these very mechanisms in the different shapes they take today. As organic intellectuals and activists, they reflect on problems of organizing and mobilizing that may provide useful insights for today's freedom fights. And as prophets who compassionately and fearlessly face both the evils of our world and the powers that be, they inspire us to do the same.

This is why we need to talk about Black prophetic fire!

—CHB

Frederick Douglass, c. 1850–1860

CHAPTER ONE

It's a Beautiful Thing
to Be on Fire

FREDERICK DOUGLASS

Our conversations on the Black prophetic tradition started in 2008 during Barack Obama's presidential campaign, when, on many occasions, the senator from Illinois would identify himself with Abraham Lincoln. And in his inauguration speech, in January 2009, President Obama strengthened the association with the sixteenth president by using the phrase "a new birth of freedom" from Lincoln's Gettysburg Address as a theme. Which Lincoln did Obama have in mind? Did Obama acknowledge the role Frederick Douglass and the Abolitionist movement played in making Lincoln the great president we remember? And how could Douglass's prophetic witness be carried into Obama's presidency?

The ascendancy of Barack Obama could easily dampen Black prophetic fire and thereby render critiques of the American system to be perceived as acts of Black disloyalty. Ironically, the incredible excitement of the Obama campaign could produce a new sleepwalking in Black America in the name of the Obama success.

We recorded our dialogue on Frederick Douglass in the summer of 2009.

CHRISTA BUSCHENDORF: Undoubtedly, Frederick Douglass is a towering figure of nineteenth-century American history in general and African American history in particular. His extraordinary ascent from a slave to the much-admired orator and prominent activist in the Abolitionist movement and the women's suffrage movement, best-selling author and success-ful editor of an influential newspaper, United States Marshal, Recorder of Deeds in Washington, and Minister to Haiti, has inspired innumerous African Americans. On the cover jacket of W. E. B. Du Bois's autobiographical essay *Dusk of Dawn* there is a photograph showing Du Bois standing before a huge framed portrait of Douglass, which seems to be a strong state-ment regarding the impact of Douglass on Du Bois. What is your general assessment of Douglass's influence on both Afri-can American and American culture at large?

CORNEL WEST: Frederick Douglass is a very complicated, complex man. I think that Douglass is, on the one hand, *the* tower-ing Black freedom fighter of the nineteenth century; on the other hand, he is very much a child of his age, which is not to say that he does not have things to teach those of us in the twenty-first century, but he both transcends context and yet he is very much a part of his context at the same time. I think that's part of the complexity in our initial perception of his influence on America, on Black America, on Du Bois and subsequent freedom fighters.

CHB: What are the factors we should consider, when you call him a child of his age, and would you say that these factors contrib-ute to reducing his status in a sense?

CW: I think that his freedom fighting is very much tied to the ugly and vicious institution of white supremacist slavery. Those of us in the post-slavery era experienced Jim Crow and other forms of barbarism, but that's still different from white su-premacist slavery, and we learn from Douglass's courage, his vision, his willingness to stand up, the unbelievable genius of his oratory and his language. And yet there is a sense in which with the ending of slavery, there was a certain ending of his high moment. He undoubtedly remained for thirty years a very important and towering figure, but for someone like myself, he peaks. It's almost like Stevie Wonder, who peaks, you know, with *Songs in the Key of Life*, *The Secret Life of Plants*, despite his later great moments. There are moments when people peak, and that peak is just sublime; it's an unbelievable peak. I don't think any freedom fighter in America peaks in the way Douglass peaks. And that's true even for Martin Luther King in a certain sense. And yet Douglass lives on another thirty years; that's a long time. Martin peaked and was shot and killed. Malcolm peaked and was shot and killed. But what if Martin had died in 1998 saying, "Well, what am I? Well, I'm a professor at Union Theological Seminary teaching Christian ethics." There are different stages and phases of their lives. So it's not a matter to reduce Douglass, but to contextualize him, to historicize him. And any time you historicize and contextualize, you pluralize; you see a variety of different moments, a variety of different voices. His voice in the 1880s is very different than his voice on July 4, 1852, July 5, 1852.

CHB: Yes, when he gave his famous speech "What to the Slave Is the Fourth of July?"[1] But while you love the militant Douglass— as did Angela Davis, for example, when she referred to him in the late 1960s[2]—others seem to appreciate him for his later development, for his integrationist policies. And often Douglass the "race man" is juxtaposed to Douglass the "Republican party man." Did he become too pragmatic a politician? Was he in his later years out of touch with the ongoing suffering of African Americans? Had he adopted a bourgeois mentality? Did his second marriage to Helen Pitts play a role in his development, as some critics claim?

CW: I think that the old distinction between the freedom fighter against slavery early on and then the Republican Party man later on might be a bit crude, but it makes some sense, because Douglass in his second stage, the later stages of his life, certainly is significant and never entirely loses sight of trying to fight for the rights of Black people and, by extension, the rights of women and rights of others. But the relevance for us

is that he is less international, he is less global in those later
years. You see, when he spends time with the Chartist Movement in Britain in the late 1840s—when he is pushed out of
the country twice, after publication of the first autobiography,
and then following John Brown's raid on Harper's Ferry—he
makes his connections in Europe, makes the connection between the planetizing, globalizing of the struggle for freedom;
whereas in the later phase of his life, Douglass became such
a nationalist and a patriot and so US centered. He is so tied
in to the machinations of the Republican Party and willing to
make vulgar compromises, and he is relatively silent against
Jim Crow, and his refusal to speak out boldly, openly, publicly,
courageously against barbarism in the South is troubling.

CHB: But what about his speech against lynching?[3]

CW: Yes, but it was a somewhat isolated thing. For example, at the
great Freedman's Memorial ceremony in 1876, when they
unveiled Lincoln's grand statue,[4] Douglass hardly makes any
reference to what was happening in the South at that time. He
says Lincoln is the white man's president, you are his children,
Black people are his step-children, seemingly beginning with
a critique. But the twenty thousand Black folk who were there
waited for him to say something about the present: nothing,
nothing. And then, you see, to allow himself to be used and
manipulated by Rutherford B. Hayes,[5] so that at the final
withdrawal of American troops he is right away appointed to
the honorable position of US Marshal of the District of Columbia, as if that were a kind of symbolic exchange, you see.

You say: "Oh Frederick, Frederick, oh my God! How
could you allow that to take place, given who you are, given
the tremendous respect that is so well earned that people
have for you, especially Black people but all freedom-loving
people, and the degree to which once you get caught in the
machinations of any political party in the United States as a
freedom fighter you are going to be asked to make tremendous concessions, compromises." The shift from prudence to
opportunism looms large. And I think you can see this also

in terms of his role in the American imperial apparatus: as he became the minister to Haiti and so on. It's just hard to be that kind of bold, free-thinking, free-speaking, freedom fighter we witness in the early Douglass when you are caught within the political system.

CHB: I agree. Yet one might still consider that the conditions for fighting for the cause had changed so dramatically that he may have decided to try whatever he could to assist Black people rising within the power system. You said in a recent interview with Jeff Sharlet, one will not find *you* in the White House.[6] But that's a decision, and once you make a different decision, you will have to compromise. Moreover, we have to historicize again, because there had not been any African American in such eminent political posts before. That in itself was highly significant and symbolic, just as today it is symbolic that Barack Obama is president.

CW: That's true. But you can also see the ways in which the political system could seize on *the* towering Black freedom fighter of the nineteenth century, absorb him, incorporate him, diffuse his fire, and make him a part of the establishment, so that the next generation that comes along would have memories of the fiery freedom fighter of the 1830s, 1840s, 1850s, and 1860s. But during those last thirty years he is an incorporated elite within a Republican Party, which itself is shot through with forms of white supremacy, not to mention male supremacy, and imperial sensibility. For example, what would a Frederick Douglass in the later part of his life have looked like and what legacy would he have left if he had sided with the populist movement, if he had sided with the working-class movement, multiracial, the way he sided with the multiracial women's rights movement in Seneca Falls in 1848? It would have sent a whole different set of signs and signals, so that the mainstream would have had difficulties incorporating him. I remember reading Michael Lind's book on the new American nationalism a few years ago, and *the* hero is Frederick Douglass.[7] He is a hero because he is a representative American;

he has got a white father, a Black mother who dies when he is seven; he's got Native American blood in his mother; he becomes the multicultural icon of America so that he can be incorporated in the latter part of the twentieth century as this patriot, nationalist, multicultural liberal. I mean, he is just tamed; he is defanged in terms of his real power and his buoyancy as a militant freedom fighter. And Michael Lind has grounds for that; Douglass provides grounds for that. Then, of course, when he marries sister Helen Pitts—he marries a white sister—all kinds of controversy break out as well. And part of it has to do with the way he manages that: he just tells the truth about his personal life—out of respect for the people who respected him. He wants some kind of rest and calm and serenity, too, a peaceful place in a luxurious mansion in Anacostia that last decade of his life. But I just wonder what kind of a multiple legacy he would have left if he hadn't taken the Republican route. Even though, you know, people are who they are and not somebody else.

CHB: And yet he is very much this heroic icon because people remember his first years.

CW: There is nobody like him. I mean, I don't know of any figure in American history whose language and oratory is so full of fire and electricity focusing on a particular form of injustice. I think Douglass stands alone in that regard. He really does. And he was somebody with no formal schooling at all, probably the most eloquent ex-slave in the history of the modern world.

CHB: Owing to these extraordinary accomplishments, he has often been considered a self-made man. In fact, in 1859, he begins delivering his successful lecture "Self-Made Men" on a tour through the Midwest.

CW: Now, his attempt to view himself as being a self-made man—a reference made famous by Henry Clay—I am also very critical of that, though. I don't like this notion of being self-made. I love the degree to which he attempts to make himself in a context where he is dependent on others, but this notion of some isolated monad or some isolated autonomous entity feeds into the worst of American ideology. I prefer Melville's notion of "mortal inter-indebtedness."[8]

CHB: Yes, American individualism is such a central facet of the American mind. But what I admire in Douglass is that, on the other hand, in his autobiographies, he seems to be quite interested in the factors that both hindered him and furthered him, societal factors that shaped him. He talks a lot about the conditions under which he grew up and which made it harder or easier for him to become what he became, and in that respect he is almost like a sociologist, I think, because he analyzes the system. He is very perceptive when it comes to revealing the master-slave relationship and power structures and so on, and in that sense, I think he is still relevant for us, because those power structures are not yet overcome, after all, even if they were cruder then than they are now. But they still exist.

CW: That's true. Yet there are two sets of issues here for me. One is what you rightly note, which is Douglass's sensitivity to the institutions and structures that serve as obstacles for his flowering as a person and, therefore, by extension the flowering of other persons. But the other side of this is, when you stress those institutions and structures but still view yourself as self-made, it can feed into the worst kind of individualism, even given the sociological analysis that is subtle. For example, you can hear Clarence Thomas talk about what he has overcome. So if he gave an analysis of Jim Crow, if he gave an analysis of institutional racism and discrimination, he would point out the fact that he overcame all of that, he is still a self-made man. There is a sensitivity to the sociological factors, but it is still him in and of himself who triumphs like Horatio Alger. For example, you notice Douglass never mentions his first wife, Anna, in terms of the crucial role she plays in his escape. She is the one who gave him money; she is the one who bought the hat and the clothes; she is the one who gave money to the chap who bore a resemblance to Douglass, who served as the person who bought the pass.

•

Now, how are you going to omit that in your narrative if you are going to be true to the social character of who you are and consequently sensitive to the social structures and the institutions of society?

There is a sense in which the Horatio Alger ideology can be sociologically astute and still ideologically backwards because of the self-made agent at its center. Douglass tends to feed into that ideology that we associate with Abe Lincoln and going back to Henry Clay all the way up to Clarence Thomas, and it's a very blinding, obscuring, and obfuscating ideology that, for me, is quite dangerous. There is a sense in which, for me, piety is central. Piety is but a way of talking about the reverent attachment that we have to those in family, in social movements, in civic institutions, in various social networks who help make us who we are. So Douglass should be the first who would have to say he was made, in part, by the Abolitionist movement. There is no great Frederick Douglass without William Lloyd Garrison. But on the other hand, he helped make the movement. There is no great Abolitionist movement without Frederick Douglass, you see. There is no great Frederick Douglass without Wendell Phillips—Phillips and Garrison, of course, the two who wrote the dedicating narratives for the first autobiography.[9] But once you take this kind of socially infused notion of piety that I accent—and I spent a lot of time on this in my memoir[10]—then you recognize what goes into that self as a supposedly self-made person, and then you are also sensitive to the structures and institutions as well; then you get, it seems to me, a much fuller and truer treatment of who we are as persons, as individuals, socially mediated persons and individuals. So that, again, I don't want to appear too obsessed with his limitations, but I'm very sensitive to his limitations given his iconic status.

CHB: In contrast to you, though, historians have emphasized the self-made man concept. I have hardly come across any comments that stressed the interrelation between the individual Douglass and society, or that underlined Douglass's own acknowledgments of what he owed to others. It is true, indeed, and it has been criticized often, that he hardly ever mentions the women who loved and supported him. Besides his first wife, Anna, and his second wife, Helen, there is, for example—

CW: Julia Griffin and the German sister, Ottilie Assing.

CHB: Right. But, nevertheless, he gives us many facts about his life recognizing circumstances where it is not due to him but to others that he can go forward.

CW: Take his name itself, "Douglass," from Sir Walter Scott's "The Lady of the Lake," from the chap in New Bedford whose name was Johnson. Remember, he says, "Too many Johnsons in town; it's too many Johnsons in town." He gives him a new name, "Douglas," and Douglass adds an "s" because he remembers a street in Baltimore. That's part of the inter-dependency; that's part of the piety in terms of acknowledging that one is indebted to and dependent on others in shaping you, and it becomes a source of good in your life, and it becomes the very launching pad for you in terms of your future, the wind at your back in the present. So, you're right that he notes those. But I don't think he accents those. I think that's one of the reasons why historians so easily assimilate him into this very narrow individualistic ideology, you see. And it could be that Douglass deliberately crafted himself in such a way that he would be acceptable to an American culture that tends to accent self-made men and later on maybe women, and that to me warrants criticism, you know, because it's just not the truth of who we became over time.

CHB: Yes, you are right. But as someone with a special interest in relational sociology, I am trying to pay attention to the analysis of the societal structures he provides, as well as to the contingent elements in his life. For example, when he is on the plantation of Master Lloyd, he happens to have frequent contact with the youngest son of Master Lloyd, Daniel, and in the first autobiography, he remarks only in passing that it was due to that contact that he learned standard English. Whereas in the first autobiography, he emphasizes that Master Daniel would protect him and divide his cakes with him,[11] and in *My Bondage and My Freedom*, he writes that Master Daniel "could not give his black playmates his company, without giving them his intelligence, as well,[12] it is only in *Life and Times*, the third autobiography, that he explains at length what to many Northerners was a mystery, namely, how he "happened to have so little of the slave accent in my speech."[13] He acknowledged then that, owing to his companionship with Daniel, he had learned the dominant language and thus was able to turn into a successful orator immediately after he had fled the South, which I doubt he could have, if he had acquired only the Black vernacular. That's just one example.[14]

CW: I like that. I think you are onto not just something, but you are onto a lot. There is probably a lot more buried in the text that has been overlooked because of the narrow lens of the ideology of self-made men that Douglass has so much contributed to.

CHB: Douglass was highly critical of "the *slaveholding religion* of this land,"[15] repeatedly castigating the hypocrisy of Christian slaveholders. But one also wonders when reading his three autobiographies, how important religion was to his own worldview. It seems to me that he is very much a man of the Enlightenment.

CW: You know, I just preached at the Mother Zion in Harlem on 138th Street. Its pastor, Gregory Robeson Smith, was a student of mine; he is the grandnephew of the great Paul Robeson. This is the church that Paul Robeson's brother pastored for thirty years. Talking about the AME Zion Church tradition that produced Harriet Tubman, Paul Robeson, Frederick Douglass, and John Coltrane, I said, "My God, even as a Baptist, we don't have anybody who was comparable to all four of them." But it raises the question of the role of religion in the shaping of Frederick Douglass and whether, in fact, he was much more secular than one would think. I was on a committee for a dissertation at Union Theological Seminary thirty years ago. It was on Douglass and Feuerbach. Douglass fell in love with Ludwig Feuerbach. That was the first set of texts that you saw in his library, both in Rochester as well as in Anacostia in Washington, DC. It's quite interesting. The first thing he wanted to do when he got to Britain was to meet Marian Evans, who was, of course, the great George Eliot, who translated *The Essence of Christianity*[16] and was also the great author of *Middlemarch* and other novels. She was obsessed with Feuerbach, too. She and Lewes, George Henry Lewes—a grand journalist—they were living together and really made a difference in the intellectual life of England and Europe. But the thesis was that even though Douglass did speak and preach in AME Zion Church, was deeply shaped by it and would say so quite publicly, that privately he was an agnostic, and that after reading Feuerbach he began to use Christian themes and motifs, narratives and stories, but did not have a cognitive commitment to the claims, and he could never really put this out in public, but he had a lot of private discussions, and so in that sense, one of the points you make, he seems much more a figure of the Enlightenment than he would be if he had remained tied to religious authority.[17] I didn't introduce all of this in my Mother Zion sermon. AME Zion Church, they still have a right to claim him, you know. But of course, Coltrane was not a Christian either; he was ecumenical and spiritual and so forth, but he was shaped by the AME Zion Church. His grandfather was an AME Zion pastor, and Coltrane grew up in the parsonage there in Hamlet, as well as in High Point in North Carolina at the AME Zion Church. This issue of how secular was Frederick Douglass deserves further investigation.

CHB: He seems to shift his position, but what to me is rather prominent are his references to humanism; as if he wanted to say, you don't really need religion; it's enough if you believe in human dignity, the right to freedom, and other values established by the Enlightenment. But as you said, he could not admit as much. He indicates it quite often, but he could not tell the public, "I'm a non-believer."

CW: Exactly. When he went to Great Britain, you know, one of the places he wanted to go was the birthplace of Robert Burns, because Burns meant so much to him,[18] and then from Burns, he goes on to say, "But my favorite of all favorites is the great Lord Byron."

CHB: Oh yes, and he quotes him on freedom.[19]

CW: Absolutely. And when you actually look closely at Byron, he really almost worships the imagination as he affirms the eclipse-of-God talk. Which is to say that there is a certain kind of secularization in such a Romantic poetic position, and I do think that Douglass was deeply influenced by Byron in that regard, freedom fighter first and foremost, and it's about the imagination, it's about transgression, it's about transformation, and not God, and yet he couldn't be explicit in the secular mode. I don't think that this dissertation on Douglass and Feuerbach was ever published. I know the professor, his name is John Grayson, he teaches at Mount Holyoke.[20] But your question about Douglass being a child of the Enlightenment or even a child of secular Romantic thinking is a very important one. Because then the question becomes, well, in the Black intellectual tradition, what legacy does he leave regarding secular thinking? I think *the* most secular thinker the Black tradition has ever produced is Richard Wright, and it would be interesting to look at Richard Wright's writings on Douglass.

CHB: In his famous speech we mentioned before, "What to the Slave Is the Fourth of July?," Douglass draws a distinct line between his white "fellow-citizens" and himself as someone "identified with the American bondman," a disparity that culminates in his words: "This Fourth of July is *yours*, not *mine*."[21] This statement is connected to the vital question of the possibility of African Americans to identify with the American nation. Even after Emancipation, the sense of belonging to the nation-state has been both a crucial and a controversial issue for African Americans. One answer is the idea of the brotherhood of men, humanity, as a community everybody belongs to and on the basis of which Black people admonish America, the nation, to come up to its promises.[22] You find this thought in many Black writers besides Douglass, for example, in Ida B. Wells's or W. E. B. Du Bois's autobiographies. What is your position on African American national identity?

CW: If you have a notion of the potential nation, of a nation that has the potential and possibility of being free, equal, and just; treating other nations with respect; and multilateral in its foreign policies, then I find the idea of African American national identity in part desirable, that's true.

CHB: "In part" means what?

CW: In part. It means that you are still a bit too tied to the most powerful ideology of modernity, which is nationalism. And I am so suspicious of nationalisms, be they potential or actual. If internationalism tied to the "wretched of the earth"[23] had become much more powerful in the latter part of the nineteenth and the early twentieth centuries, the twentieth century would have been less barbaric, less fascistic, less chauvinistic, you see. And even these days, when globalism and internationalism are much more popular, more buzzwords, they tend to still be easily colonized by capitalism and a lot of other more mainstream ways of looking at the world.

CHB: But isn't the notion of humankind, humanity, the counter-notion to what you are criticizing? Or what would you say? What is your solution if you want to avoid the nationalisms?

CW: Well, for me, the three major counter-voices against the nationalisms, be they potential or actual, would be Marxism, radical democratic movements and views, or a prophetic religious view. So, in the Marxist tradition, you have at the center an internationalism and a globalism that are always tied to working-class movements and so on. That is one of the reasons why I resonate so deeply with that tradition. And the second, the radical democratic one, you're still concerned with everyday people, no matter where they are, no matter what the national context, no matter what boundaries they find themselves in terms of land and space. And in terms of prophetic religion—but for me, especially, prophetic Christianity—you've got the symbol of a Cross, which is the catastrophic, the mutilated body of this particular Jew in the face of the Roman Empire, that is tied to a love, connected to a concern for the least of these, and every flag is subordinate to that Cross; every nationalism, every ideology, even, is subordinate to that Cross; and that Cross is nothing but the scandalous, the calamitous, the horrendous, the catastrophic in the human condition, which is suffering. And how do you transfigure that suffering into some voice, some vocation, some vision to empower the least of these (as in the twenty-fifth chapter of Matthew)?[24] So, for me, all three are intertwined; so the Marxism is indispensable, and the radical democracy is indispensable.

CHB: But I wonder why you do not include the Enlightenment ideas of human brotherhood, of universalism. Is it because they are too optimistic in that the belief in progress comes with that particular historic movement of Enlightenment and the rationality that is also part of it, and that you would consider too one-sided?

CW: Well, it depends on which particular figures. When you're thinking of Voltaire's *Candide*, you don't get a deeper critique of optimism, Pangloss and so forth. It would also be true of *Rameau's Nephew*, of Diderot. I think that the greatness of the European Enlightenment was precisely the shattering of the tribalism and clannishness, the nationalism, to turn instead to grand visions of justice, and I see that in Voltaire; I see it in Diderot; I see it in Kant, in his own very complicated conceptions of autonomy and rationality; I see it in Lessing.[25]

CHB: But what is your apprehension, why don't you include it in your list—except if you claim that it is in Marx anyway?

CW: Yeah, I think, Marx, for me, would be one of the grand fruits
of the Enlightenment but also of a certain Romanticism. I
don't want to downplay Romantic thinkers; I think the Byrons
and Shelleys are magnificent. Shelley died for Greek independence, but it was an independence of Greeks that was tied
to the call for the independence of all peoples who are under
forms of the yoke of oppression. So I don't really want in any
way to disparage the best of the Enlightenment or the best of
Romanticism. Of course, I don't know enough about the East,
Islam. I'm sure they have great humanist traditions too. So,
I'm with you on that.

CHB: In an essay on Douglass, John Stauffer comments on Douglass as an intellectual as follows:

> Throughout the book, Douglass quotes or paraphrases
> famous white writers: Coleridge, Sir Walter Scott, Shake-
> speare, Lord Byron, Aristotle, Milton, Martin Luther,
> William Cowper, Longfellow, and Whittier; and there
> are at least thirty-five separate biblical references. These
> references reveal not only Douglass's growing intellec-
> tual powers, they highlight his efforts to break down the
> color line. He anticipates W. E. B. Du Bois, who declared
> in *The Souls of Black Folk* (1903): "I sit with Shakespeare
> and he winces not." Like Du Bois, the Douglass of *My
> Bondage* seeks to become a "co-worker in the kingdom
> of culture," dwell above the veil of race, and merge his
> double self—a black man and an American—into a better
> and truer self.[26]

But there are others who would think of Douglass more as
an activist than an intellectual. You have written on the pre-
dicaments of Black intellectuals. What kind of an intellectual
was Douglass? You have propagated the Gramscian concept
of the "organic intellectual."[27] Would you call him one?

CW: He is definitely an intellectual. He is not an academic, but he
is certainly an intellectual. Douglass, I think, represents the
height of modern eloquence, what Cicero and Quintilian call

"wisdom speaking," or a memorable and moving utterance that touches not just mind but also heart and soul, both to think and act, and I can't think of someone who is able to do that and not be an intellectual in a certain sort. Absolutely. I think he is also an organic intellectual. He is an intellectual who was shaped by a movement, the Abolitionist movement, one of the greatest social movements in the history of America, maybe even of modern times, the nineteenth century certainly. To have someone who was molded, shaped, and formed in that movement—you can just see it over time, the intellectual exposure, the readings of a variety of different thinkers as he is trying to promote the cause of the movement, the cause of freedom and justice. I mean, it's very rare that you have a kind of Gramscian-like organic intellectual who does not go to school, who learns how to read and write and think in a serious way in the context of a movement. That's a rare thing, you know. It's not even true for Marx himself. When he is writing his dissertation on "The Difference Between the Democritean and Epicurean Philosophy of Nature," he's not part of a movement at all, not as of yet.

As to Douglass, one wonders whether he is reading William Cobbett, one of the great cultural social critics who was tied to working-class, populist concerns.[28] I don't know if he's reading Hazlitt.[29] I don't know if he's reading Ruskin.[30] Did he read William Morris?[31] One wonders. We know he loved Carlyle. This is very interesting. Carlyle's book *On Heroes and Hero Worship* meant a lot to Douglass, and the Carlyle between *Sartor Resartus* up unto maybe *The French Revolution* does have some very important things to say in terms of his critique of society. He later became much more conservative, and by the time we get to the pamphlet on niggers, Carlyle is really degenerated.[32] I'm telling you, sometimes it is best just to die early.

CHB: Well, there is a link to Emerson, I would think, because Emerson liked Carlyle, too.

CW: Absolutely, absolutely. Do we have evidence, though, of Douglass reading Emerson?

CHB: Yes, yes.

CW: Widely, though?

CHB: Oh, I can't tell you. For example, there is the idea of representative men, which James McCune Smith takes up in his introduction to the second autobiography. He explicitly alludes to Emerson's *Representative Men* by claiming that Douglass himself is "a Representative American man—a type of his country men."[33] I remember Douglass read *English Traits*, but that was later in his life, in 1886.[34]

CW: I wonder how widely, how deeply. But I know that they were on platforms together for the celebration of British emancipation of slaves in the West Indies; I remember they are mentioned in the Gay Allen biography.[35] Historians make much of that, as my dear friend at Harvard, Lawrence Buell, who wrote that wonderful biography of Emerson, did.[36] You can see the overlap there with Douglass, but it's not tight; it's not close. Emerson wasn't close to anybody, including his wife. But it would be interesting, if they had spent more time together. But, you know, this recent work[37] that you note between Douglass and Melville . . .

CHB: Yes, it is quite fascinating to see how many scholars have considered comparing the two.

CW: Well, I haven't read the new collection; I know Sterling Stuckey and others had talked about the Black elements in, as well as Black influences on, Melville in *Moby-Dick* and other texts, but Douglass and Melville, wow, I'd be quite interested.[38] There is nobody like Melville in American literature, I'm telling you. There is this new book by William Spanos on Melville. That is powerful. On Melville's critique of American imperialism. He's got a Heideggerian reading, too, and a critique of the metaphysical tradition and the openness to concrete, lived experience not being subsumable under any kind of philosophical system. But William Spanos, my dear brother, he was a teacher of Edward Said at Mount Hermon, when Said was a prep school student,[39] and, you know, Spanos founded *Boundary 2*, the first postmodern journal. I was blessed to be on the board together with Paul Bové, Jonathan Arac, Donald Pease, and the others. But Spanos has got two huge volumes out on Melville, one just on *Moby-Dick*, and the recent one is on the later fiction. It is called *Herman Melville and the American Calling*,[40] and it is about Melville's resistance to the American call for nationalist, chauvinist, exceptionalist discourse. It's a fascinating read. But Melville is just so profound, and to juxtapose him with Douglass, who has his own kinds of profundities but is very, very different, is a complicated matter.

CHB: One possible aspect of comparison would be their concepts of power, how they describe power relations, and I think in that respect they would be equal.

CW: That's interesting.

CHB: Of course, the other reference would be their ways of being prophets.

CW: Oh yes, that's true. That's very true.

CHB: As you defined it, to be a prophet is not about predicting an outcome but rather to identify concrete evils, and both did.[41]

CW: Absolutely, in that sense both would be deeply prophetic. And yet, Douglass was such an activist, and Melville was hardly an activist at all, or not a political activist. You could say he was an activist in language, and, my God, identifying those concrete evils was a form of activism. I'm quite intrigued by how these folk are connecting Melville and Douglass.

CHB: But to come back to the question of nationalism, there is another interesting recent study on Douglass, a chapter in

a book by one of the editors of the collection of essays on
Douglass and Melville, Robert Levine: *Dislocating Race and
Nation*.[42] Levine investigates the critique of Douglass that
you share as to his commitment to the nation in the later
years, to American patriotism and so on. One of the issues
usually mentioned in this context is the annexation of Santo
Domingo, later known as the Dominican Republic. Douglass was involved in exploring the possibilities of an annexation, that is, he was a member of a government committee
that went there and interviewed the people, and he is always
criticized in that he seemed to encourage the annexation in
dialogue with President Grant. Levine takes a close look at
the contemporary debate and shows that those people, for
example, Charles Sumner or Carl Schurz, who were against
the annexation, were against it partly for the wrong reasons
from Douglass's point of view.[43] Their arguments based on
climate theory were racist in fearing that annexation would
add "tropical" Blacks, who allegedly were unfit for civilization to the US nation. According to them, certain regions of
the earth were preserved for specific races and one should not
mix them.

So, their anti-imperialist arguments seem to be progressive, but they were racist as well. In contrast, Douglass argued
for the annexation, granted that the Blacks of Santo Domingo
would consent to it, and he believed they would. As you know,
it never came about, but it was a very concrete plan at the
time, and Levine tells a much more complex story than most
historians who complain about Douglass, asking, "How could
he ever be in favor of the annexation?"

CW: Well, I think that even if Douglass had his own good reasons,
if he's acting as an agent of the US government, there is a
good chance that the US government does not have the same
reasons that he does. And in the end their reasons will prevail
in terms of the effects and consequences of the policy.

CHB: That's right. But Levine goes into the papers of the president,
and there is a "Memorandum" in his personal files, a list that

he made for himself of "Reasons why San Domingo should be annexed to the United States."[44] Well, what are his reasons? What are good reasons for the annexation? You're right, they are economic reasons.

CW: Absolutely. Resources.

CHB: Exactly. But the interesting thing is that, in this list, there is also the issue of race and, for example, the reflection that it would be favorable in terms of fighting slavery that still existed in Brazil if the US were less dependent on Brazilian goods.

CW: That's interesting. No, that's true. It's very true, because we have to keep in mind that Douglass had encountered some very ugly racism within the Abolitionist movement himself, you know, reducing him from person to symbol and spectacle and "stay away from philosophy, you just give the facts," as John Collins used to tell him all the time.[45] Now, it's true, people like William White saved his life, so that there's a white brother and a Harvard grad who really sacrificed himself to save Douglass's life, and Douglass almost got killed in Pendleton, Indiana.[46] So he had some white comrades who he knew cared for him. But the racism within the Abolitionist movement was something he was quite sensitive to. And, therefore, you can understand how he would also be sensitive to some of the anti-imperialist arguments that were also racist. It's true that those kinds of complications always need to be acknowledged, even though in the end, I would want to come down on the anti-imperialist side with good reasons rather than on the US government side with good reasons. See, Douglass situated himself historically on the wrong side. It reminds you of James Weldon Johnson in Nicaragua, who wrote *The Autobiography of an Ex-Colored Man*.[47] Remember, when he is in Central America—that's where he writes that novel—he's an agent of US imperialism. He's pushing, supporting the companies down there, and then still reflecting on various forms of oppression in the metropole, in the US itself. So it's interesting how you get those kinds of contradictions. But, I guess, we're all shot through with contradictions.

CHB: Let us talk about the significance of Douglass in this particular historical moment. In a recent interview with Tavis Smiley on Public Radio International, you talked about Douglass's attempts to influence President Lincoln, trying to push him toward more forceful action with regard to Emancipation. Discussing the prospects of the Obama presidency, you suggested that we need a Douglass today as well, a Douglass who would put pressure on President Obama as to the recognition of today's problems of African Americans—and, by extension, Americans of all colors who suffer from the effects of neoliberal politics. Obama refers to Lincoln and to Douglass.

CW: Yeah, I think my dear brother Barack Obama has got the wrong Lincoln in mind. And Douglass could help him here. And I think by keeping track of Douglass, when Douglass called Lincoln a representative of American racism or when Wendell Phillips famously called Lincoln the "slave hound from Illinois," you wonder what is going on here. You see what I mean. That's not the Lincoln that people want to take seriously, but it is the Lincoln who is part of the historical record. So that when I say Obama has got the wrong Lincoln, you know, he thinks that is the Lincoln who is concerned with reaching out to rivals, especially on his Right. So you bring in people from the opposite political party or the opposing political group or constituency, and you don't recognize that Lincoln was not only a child of his age but that one of his heroes was a slaveholder, Henry Clay, from Kentucky; his best friend is a slave-trader, Joshua Speed, with whom he sleeps in the same bed for four years, visits him over and over again. Lincoln has his own slave that Joshua Speed gives him when he goes and spends time with him in Kentucky.

That is not to say that Lincoln didn't hate slavery, but it is to say that he was quite complacent and willing to defer. He doesn't oppose the Black Codes in the State of Illinois, where Black people had to pay money in order to enter the state. We know his history of voting for the slave trade in Washington, DC, in the House; we know of his strong support of the Fugitive Slave Act of 1850. That was really, one could say, the straw that broke the camel's back for the Abolitionists. We know that in the first inaugural address he talked about supporting the first proposed Thirteenth Amendment, which was to make slavery permanent in the South as a concession to the South, the unamendable amendment. He said, "Yes, I will accept that." And Douglass, of course, was ready to go to Haiti because of that. That's one of the moments when he calls Lincoln the pro-slavery president.

Most historians don't deal with that Lincoln. They don't want to deal with that Lincoln. Well, Obama needs to recognize that that is an integral part of the Lincoln that he is crazy about, and that the Lincoln Douglass calls pro-slavery goes on from that: he is the Lincoln of colonization; he supports not just either going to Liberia or Cow Island—where he provides the money and over three hundred Black folk die—or to Columbia, which is now Panama, the isthmus there; Lincoln supports colonization. The Lincoln that most of us really cherish is the Lincoln of just the last two and a half years of his life, and that's because of the Abolitionist movement; it's because of Harriet Beecher Stowe; it's because of Wendell Phillips; it's because of Charles Sumner, and Frederick Douglass at the top. So that you say to President Obama, "Now, wait a minute, you not only support the Republican ambassador to China, you got him in your Cabinet. You feel like you got your team of rivals in this little truncated, domesticated, tamed version of Lincoln." You say, "No, there is no great Lincoln without the social movement," and Barack Obama is very, very suspicious of social movement people. He is mesmerized by the establishment. He wants to reassure especially the financial establishment; he is mesmerized by Wall Street; he is seduced by these neoliberal economists, by the economists who have been rationalizing elite interests for the last fifteen or twenty years. And, you see, the great Lincoln was not mesmerized by these kinds of people; he really wasn't. The great Lincoln would say: "Frederick, you got a point. Harriet, you are the one who got us into this mess. Sooner or later I've got to take you all seriously, you know. I'm not an Abolitionist, but I do hate slavery. I didn't believe that we could overcome white supremacy and create a multiracial body politic until the last few days of my life, but I am influenced by the social movement." And you say, "OK, but which social movements influence Barack Obama?" The green movement, that's the one movement. I think, he is very good on green issues; he really is.[48] But when it comes to the Black freedom movement, he is trying to neutralize if not tame it, you see. He's got a very, very ambivalent relation to it, he really does.

CHB: And you think it is more than just strategy, because you might realize as an American politician, and especially as a president, that your means are limited, that if you go too far, especially too far to the left, that that's the end of you. So how do you steer in-between?

CW: I think, in the end, it's fundamentally a question of style, and here, as Frantz Fanon used to say, style does help to define who you are and help to define your being. Barack Obama is someone who likes to be liked by everyone, and he likes to be able to create some kind of middle-ground synthesis that brings people together without really coming to terms with the deep conflicts. Here he could learn a lot from Douglass. He might quote Douglass all day and all night about power conceding and so forth, but Douglass understood the depth of it, that you don't find truth in the middle of the road; you find truth beneath the superficial, mediocre, mainstream dialogue, and the truth is buried, is hidden beneath that, and when you connect with that truth, you have to take a stand. When you take a stand, you're not going to be liked by everybody; people will try to crush you, people will try to lie on you, people will try to kill you. Now, Obama still gets assaults in the media all the time, but I think he really doesn't want to be someone who just takes a principled stand and risk and is able to withstand all those bows and arrows. That's not his personality. I would argue that the Black freedom movement has produced a lot of different styles and strategies, but the great figures in the Black freedom movement, like Douglass, know they can't be liked by everybody. When you think of figures like Martin Luther King, Fannie Lou Hamer, Ella Baker, Malcolm X, that's not the strand that Barack Obama is comfortable with at all.

CHB: There is this great statement by Douglass you just alluded to from which Obama takes these famous lines: "Power concedes nothing without a demand. It never did and it never will."[49] But in the same speech Douglass also says: "Those who profess to favor freedom and yet deprecate agitation are men who want crops without plowing of the ground; they want rain without thunder and lightning."

CW: That's powerful. So Douglass understood.

CHB: And he goes on to say, "Find out just what any people will quietly submit to and you have found out the exact measure of injustice and wrong which will be imposed upon them, and these will continue till they are resisted with either words or blows, or with both. The limits of tyrants are prescribed by the endurance of those whom they oppress." If that's not powerful . . . But Obama doesn't quote it.

CW: He didn't go that far. No. Well, you see, some of those particular words are not part of the soul of Barack Obama. And, you know, everybody is who they are and not somebody else.

CHB: But you could say that he wouldn't be where he is if they hadn't been who they were.

CW: That's right. Absolutely. He wouldn't be head of the American empire as a Black man if he followed the fiery Douglass. That's absolutely right. And that's both the strength as well as the severe limitation of Barack Obama.

CHB: And the system wouldn't allow it either.

CW: That's exactly right. In fact, that's probably the most important thing. the system that wouldn't allow and concede his ascendency, which is still historic, and that's the reason why I supported him. But we ought to be honest, the truth that led many of us to support him is the same truth that lead many of us to criticize him and the system, and I think that's something that the early Douglass would understand, though, later, Douglass could be appropriated by Obama and would be very consistent. In a certain sense, he's heading the very system that was appointing Douglass.

CHB: Maybe one more thing. In his autobiography Douglass emphasizes the moment when he fights against the slave breaker Edward Covey, and he says one of the preconditions was that he was ready to give up his life. He refers back to Revolutionary times and that famous phrase "Give me liberty or death."[50] So to be ready to give up your life for freedom is also a thought that Douglass cherishes, and it is like a red thread in his work, at least its first part.

CW: A deep commitment.

CHB: Yes, and I thought it was interesting because you refer to something like that yourself.

CW: Absolutely. But this sense of giving up one's life was the ultimate cause, but there's also a penultimate cause in the life you live before you die, and that to me is just as important a question, you know. How do you use your time and your energy? And the time and energy that you have available to you before death puts an end to the whole thing, and there again you got this creative tension between truth and power and a commitment to telling the truth, bearing witness to the truth and yet easily being marginalized versus trying to gain access to political power, economic power, cultural power, and oftentimes easily being absorbed and incorporated, and how do you deal with that to and fro, moving back and forth. It is like the early Ralph Bunche, you know—Marxist, leftist, powerful critic of US capitalism—and the later Ralph Bunche, who is

one of the Black bourgeoisie to the core, Nobel Peace Prize
winner hanging out in the upper-middle-class circles in Black
and white DC, caught up in the establishment. We see a similar shift in Douglass: Shakespeare Society on the fifteen-acre
Cedar Hill that looks like the White House in Anacostia, all
of the different teas there, having the very genteel dialogues
about a variety of delicate subjects while Jim Crow is raining
terror on Black folk.

Did you see this new book called *Slavery by Another
Name*?[51] It's a hell of a text. The author is actually the Atlanta
bureau chief of the *Wall Street Journal*, and he is a white Southern brother and his name is Blackmon. Fascinating ironies of
life. But he is a kind of centrist guy who follows the white
and Black members of the family of Green Cottenham in a
book of about five hundred pages that won all these awards.
I couldn't put it down because this guy really concludes that
Jim Crow was a form of slavery, a view confirmed by many
Black and progressive scholars years ago, for instance, Leon
Litwack's book *Trouble in Mind*, which is still the best thing
ever written on Jim Crow.[52] People were saying nothing has
been written since Litwack—that's not true—but this guy
says something like, "This is slavery by another name, this is
the most vicious form of terrorism I could conceive alongside
slavery," and he's telling a story beginning in the latter part
of the nineteenth century of the white and Black members of
the Cottenham family, how their lives are intertwined. The
Black members of the family get caught in this Jim Crow
system, and it is quite ugly. The book focuses on the human
dimension to it. It is not an analysis solely, but Blackmon
is telling the archetypal story of what happened generation
after generation. And you say to yourself, Douglass is dead in
1895, but by the 1870s, it is beginning to take shape, crystal-
lizing in the 1880s, legalized in the 1890s, and was in place
until the 1960s, and you say, well, where is the voice of that
early Douglass in the nation as Jim Crow is developing in the
1870s and '80s?

CHB: But even so, someone like Ida B. Wells speaks out for Douglass and acknowledges him in this respect. I don't know whether she idealized him, but she takes him seriously as a fighter for the cause, even in the later years.

CW: Yes, that's true. And you couldn't get a grander crusader for justice than Ida in the face of American terrorism as manifested in Jim Crow.

CHB: And she was the person who convinced him that the reasons given for lynching were not the true ones. As you know, she studied the statistics and specific cases, and she told him, and that made him aware that he should not stick to the propaganda, and he changed his mind, and then he gave this speech, which you mentioned earlier.

CW: I mean the last speech that he gave, "Lessons of the Hour," 1894, that's a great speech. A powerful speech, there's no doubt about that. I remember when I first read it. He is looking back; it is almost a self-critique too. He is looking back saying, "Don't be duped by this kind of false bread of freedom given to emancipated slaves. We got new challenges. America, you either have to come to terms with this or you are going under." But what I think Ida B. Wells has in mind and what Du Bois has in mind—and you pointed out that on the cover of Du Bois's *Dusk of Dawn*,[53] he is standing before a portrait of Douglass—is that it is inconceivable to be a freedom fighter in the United States and not have Frederick Douglass's spirit as integral to what you are doing. That is part of the grand achievement of those twenty-three years. And that is just there. He could have gone off and played golf after Emancipation like William Lloyd Garrison and a lot of the others. For them it was over.

CHB: And that is what, for a moment, he had thought about. Why not go to a farm and lead a quieter life?[54] Haven't I done enough—

CW: —Enough in one lifetime. You can understand that. Absolutely right. Even though you can't ever conceive of Martin
or Malcolm doing that in their later lives. You just get the
impression that they were so on fire that they would have just
burned till the end, no matter what, till sixty-five, seventy, and
Du Bois was like that too. At ninety-five he is still on fire, you
know. There's no doubt about it. Very much so. It's a beautiful
thing to be on fire, though. It really is.

W. E. B. Du Bois, 1918

CHAPTER TWO

The Black Flame

W. E. B. DU BOIS

With a Black president in the White House, the question arose as to what this meant for the Black prophetic tradition. Was it possible that Black people would mistake this symbolic achievement for a wholesale victory? Could it be that, overjoyed by the iconic recognition of Blackness, they would ignore—notwithstanding the undeniable effects of the financial crisis—the continuing or rather growing inequality between whites and Blacks, rich and poor in terms of decent income, housing, education, health care, jobs? In this situation, the incorruptible voices of the Black prophetic tradition needed to be heard. We decided to continue our dialogue, and W. E. B. Du Bois, as undeniably the most important Black intellectual of the twentieth century, was the obvious choice. We agreed to explore the more radical facets of his thinking and expose his uncompromising critique of the United States, which has often been considered too painful to become part of the American (or even African American) collective memory. The title of this chapter, "The Black Flame," refers to Du Bois's little-known trilogy of historical novels, which he wrote in the last decade of his life.[1]

CHRISTA BUSCHENDORF: Given W. E. B. Du Bois's long and eminent career, his versatility and productivity, any assessment of his life work is a challenging, if not daunting, undertaking. It seems to be appropriate to start out by evoking some of the

points you have made in your own writings on Du Bois. You
have written extensively on Du Bois. In your study on American pragmatism, you characterized Du Bois as "the Jamesian
organic intellectual,"[2] and in your essay "Black Strivings in
a Twilight Civilization," you called him "the towering black
scholar of the twentieth century"[3] and "the brook of fire
through which we all must pass in order to gain access to the
intellectual and political weaponry needed to sustain the radical democratic tradition in our time."[4] In addition, you put
forth an extended critique of some of Du Bois's basic tenets.

CORNEL WEST: Absolutely. Let me start off by saying that W. E. B.
Du Bois, alongside John Dewey, is *the* towering public intellectual in the first half of the twentieth century in the American empire. And when looked at through the international
lens, he is even more important than Dewey, because Du Bois
understood the centrality of empire, and he understood the
centrality of white supremacy and the shaping of the US empire in a way that John Dewey did not. And when we look
fifty, a hundred, a hundred and fifty years from now, when the
American Gibbon puts pen to paper to the "Decline and Fall
of the American Empire,"[5] it will be Du Bois's work that will
be seen as most insightful, as opposed to Dewey or even William James or some of the other great figures that we know.
And so in that sense we may not even be yet in a position to
fully appreciate the breadth and the scope and the depth of
W. E. B. Du Bois as a scholar, as a public intellectual, as well
as an activist, as someone who offered an astute critique of
capitalism and class hierarchy and understood the latter's in-
timate relation to white supremacy and racial hierarchy. And
so I think we are still very much in the early stages of the kind
of appreciation of Du Bois's contribution to our understanding, especially, of a post-American world or a world in which
the American empire is no longer at the center. And in that
regard, I think, we have to proceed very tentatively, provi-
sionally, and yet also firmly to try to understand the variety
of different dimensions and aspects of this towering genius.

CHB: It's interesting that it took him a while to get to the internationalization of the problem, as he mentions in his autobiography, *Dusk of Dawn*.[6]

CW: That's true. I think it is the 1915 book *The Negro* where he really begins to understand the centrality of empire and again race in the US empire.[7] You can just see him beginning to become awakened, and any time he becomes awakened there are two fundamental consequences. One is the radical character of what he has now to say, and the second is the problem of how to come to terms with the marginal status of such a radical perspective. After all, most of America, and especially the American academy, is just not ready. They can't assimilate, they can't incorporate, they can't render intelligible the radical message that Du Bois is putting forward. I think this is going to be true for a whole subsequent slew of figures, including myself.

CHB: It certainly was true during Du Bois's lifetime, when he was not recognized adequately in the academy, though he was one of the foremost sociologists of the time, a man who came up with a new method: interdisciplinary empirical studies.[8] If he had been a white man, this breakthrough would have been celebrated, and he complains that he was not even published, and that when his book on the Negro in Philadelphia came out, there were no reviews.[9]

CW: Yes, the 1899 classic *Philadelphia Negro*, it's true. But I think that even if Du Bois had been white, his radical view would still have been very difficult for mainstream America and most difficult for the American academy to come to terms with. Being Black made it even more difficult. There is no doubt about that. So the response has been to domesticate Du Bois, sanitize and sterilize him, and to make him part of a kind of a domesticated view about Black Nationalism on the one hand and integrationism on the other hand. And of course, there was the issue of his dispute with Booker T. Washington, especially Washington's reluctance to promote civil rights, voting rights, and liberal education for Blacks. And those are part and parcel of who he is, but they are just small slices of what his project was, and I think in the twenty-first century, it's up to us to begin to see what he was actually about. How is it possible for this emerging cultural freedom—that comes out of an enslaved and Jim-Crowed people—to present a challenge to an imperial power with very deep roots in white supremacy, one driven by a capitalist project or driven by capitalist forces and tendencies? For Du Bois, this becomes the central problematic, and it very much is our problematic today. I think there is a sense in which W. E. B. Du Bois is the most relevant figure from the twentieth century for us in the twenty-first century, and we ignore him at our own peril. Very much so. And in that sense, you know, we all stand on his shoulders. When I had written fifteen years ago that he is the towering Black scholar of the twentieth century, there was no doubt about that, and I'm more convinced of that fifteen years later than I was then.

CHB: You have just remarked that it is from the position of an outsider, or, as he himself calls it, a "group imprisonment within a group,"[10] that he could analyze the empire, and actually, I think he is of the conviction that it is *only* from the margin that one can criticize society because of the distance one necessarily has from it.[11] One does not fully identify with it. So that though, in general, there is a great disadvantage in being at the margin, in this one respect there is an advantage in marginality, and I would think that you have that view on your own condition as well.

CW: Yes, I think that's true. Of course, you can be marginal and an outsider and still get it wrong. But in terms of those who are willing to tell some of the most painful truths about the emergence and sustenance of the American empire alongside the precious American democratic experiment within the American empire and the tension between those two, certainly being on the margins or an outsider is almost a precondition. I think he is right about that. The problem is when it comes to solidarity and its preconditions, which is to say the conditions under which collective insurgency can emerge, the conditions under which agency among the oppressed can emerge, oftentimes it becomes a rather depressing matter because, you see, it seems as if there is a relative impotence or relative powerlessness. The emergent agency is so often pacified, and folks suffer generation after generation with unjust treatment, unattended to, and then layers of suffering begin to mount, just like in the ninth thesis of Walter Benjamin's "Theses on the Philosophy of History," that history of catastrophe, the piling of wreckage, generation after generation, all of those precious lives lost, wasted potential, witnessed generation after generation.[12]

One wonders how Du Bois, who lived ninety-five years, was able to witness that wreckage, see the US empire shipwrecked at the very moment when it viewed itself as victorious and sailing uncontested in the sunshine. You can imagine what a tearing of the soul that must have been for him. Of course, he began as a much more naïve Enlightenment figure, naïve Victorian figure, who was initially tied to empire and tied to the West in its contemporary incarnation. He never gives up on the West; he never gives up on the Enlightenment; he never gives up on the Greeks; so the legacy of Athens, the legacy of Jerusalem, the legacy of the Enlightenment mean much to him. But once he really discovers the Marxist critique of capitalism, once he discovers the variety of critiques of empire and weds it to his profound resistance and critique of white supremacy, he's in a different space. I think he began to realize that after the lynching of Sam Hose.

CHB: He acknowledges himself that he was naïve and that he had to go through stages.[13] In the beginning, he thought you just have to teach people; you just have to tell them the truth, and they will accept it and they will change. But then he acknowledged that there was irrationality, that there was habit you have to cope with.[14]

CW: Absolutely, the cake of custom and the gravitas of habit. I think in a certain sense the early Du Bois had a naïve conception of evil—evil as ignorance, evil as not knowing the facts—as opposed to the later Du Bois, who saw evil being tied to interest, evil being tied to power and privilege within various social structures that have to be contested politically, organizationally, collectively. And, you know, *that* Du Bois is the Du Bois that remains *our* Du Bois; he is a figure of our times. I mean, it's amazing that it has taken American history fifty, seventy-five years to begin to catch up with Du Bois in terms of this problematic of the US empire that will decline as political system, will be broken as culture, will decay, if it does not come to terms with the kind of very deep democratic reforms and structural transformations required for that empire to revive and become something that's worthy of affirmation.

CHB: One of his ideas of how to try to accomplish that was that he believed in a special role for African Americans. He believed, maybe idealistically, naïvely—I wonder what you think about that?—that due to their tradition, due to roots in Africa and the communal spirit that he thought derived from that African culture and was in a way transposed to the New World, that African Americans could and actually should be a counterforce to American capitalism by forming communal and economic projects by deliberate separatism—a controversial word, of course. His ideas remind me of Malcolm X's notions of how African Americans should create their own businesses and keep them separate so that whites would not be able to further exploit and profit from their labor, suggesting that anti-capitalist forces might be based on the African American community, something not often taken up, I think.

CW: Yes, I've never been convinced of that aspect of Du Bois or Malcolm in that regard. It seems to me that these Black businessmen and -women tended to be just as deferential to capitalist forces and just as ready to embrace the market forces on the capitalist conditions as anybody else.

CHB: But maybe there is a difference between Malcolm X and Du Bois in that the latter really means no compliance with the capitalist system but introducing a communist—Du Bois didn't call it that—but a communist way of doing business, without profit; you know, oriented toward the community and its needs without giving in to capitalism.[15]

CW: Yes, at the normative level I can see Du Bois putting that forward. It reminds me in some ways of the Honorable Elijah Muhammad, whose economic cooperatives were going to be different than the competitive capitalist models. And yet, when you actually look at the practice of Black businessmen and -women, some of whom may have partly even been influenced by Du Bois—very few probably, but those few who are—they still find themselves caught within the ravages of the capitalist market. And therefore, at the aspirational utopian level it may make sense, but it's just hard to see how that's translated on the ground. I do think that one of the most important texts Du Bois ever wrote is *The Gift of Black Folk* [1924]. It's a classic that tends to be overlooked and underappreciated like so much of Du Bois's magisterial corpus, and there, I think, he is on to something. He talks about the gift of Black folk to America and the world as being a reconstruction of the notion of democracy looked at from the vantage point of enslaved or Jim Crowed people, or a reconstruction of the notion of freedom from that vantage, and then a cultural gift as well, in song and story and tradition and art. Each one of those contributions is quite powerful, and they certainly constitute counter-hegemonic forces in making American capitalist democracy a more fully inclusive capitalist democracy; there is no doubt about that. The question is how these gifts did become counter-hegemonic in a more radical way, you see.

Now one of the things that has always fascinated me about Du Bois—and I have been quite insistent in my critique of Du Bois—is that when it comes to popular culture, he was in love with the "sorrow songs," to use his wonderful phrase in the last chapter of *The Souls of Black Folk*. He was in love with the spirituals. But I've never been convinced that he had an appreciation, let alone a deep comprehension, of the blues and jazz. We know he was very, very suspicious of blues and jazz; he distanced himself from them. And yet, for me, they constitute crucial, indispensable counter-hegemonic forces in terms of keeping alive ideals of humanity, ideals of equality, ideals of humility, ideals of resistance and endurance in the face of the catastrophe that the US empire has always been for the masses of Black people, be it slavery, Jim Crow, or be it the new hyper-ghetto that our dear brother Loïc Wacquant has written about better than anybody else,[16] or the hyper-incarceration that has targeted poor people, specifically Black men. When you look at the forms of agency of those particular brothers and sisters, the music has been central, and it's not spirituals for the most part, because they are unchurched, most of them; most of them are un-mosqued and un-synagogued; they don't have any ties to religious institutions at all. So it's fascinating to me that there is still a certain relic of cultural elitism in the radical democratic, anti-capitalist, anti-imperialist project of Du Bois, and this creates a tension for me.

CHB: The reason I see for why he was so distanced from that part of the African American tradition is that he was so much afraid of hedonism, of entertainment as something that is just distraction, part of capitalist consumer culture, distracting people from what they should try to become, and he probably didn't see the serious contribution to cultural work that jazz and blues ultimately makes.

CW: I think that's a very good point. There is an irony here, because you know the great August Wilson used to say that Black people authorize reality by performance, that performance in a communal context, where call and response is central, creates a form of agency, creates a form of self-confidence and self-respect that are preconditions for the creation of new realities. You see that in churches in the past under slavery. We've seen it in communal artistic practices under Jim Crow, and we see it today in hip-hop. They are not revolutionary forces, but they do constitute spaces, spaces that are very rare, because most of the spaces in the US empire are already colonized. But to have certain spaces by means of performance can provide a view of a different sense of who you are: You're human as opposed to subhuman. You're human as opposed to being a commodity. You're human as opposed to being an object. You're human as opposed to being an entity to be manipulated. And that's, again, the profound role of Black music, especially within those communal contexts. I'm not sure Du Bois understood that because of his fear of hedonism and cheap entertainment and the stereotype of Black people as, you know, born singing, born dancing, born moving, and so forth and so on.

CHB: And another point might be his own upbringing. He was from New England, and it's really funny to read his account when he first came to the South and was overwhelmed by how his people—and he calls them "his people"—behaved. But he is completely alien to their traditions, for example, in church.[17] It was difficult for him. This reticent gentleman, he had problems; he embraced the culture, but it never became part of his own habitus.[18]

CW: Absolutely. One of the great ironies of W. E. B. Du Bois is that he is the greatest—and will probably always be the greatest—Black intellectual ever to emerge out of the US empire, and the problematic that he ended up wrestling with about the US empire—the centrality of race and class and gender, but especially the capitalist core—needs to be hit head-on. But he was not the spiritual extension or the spiritual property of the very people that he was willing to give his all for, the very people he was willing to live and die for. Billie Holiday would have scared him to death; James Brown would have sent him into conniptions; and he just would not have been able to fully embrace brothers George Clinton and Bootsy Collins. And the Funkadelics would have generated a heart attack. If he had shown up at a Parliament-Funkadelic concert, with Garry in diapers and brother George and all his colors,

Du Bois would have gone crazy. Or if he had listened to a Reverend C. L. Franklin sermon when the whooping began, he would have been ashamed, you see. You would want to say, "Du Bois, this is the spiritual genius and part of the very people you're talking about." And yet at the same time we know that there could be no Franklin, there could be no Clinton, there could be no Funkadelics without the genius of W. E. B. Du Bois, because he has given his all, his intellectual wherewithal, his political activism, his time, his energy to affirm the humanity of the Clintons and the James Browns and the C. L. Franklins and the Jasper Williams and Manuel Scotts and all of the great cultural geniuses, the Cecil Taylors, and so forth. So that's a fascinating irony.

One of the things that I have been able to really both revel in and benefit from—and you see it probably more in *Democracy Matters* than in anything else[19]—is trying to unite this radical intellectual legacy of Du Bois that hits the issue of empire and white supremacy with the popular cultural expressions of genius and talent—be it in music, be it in dance, be it among the younger generation or older generation—so that you actually have a kind of an interplay between, on the one hand, Du Bois's radicality and militancy when it comes to politics and economics, empire and race, and, on the other hand, the antiphonal forms of call and response, the syncopation, the rhythm, the rhyme, the tempo, the tone that you get in the best of Black cultural forms that are requisite for sustaining Black dignity and sanity, sustaining Black people as a whole.

CHB: He was so afraid of "uncivilized" behavior, he would probably have taken much of what you are talking about to be just that. And his concern with education—and maybe we could talk about his idea of the Talented Tenth—was quite different from any attempts at grassroots political socialization or education in general.

CW: Absolutely. Of course, Du Bois should consider Louis Armstrong, Ma Rainey, or Bessie Smith part of the Talented Tenth, you see. Bootsy Collins, George Clinton, Aretha Franklin, they are certainly part of the Talented Tenth. Stevie Won der is part of the Talented Tenth, but given Du Bois's elitist conception of education, they would be considered mere entertainers. So I do resonate with his need for a conception of education that has to do with awakening from sleepwalking, with wrestling with reality to transform it so that that illuminates and liberates. I do resonate with that. But because of his conception of who would be candidates for that, it seems to be still too narrow for me. The irony is that for Du Bois, the nonliterate or illiterate slaves who created the spirituals would probably be candidates for the Talented Tenth, because when we look closely at his readings of their products, their songs, their expressions, he sees their genius. He really does!

CHB: In the expression of suffering.

CW: Yes, yes.

CHB: It is here that his empathy shows. There is a piece, a conversation Du Bois has with a white person, I think, who does not understand what Jim Crow is like, even in 1920.[20] And he explains it in terms of his own daily experience and how humiliating it can be. This is his way of expressing the suffering of the people under oppression.

CW: Very much so. You could be alluding to what I consider to be one of the most powerful essays that he wrote—and he wrote so many powerful essays and texts—but "The Souls of White Folk" is probably the most militant, radical, illuminating, and counter-hegemonic text that we have.[21] I know it was a favorite of the great John Henrik Clarke, who was a great Pan-Africanist and who viewed Du Bois as one of his precursors, but again fascinating that John Henrik Clarke viewed Du Bois as a precursor in the same way that William Julius Wilson, concerned about class but more about integration, would view Du Bois as a precursor. In the same way, an NAACP liberal integrationist would view Du Bois as a precursor, so that Du Bois is rich enough and his work polyvalent enough, subject to multiple interpretations enough, that he ends up with all of these different progeny. But that essay, "Souls of White Folk," is a devastating thing. I remember the first time I read this, I said, "Oh my God, this is a Du Bois we don't really get a chance to look at too closely." He writes:

> It is curious to see America, the United States, looking on herself, first, as a sort of natural peacemaker, then as a moral protagonist in this terrible time. No nation is less fitted for this rôle. For two or more centuries America has marched proudly in the van of human hatred,—making bonfires of human flesh and laughing at them hideously, and making the insulting of millions more than a matter of dislike,—rather a great religion, a world-war cry: Up white, down black; to your tents, O white folk, and world war with black and parti-colored mongrel beasts![22]

That's just one moment.

CHB: There is yet another one, where there is the perspective of the daily life of Blacks and their suffering from discrimination, etc. He exposes that in a dialogue that is really powerful. Which brings me to another point, namely, that within the limits of his concept of culture, he, in principle, would have agreed with you that it is not enough to explain something scientifically but that one should also try to express it by other means, in different styles. This is what he did in his work, be it in his novels or in his very early essays in *The Souls of Black Folk*, where he combined scientific essayistic writing with the poetic. And the reason for this was really that he wanted to reach out. He knew he could not reach people otherwise, though one would doubt that he could reach them today with his at times lyrical *Suada* [German for "harangue"].

CW: No, but there would be other artists who would appropriate his work and make it more popular, because they could see the genius at the center of it. One of the things that makes me smile is Du Bois putting on these pageants, these plays, you know, thousands of Black people, trying to get them to see the greatness of African civilization, hundreds of actors and so forth. I mean, that's popular culture at its core, and it's, again, his attempt to reach out. I love his passion to communicate by any means relative to what he thinks are going to be the most effective means.[23]

CHB: True, and also, as to media, in his time he was avant-garde as an editor of the *Crisis*. This is what he could do as an activist.

CW: Absolutely. That was popular. Any of us who try to expand the public spheres into film and music and books and magazines and some of television and, of course, radio—I think we're building on Du Bois, even if we have slightly different conceptions of culture. I think that in an interesting kind of way, Du Bois was an indisputable radical democrat in his ideology—though I'm not so sure he was an indisputable radical democrat in his temperament, in his personality. I think he was shaped at a time when his temperament and personality were much more rooted in a kind of elitist formation essentially, and yet he never allowed that to impede or obstruct his sensitivities and his inclusivity when it came to the suffering of other people. That is part of his greatness to me, even though I tend to accent a much more radical democratic temperament, personality, and way of being in the world.

CHB: Again, he saw the problem himself. He revised the concept of the Talented Tenth, because he wondered about it. He again admitted that he had been naïve, idealistic, because what he had counted on was character, and he had become aware of the fact that you could not count on that. So when he revised his concept of the Talented Tenth, he was contemplating how to actually realize his concepts and how to solve the problem of organization.[24] And this essay shows to me that there was a certain helplessness on his part, but then, aren't we all at a loss when it comes to organization? It is so difficult a task.

CW: Oh absolutely. Yes, I think it's true. And I do think that at the center of his conception of the Talented Tenth was an ethos of service to the poor, service to those who have been left behind, as it were, or in the religious sense, service to the least of these—echoes of the twenty-fifth chapter of Matthew—and I like that core very much. It's just that early on in 1903, when he put forward that notion, it was deeply bourgeois and elitist. In the 1940s, when he revised it, he had been radicalized by Marxism; he had been radicalized by the Communist movement. And so he knew that that ethos of service had to be now cast in such a way that the class elitism of 1903 had to be rejected, and also the sexist elitism.

CHB: He was a nineteenth-century person in that regard, but he moved forward.

CW: Yes, he had come a long way from where he was in the early part of the twentieth century. Of course, you are absolutely right, "The Damnation of Women" from *Darkwater* is a good example. I was blessed to take courses with his second wife, Shirley Graham Du Bois. She was an intellectual powerhouse. She was on fire for justice and would not put up with any kind of patriarchal mess from anybody. She taught at Harvard in the early 1970s. She was something, and she had wonderful memories and reminiscences of her husband.[25]

CHB: And Du Bois then writes in *Darkwater* about servants, female servants.

CW: Yes, yes. Absolutely. "The Servant in the House"; that's powerful.

CHB: What I appreciate is his self-reflexivity on his own development, his self-criticism. It is very honest.

CW: Yes. You wonder, though, whether the major reception of Du Bois's corpus will be providing the launching pad for that American Gibbon I was talking about, i.e., a turning away from Du Bois's challenge and the escalation of the refusal of the deliberate ignorance, the willful evasion of the realities Du Bois was talking about at the level of empire and white supremacy that will constitute the downfall of the American project. America slowly but surely moves toward a second-world, maybe even a third-world status, with ruins and relics of its great democratic past being completely trampled by the kind of neoliberal obsession with unregulated markets and indifference toward the poor and polarizing politics of scapegoating the most vulnerable. And Du Bois's magisterial corpus sits there and says: "You should have listened. I've spent my whole life trying to get you to listen, to wake up, to heed the challenge that I was talking about because I was concerned both about you but first and foremost about my people that you've been trampling." And there is a very, very good chance that that's where we are headed. The irony would be that the indisputable relevance of Du Bois was not heeded: we didn't listen; we didn't take him seriously. Shame on you, America! Shame on you, the American academy! Shame on you, the American intelligentsia, that your narrow individualism, your truncated rapacious marketeering, your deep dedication to paradigms and frameworks that are too truncated to come to terms with the realities that were undermining your democratic experiment have led to the need for the American Gibbon. That's very much where we are right now.

CHB: Yes, but it is really a question of bringing the more radical Du Bois to the fore. Before I had read more of Du Bois, I used to focus on *The Souls of Black Folk*. That is not to say that this is not a great work, with all the metaphors that have shaped academic discussions such as "the veil" and "double-consciousness." But I am also deeply impressed, in *Dusk of Dawn*, by his metaphor of the cave, which is describing the same caste system[26] but in much more radical terms; or rather, it's darker, more pessimistic, and you hardly ever see it referenced. He plays on Plato's cave, I think.

CW: Absolutely. Straight out of *Republic*. No, it is darker here. It is darker here. He writes:

> No matter how successful the outside advocacy is, it remains impotent and unsuccessful until it actually succeeds in freeing and making articulate the submerged

caste. [. . .] This was the race concept which has dominated my life, and the history of which I have attempted
to make the leading theme of this book.[27]

And yet he is one of those who emerges out of the pro-
vincialism, he shatters the narrowness and becomes the grand
cosmopolitan and internationalist that we know him to be. I
mean, that's one of the reasons why in my own classes I assign
Souls of Black Folk, but I also have students read *Reconstruction*, the 1935 classic, especially the more literary, more metaphoric sections of that text alongside the analytical sections,[28]
because by 1935, he has become someone wrestling with the
legacies of Marx and Freud, wrestling with Lenin's conception of imperialism based on Hobson[29] and others, and that is
a different Du Bois. I mean, there are continuities, but it is a
very different Du Bois.

CHB: When I was thinking about the issues we would be talking
about, I thought your perspective might be that, in the end,
he is just too dark. Where is the hope that you would insist
on? But in contrast, one of your points of criticism in *The Future of the Race* is that you think he partakes in American optimism.[30] So you probably meant a different phase. But what do
you think about Du Bois's optimism or pessimism?

CW: Remember, when he was on the boat and he looks back he
says: "The Negro cannot win in America. I must go international, got to go to Ghana," linked to China, the Soviet
Union, and so forth.[31] I'd have to rethink what I had in mind
when I talked about American optimism. That was certainly
part of his earlier phase. I think the later phase is closer to the
darkness that I was talking about. One of the things that has
always disturbed me about the great Du Bois is that I've never
encountered in his grand works a substantive wrestling with
Chekhov, or I would even say with Russian literary tradition
as a whole: Tolstoy, Gogol, Leskov, Turgenev, Dostoyevsky,
and we could go on and on.[32] And I believe that would have
shattered any cheap optimism or any American optimism that

informs earlier stages of his work. I'm just amazed that there is no wrestling with Kafka; there is no wrestling with even Beckett in the 1950s, from a radical democratic point of view. I want him to hold on to his militancy and radicality in terms of the talk about empire and white supremacy. But I think there is a connection between him running from the blues and him running from Chekhov and running from the Russian literary tradition and running from Kafka and from Beckett. And yet he has his own kind of darkness at which he arrives on his own.

CHB: By way of analysis, on the basis of his sociological training.

CW: Yes, exactly. When he looks at the structural and institutional forces in play vis-à-vis poor and working people, and those Frantz Fanon called "the wretched of the earth,"[33] I think of the Chekhovs and the blues sitting there waiting for him. And yet he arrives on his own, so in that sense I'd have to revise my critique if I was implying that American optimism actually held through all of the phases of his thinking as opposed to just the earlier phases.

CHB: I wonder what he read in terms of literature, since, he quotes in *Souls of Black Folk*—

CW: —A lot of Shakespeare, Balzac.

CHB: Yes. His famous quote: "I sit with Shakespeare and he winces not."[34]

CW: Oh, we know his favorite was Goethe. That's one of the things that I hit him hard on, you see.[35]

CHB: Well, after all, he had spent some time in Germany.[36]

CW: Yes, he was deeply shaped by the German conception of *Bildung*, and at that time—and understandably so—the major stellar figures were Goethe and Schiller, who actually mean much to me, too.

CHB: It's the idea of humanism, I think, that shapes him.

CW: Yes, absolutely. Yet you don't get a serious wrestling with modernist texts at all in his work. There's little Joyce, there's little Proust, there's little Kafka.

CHB: What I wonder is, did he really not read any of them, or did he choose not to comment on them because they were alien to his thinking?

CW: It's a good question. My hunch is that he was certainly aware of them. He was too cosmopolitan and intellectual not to know that Joyce, Eliot, Pound, Proust, Kafka, and Mandelstam and others were around. He may have read Hermann Broch's *The Death of Virgil* [1945] in German, but we have very little evidence for this, and it would be the same in terms of modernist movements and in Afro-American life. What did he think of Charlie Parker? Was he moved by the pianistic genius of Art Tatum? I would like to know.

CHB: And what about Richard Wright and writers of his time?

CW: I think he did read Wright. I recall reading a review of Richard Wright, especially given the Communist overlap, both being members of the Communist culture.[37] Wright was actually a member of the party. Du Bois was not, but they overlapped for a little while before Wright left the party. And what did Du Bois think about Ralph Ellison? I think he did actually write about Ellison, too. So, again, I mean this not so much as a brick thrown at the great Du Bois but as a matter of trying to see what constitutes his edifice and which bricks are missing in the building that he was working on. And I think this again resonates with the concerns about popular culture, the contemporary cultural expressions of his day, and the concern about popular culture as a whole.

CHB: There is a heated debate about religion in Du Bois's work, and most of his biographers think he was an agnostic, if not an atheist, due to his Marxism. There are comments that he makes from which you could conclude that. But then there is an interesting book by Edward Blum, *W. E. B. Du Bois:*

American Prophet, who argues that Du Bois, though certainly not an orthodox Christian, was religious in a way and kept it up.[38] In his view, Du Bois did not just do some window dressing using religious phrases, examples from the Bible, but there was a, let's call it, spirituality that shaped him throughout his life.

CW: I think that Du Bois had a self-styled spirituality that was not wedded to cognitive commitments to God talk. He was very similar to his teacher George Santayana. Santayana used to go to Mass, shed tears weekly as a lapsed Catholic, and would say, "The Mass was too beautiful to be true." So he was moved by the passion and the perceptions and the purpose in the Eucharist but could not make cognitive commitments to any of the claims. Ludwig Wittgenstein was the same way, and I think Du Bois is part of that particular coterie of secular figures who are profoundly religiously musical, to use Max Weber's words; people who resonate deeply with the issues that religious people are wrestling with—what it means to be human, how do you engage in a virtuous life, what kind of character do you cultivate, what kind of sensitivity, what kind of compassion, what conceptions of justice, the centrality of love and empathy—without being religious in terms of belief in God, in the rituals of faith.

And I have a great respect for Du Bois's spirituality, even as a Christian, which makes him in some ways even more of a prophet than most Christians or religious Jews or religious Buddhists and so on, because it means that he was able to sustain himself spiritually without the help of the religious apparatus of tradition. He also didn't fall into the kind of narrow reductionist traps of scientistic, positivistic ties to science, the kind of narrow Darwinism that you get today among the number of the more sophomoric atheists like our dear brothers Christopher Hitchens, Richard Dawkins, and others, who reduce the rich Darwin to narrow scientism. Darwin is the brook of fire through which we all must pass. But you can be religiously sensitive without being religious, and Du Bois certainly was one of the most religiously sensitive of the secular thinkers.

CHB: Du Bois wrote an essay entitled "The Revelation of Saint Orgne"—i.e., Negro—"the Damned," and there is a concept of a new church which, according to Du Bois, should be based on the "word of life from Jeremiah, Shakespeare and Jesus, Buddha and John Brown."[39] And it's a church organized "with a cooperative store in the Sunday-school room; with physician, dentist, nurse, and lawyer to help serve and defend the congregation; with library, nursery school, and a regular succession of paid and trained lecturers and discussion; they had radio and moving pictures"—now: mark that!—"and out beyond the city a farm with house and lake."[40] That's his—Orgne's—concept of a church, and what I think is so interesting about it is what is joined here: not just the secular and Christian traditions but body and soul, mind and body; that is what the church would have to offer to help people come to combine the two, to provide food for body and soul. I have noticed that this concept appears in several of Du Bois's writings, and I'd like to follow up on that because I don't think it has been much commented on, though it seems to be part of his later thinking. At first Du Bois counted on the mind exclusively, and then he changed and said, "No, that's not enough," and although he does not go as far as you wished him to—namely, to take into account the physical expression in dance and music and so on of the African American tradition—as a concept he expresses it in that new church that he thinks is needed to raise people to a higher level.

CW: I think you are right about that. It reminds me of one of my own favorite figures and thinkers, Nikos Kazantzakis, where you have this kind of self-styled spirituality that appropriates Jesus, Buddha, Lenin, Shakespeare. I mean, it's quite a heterogeneous coterie of chaps—not too often women actually—who become part of a kind of ecumenical exemplary group of those who constitute grand examples of high-quality living.

So it's the beauty of life, it's the quality of life, it's the courage, the freedom that these people exemplify.[41] You can go from Socrates to Shakespeare in that regard. And there's something that I've always found fascinating about that, I must say. Again, it has a lot to do with Du Bois's humanism. He is a thorough-going radically democratic humanist drawing on the Renaissance, on the Enlightenment and the Victorian critics. William Morris was probably the most revolutionary of them, but Ruskin played a role, and certain moments in Arnold, certain moments in Carlyle, certain moments in Hazlitt; those are Du Bois's intellectual ancestors. I do think that Du Bois would be again relevant for our day because the religious traditions—be they Christian or Islamic or Judaic—if they are not radically Socratized and humanized, then the fundamentalist wings of all three are going to push us into a living hell, which is to say, radically anti-democratic, radically sexist, racist, xenophobic, capitalist hell. Well, I shouldn't say that radical Islam would be capitalist, though. The fundamental Christians would be capitalist, but not the fundamental Islamic folk; they are just theocratic. Now the fundamentalists in Judaism, that's interesting. They tend to be free-marketeers, too, in general, though there are theocratic manifestations of it, too.

You can just see how badly we need Du Bois today in the midst of our catastrophic circumstances. There is no doubt about it. We need the rigor of his structural and institutional analysis, the religiously musical sensitivity to the things that religion is wrestling with as opposed to simply the truth claims of the God belief or the truth claims of the faith appropriated by religious people, and, probably more than anything else, his acknowledgement of subaltern peoples and voices, and just how crucial those voices are in helping us come to terms with our crisis. There is a sense in which Du Bois's witness is such a thoroughgoing indictment of the transatlantic intelligentsia. It really is. If you were to examine much of the intellectual work of the transatlantic intelligentsia—from Europe and the US—there is not just a relative silence around Du Bois's work but a relative silence about the issues and problematic that Du Bois is coming to terms with. It's a very sad state of affairs when you look at the kind of pre–Du Boisian condition of much of the transatlantic intelligentsia. And it says much about how far we have *not* come; how cowardly, how deferential, how careerist, how narrow so many of our beloved colleagues in the academy can be.

CHB: Well, you pay for it. And he paid for it.

CW: Absolutely. There is a cost to be paid. But I love Martin Luther King Jr.'s remarks in his "Honoring Dr. Du Bois" address.[42] I recall talking with John Hope Franklin before he died about his decision to attend this event, because when they had the celebration of Du Bois's birthday at Carnegie Hall, most of the intelligentsia, including Black intellectuals, would not come within a mile or two miles of the gathering; they were just scared. They were afraid; they didn't want to be tainted with the Communist brush during the anti-Communist hysteria and frenzy that was then taking place. But, thank God, Martin Luther King Jr., along with John Hope Franklin and a few others, had the courage to attend. This is when brother Martin laid out his statement:

> We cannot talk of Dr. Du Bois without recognizing that he was a radical all of his life. Some people would like to ignore the fact that he was a Communist in his later years. It is worth noting that Abraham Lincoln warmly welcomed the support of Karl Marx during the Civil War and corresponded with him freely. In contemporary life, the English-speaking world has no difficulty with the fact that Sean O'Casey was a literary giant of the twentieth century and a Communist or that Pablo Neruda is generally considered the greatest living poet though he also served in the Chilean Senate as a Communist. It is time to cease muting the fact that Dr. Du Bois was a genius and chose to be a Communist. Our irrational obsessive

> anti-Communism has led us into too many quagmires to be retained as if it were a mode of scientific thinking. [. . .] Dr. Du Bois's greatest virtue was his committed empathy with all the oppressed and his divine dissatisfaction with all forms of injustice.[43]

This is powerful stuff. This is very, very powerful stuff. King is right. Martin King is absolutely right. Good God Almighty.

Martin Luther King Jr., 1964

CHAPTER THREE

Moral Fire

MARTIN LUTHER KING JR.

After having spoken about the two towering male figures of the Black tradition of activists and intellectuals in the nineteenth and first half of the twentieth centuries, Frederick Douglass and W. E. B. Du Bois, we decided to focus next on Martin Luther King Jr. Du Bois died aged ninety-five on August 27, 1963, that is, on the eve of the famous March on Washington for Jobs and Freedom, passing on the baton, as it were, to King, who delivered his celebrated "I Have a Dream" speech before the Lincoln Memorial.

Though our exchange had been motivated by politics from the very beginning, the dramatic political events of 2011—with the anti-government protests in Spain, the Arab Spring, and the emerging Occupy Wall Street movement in the United States—brought an urgency to our transatlantic conversations. We knew that if we wanted to bring the precious Black prophetic voices into the current debates and struggles for freedom, justice, and economic equality, we would have to wrest them from a collective memory that had reduced their radical messages to inoffensive sound bites. The most evident example of a sanitized national icon was Martin Luther King Jr., a fact that strengthened our decision to select him for the subject of our next talk, which took place in August 2011. Our project gained further momentum when the dialogue on King was accepted for publication in the German journal *Amerikastudien/American Studies*.[1] The idea of a book took shape—and we sped up.

CHRISTA BUSCHENDORF: You consider Martin Luther King Jr. the "most significant and successful organic intellectual in American history."[2] Your claim that "never before in our past has a figure outside of elected public office linked the life of the mind to social change with such moral persuasiveness and political effectiveness" seems to be based on the following interconnected assumptions: first, that the vocation of the intellectual is to "let suffering speak, let victims be visible, and let social misery be put on the agenda of those in power,"[3] and, second, that "moral action is based on a broad, robust prophetism that highlights systemic social analysis of the circumstances under which tragic persons struggle."[4]

The following quotation by Martin Luther King Jr. is particularly pertinent in view of the present global crisis of capitalism, which drives more and more people into poverty:

> I choose to identify with the underprivileged, I choose to identify with the poor, I choose to give my life for the hungry, I choose to give my life for those who have been left out of the sunlight of opportunity. [. . .] This is the way I'm going. If it means suffering a little bit, I'm going that way. If it means sacrificing, I'm going that way. If it means dying for them, I'm going that way, because I heard a voice saying, "Do something for others."[5]

"Let us march on poverty," King suggested in 1965.[6] To highlight the increasing plight of the poor in the United States almost half a century later, Tavis Smiley and you recently undertook the "Poverty Tour" through eighteen cities, talking to Americans of all colors who struggle to make ends meet.[7] In his mission statement, Tavis Smiley quotes from King's declaration, thus it seems to be particularly apt to speak about Martin Luther King Jr. at this very moment—his historical significance to America and his relevance in the present.

CORNEL WEST: One of the great prophetic voices of the twentieth century, Rabbi Abraham Joshua Heschel, said that the future of America depends on the American response to the legacy of

Martin Luther King Jr.[8] Martin himself had said that the major issues in the America that he would soon die in—what he called a "sick country"—were militarism, materialism, racism, and poverty. Those four, for him, were going to be the fundamental challenges. And I think he was prophetic in this sense: when we look at the role of the military-industrial complex—the role of the Pentagon, the share of the national budget, the ways in which militarism has been routinized and institutionalized and recently outsourced; then the materialism, which is really very much tied to corporate media in the various ways in which it produces its weapons of mass distraction that try to pacify and to render the citizens sleepwalking by means of stimulation and titillation; then when you look at racisms, beginning with the "new Jim Crow" that Michelle Alexander talks about[9]—with the prison-industrial complex in ways in which legacies of white supremacy are still very much operative, even though in some ways more covert than before; and then the last one—poverty—which is very much tied to the Wall Street oligarchic and plutocratic complex—so, when you think about the military-industrial complex, the corporate-media multiplex, the prison-industrial complex, and the Wall Street oligarchic and plutocratic complex, those four complexes have really squeezed most of the juices or sucked most of the life out of the democratic experiment. And this was what Martin was talking about.

So, I think, in fact, when brother Tavis and I were on that Poverty Tour and said, "Look, we are trying to make the world safe for the legacy of Martin Luther King," that it was really responding to Heschel and saying, "You know, since 1968, what has been the response of the country to Martin on all four issues?" When we look at wealth inequality increasing, hyper-incarceration; when we use brother Loïc Wacquant's language, from his brilliant book *Punishing the Poor*[10]—the kind of emptying of souls given the debased and decayed culture that is produced day-in and day-out by the corporate media, Martin's characterization of America as a sick country really makes more and more sense, and I think more and more people are seeing that. Part of the problem is, I think, the death of Martin in some sense signified that America was in deep need of a revolution. He used the language of revolution, the need of a revolution in priorities, revolution in values, the need for a transfer of power from oligarchs to the people. America was deeply in need of a revolution, but he wondered whether America was only capable of a counter-revolution, and therefore all he could do was just bear witness and be willing to live and die for what he understood at the end of his life as democratic socialism or kind of a radical redistribution of power and wealth, as he put it. He used to say, over and over, every day he would put on his cemetery clothes. That was all he could do. And in some ways I think he was right; you just have to be coffin-ready for this bearing of witness and struggle in the midst of a very sick country run by greedy oligarchs and avaricious plutocrats whose interest is very entrenching, whose power is mighty. It's not almighty. Rebellion could make a difference; civil disobedience could have some impact. But the kind of fundamental rise of a revolutionary social movement is very, very unlikely given the powers that be.

CHB: It was a long process for him, too, to discover what you were just talking about: the power of these forces.

CW: But it's funny, though, because it's two things about Martin people tend to overlook. Coretta Scott King told me one time that when she went out with Martin on their first date, it was the first time in her life she ever met a Socialist, that Martin was already calling himself a Socialist and was part of the intercollegiate Socialist movement.[11] The other interesting thing is that when Martin was called by the Nobel Prize committee and told that he had won, he said that he didn't deserve to win if Norman Thomas had not yet won. Norman Thomas, of course: Princeton undergraduate, Union Theological Seminary grad, left the church, became head of the Socialist Party, ran for president six times—three times against Franklin Roosevelt—and actually was supported by John Dewey.[12] So that even as a very young man, especially under Chivers—there was a professor named Walter Chivers at Morehouse who was a Socialist—[13]

CHB: And sociologist—

CW: And sociologist too, absolutely. So they read a lot of Marx, and Martin was very influenced by this brother. So that in an interesting kind of way—even though a lot of people think that Martin really began as a liberal and was radicalized as a result of the movement and the pressures of Stokely Carmichael and the pressures of those in SNCC[14] and, of course, Stanley Levison, who had been a Communist, and Bayard Rustin, who was a Socialist[15]—in fact, as Coretta has suggested, he actually began early on as a Socialist but knew that he could never use that language in the Jim Crow South or even America. And so it became a matter of a kind of confirmation of what Norman Thomas and others had been talking about in the thirties and forties. Even in the early sixties, Norman Thomas was one of his great heroes. Martin is a very fascinating figure in that regard. He really is.

CHB: But don't you think there was a change in him, after all? At least I think he talks about that himself—that once he went to Chicago and lived there among the poor, that this was yet another dimension to him. Or was it just that when he was confronted with that situation in the ghetto, he thought he had to speak out, that he had to be more explicit, that he had to drop his careful distance in rhetoric to socialist or Marxist phrases in order to get his message across. Or is it both?

CW: I think there were two things going on when he moved to 1550 South Hamlin Avenue in Chicago. I was just there at the apartments with brother Tavis in the very room where he and Coretta lived, and then when we met Bernice and Martin Luther King III and laid the wreath a couple of days later, they talked about living in Chicago—because he brought the kids with him to Chicago—that, on the one hand, Martin had little experience in the North. Boston and Philadelphia had been the only places where he had spent time, and Boston in some ways was an aberration as opposed to Chicago and Detroit, as opposed to even Los Angeles or New York, with high concentration of Black folk, even Washington, DC. To move to Chicago was to recognize that the ways in which Jim Crow Jr. in the North operated, as opposed to Jim Crow Sr. in the South. The dynamics were different. It was more entrenched in the North in terms of getting at some of the economic causes, but it was much more visible in the South, because the apartheid was right in your face, you know, and the violence was right in your face. And so he knew he had to come to terms with class issues in the North in a way that he just didn't in the South. But in addition, I think—and here, of course, it goes beyond Norman Thomas—that when Martin became a critic of American imperialism—because that happened roughly at the same time: he moves to Chicago in '66; he is already being pushed by SNCC to come out against the war; then he reads *Ramparts* magazine and sees the bodies of those precious Vietnamese children, and decides he must speak out: he can't be against violence in Mississippi and not also be against violence in Vietnam—that being forced to come to terms with class in Chicago and forced to come to terms with empire in Vietnam does in fact change him and sharpen his analysis, even given his earlier socialist sensibilities and sentiment. It really does. But it's in the heat of battle, it's in the context of intense struggle that Martin begins to have this clarity, and, ironically, it's the clarity that intensifies his dance with mortality.

CHB: And toward the end it becomes a battle not just against all these forces you mentioned but against his own activist groups, because they become anxious that he is going too far. And he is very isolated.

CW: Absolutely. At the time he is shot dead, 72 percent of Americans disapprove of him and 55 percent of Black Americans disapprove of him.[16] He is isolated. He is alienated. He is down and out. He is wrestling with despair. He is smoking constantly; he is drinking incessantly. He is, in many ways, more and more—not so much distant but having more difficulties with Coretta, who was heroic in her own ways. His relations with the various women and so forth are increasing as a way of what he called dealing with his anxiety, getting relief from the deep anxiety of living under the threat of death and all of the vicious attacks and assaults on his character by Black writers like Carl Rowan[17] and leaders like Roy Wilkins and Whitney Young[18] and within his own organization, the Southern Christian Leadership Conference,[19] people seeing him becoming more radical.[20] And that too is something that's not talked about as much as it should: that Martin King started very much as a patriot, that he was part of that generation of the Black bourgeois formation, where the Declaration of Independence had nearly the same status as the Bible, not as much, but it nearly did.

CHB: The American civil religion.

CW: Exactly. It's just so tied into his own Christianity.

CHB: But the interesting question here is, to me, is it patriotism or is it some kind of universalism? Because what he appeals to when he refers to the Declaration of Independence is the declaration of equality of people. So often in the past, as we have seen in Douglass and Du Bois, there was a conscious reference to those values that, at the same time, are values of the United States of America, and thus there is an interrelation between universalist values and patriotism, because you might be proud of your country if you believe that it represents those values.

CW: That's true. But I think—maybe I could be wrong because I am fundamentally opposed to any version of American exceptionalism—American exceptionalism is not just self-justifying but one of the most self-deceiving concepts in the history of the nation. There is a distinctiveness to the American democratic experiment, but America is in no way a nation as chosen, in no way a nation that God smiles at and winks at and shuns others. I think Martin King, early in his career, did subscribe to a form of American exceptionalism, and in that sense, there still is an interplay between universal values and the fact that America enacts or embodies those values at their best.

But I believe at the end of his life he felt that American exceptionalism was a major impediment for the struggle for justice in America and around the world; he had discovered that it was Gandhi that had influence; he had discovered that South African struggles for democracy were as inspiring as anything Thomas Jefferson had to offer. Maybe it was a matter of growing and maturing and recognizing that internationalism was the only way to go. I recall listening to a sermon of his in '68, '67/'68, where he says that he has to recognize now more than ever that his commitment is fundamentally to a struggle for justice that doesn't just transcend the US context but views the US context alongside of the international context. You see, when he began in '55, '56, '57, that's not his language. Now, you would think as a Christian preacher—which is his fundamental vocation—every flag would be beneath the Cross. And Martin did always believe that the Cross was about unarmed truth and unconditional love. Those are the two pillars that he always talked about: unarmed truth and unconditional love, across the board. And that is an internationalism; every flag is beneath that. But that American exceptionalism, you see, sneaks back in again, and lo and behold, the United States becomes that very special case that embodies it more than anybody else. And the next thing you know—going back to American civil religion—it's providential. And even if America somehow died out, it would undoubtedly bounce back, rooted as it was in that heroic errand into the wilderness—an American jeremiad that our dear brother Sacvan Bercovitch talked about with such an insight.[21] And Martin was a part of that for much of his calling and career. But I think at the end he was beginning to let that go. Malcolm X had already let it go a long time before, though we must not forget Martin reaching out through his personal lawyer Jones[22] to Malcolm, joining him in his efforts to put the United States on trial at the UN for the violation of the human rights of Blacks.

CHB: But it was easier for Malcolm X to see through the deception because of his upbringing that left him no—or hardly any—illusions to begin with, whereas King rose in the academy and had a successful career, and so it's the upbringing that very much shaped him.

CW: That's exactly right. Even in fraternity—Martin King was an Alpha like myself, as were W. E. B. Du Bois and Paul Robeson and Duke Ellington, Jesse Owens, Adam Clayton Powell Jr., Donny Hathaway, John Hope Franklin.[23] All of these were Alphas—and we Alphas do tend to move in patriotic ways. But you look at Du Bois: he swerves from US patriotism; Robeson: swerves; and Martin at the very end: swerves. That's what's fascinating. That's a very difficult thing to do, to break like that. Someone like myself, I had the privilege of building on their breaks, you know, with the Black Panther Party and others. I had already learned lessons as a young lad that America didn't have this special providential role in the history of the world, ordained by God to embody democracy, given its history of what it did to indigenous peoples and crushing the workers, enslaving Black folk, and so on. But there is something about that Black middle-class incorporation and formation in the South as a "PK," as a preacher's kid, that made it much more difficult for Martin to break and made his break more heroic. Very much so. Martin—there simply is no one like him in the history of the American experience because he really is an intellectual, but he never really has a lot of time to meditate and reflect. But he has a deep tie to the life of the mind, and his calling is rooted in his Christian faith, unlike Douglass and unlike Du Bois.

CHB: How did he talk about the possibilities of combining religious faith and socialism? It was not really a problem for him, or was it?

CW: I think that because he was part of the Black prophetic tradition, he always connected religious faith with social change, and socialism just became one particular end and aim of social change that he began to take very seriously. Black prophetic tradition has always rooted spirituality and religiosity with social transformation. And this is where you can show that present-day America is so profoundly decadent, especially in the age of Obama—it is demeaning, devaluing, and marginalizing the Black prophetic tradition, which has been the primary tradition that has contributed to the renewal and regeneration of American democracy.

ChB: Could it be that this moral change is based on a change of social conditions that people are confronted with, so that something like the hope that is embodied in Christian prophetic faith is hard to maintain, hard to sustain, when in your social conditions you see hardly any future for your kids, for yourself?

CW: Yes, but you think through 244 years of slavery, that kind of American terrorizing and traumatizing and stigmatizing of Black folk, and we still kept the Black prophetic tradition alive. You are right. I think the social conditions that you are talking about have as much to do with the changes in the culture, with market forces so fundamentally undermining family and community, with corporate media filling the void with narcissism and materialism and individualism and those distractions. So that during slavery we could keep the Black prophetic tradition alive by lifting our voices—music was fundamental in sustaining Black dignity and sanity—and families still had networks, even given that the slaveholders attempted to destroy the Black family. Whereas in contemporary late-capitalist culture, there is such a distraction from empathy and compassion and community and non-market values as a whole, and you cannot have the Black prophetic tradition without non-market values. I mean, one of the problems since Martin's death is when it comes to leadership. You have either the fear of being killed because the FBI, the CIA, and the repressive apparatus of the nation-state might kill you quickly—as was the case in the 1960s—not just Martin but Fred Hampton, Bobby Hutton,[24] and a lot of others—or the other alternative is just buying people, so that you end up with

Black leaders today, most of whom are just up for sale. All you got to do is just give them a bit of money, give them access to corporate position, give them access to the White House, give them access to whatever status they want and they are paid off. So you either get killed or bought. And Martin, I mean, one of the reasons why he stands out so is that there was no price that he was ever willing to accept to be bought—and in that he was like Malcolm and like Fannie Lou Hamer.[25] He was not up for sale, and that's just so rare. It's almost alien to us, really; it's alien to us that corporate America couldn't buy off everybody. The White House couldn't incorporate him. He supported Lyndon Johnson intensely when LBJ helped to break the back of US apartheid, and then two and a half years later, LBJ was calling him a nigger preacher he wished would go away because of Martin's opposition to the war. And Martin refused to support him in '68, and LBJ decided to withdraw from the race. You see, that's something. Even among the Black intelligentsia, Black leadership, and the Black community as a whole, many were talking about Martin like a dog. Here he is willing to die for folk, and they are still talking about him so bad. He refuses to be bought, you know. He doesn't want to be popular in the community if he can't have integrity. It's a very rare thing.

CHB: And now he is no longer able to defend himself, because in public memory he has not been turned into a radical leader, but as you always say, he has been sanitized, and it's that sanitized King that has survived, and it is the radical King that has disappeared. Or maybe, due to the increasing suffering and the increasing crisis of capitalism, he is being rediscovered. One instance I noticed recently was when Tavis Smiley talked on National Public Radio about King's speech "Beyond Vietnam," which is not very well known.[26] It is interesting to juxtapose the "I Have a Dream" speech with the "Beyond Vietnam" speech, but the latter is the forgotten or repressed Martin. I wonder how you see it, whether the more radical Martin has a chance to be rediscovered now.

CW: The radical Martin is highlighted in what brother Tavis Smiley has done in the National Public Radio show on the "Beyond Vietnam" speech. And *that* Martin cannot but come back. So that the kind of, as you say, sanitized, sterilized Martin, the deodorized Martin, the Martin that has been Santaclausified,[27] so that the Santa Claus that he now becomes, jolly old man with a smile giving out toys to everybody from right-wing Republicans to centrists to progressives, is opposed to the version of King who took a stand on the side of a class war and of an imperial battle, which is actually closer to the truth. He really did take a fundamental stand: "I choose to identify with the underprivileged, I choose to identify with the poor." That sounds like Eugene Debs; that sounds like Jim Larkin of the Dublin working-class 1913 strike; it sounds like all of the great freedom fighters of the last hundred and fifty years in modern times.[28] Now *that* Martin is so scary; *that* Martin requires so much courage; *that* Martin requires all of us to pay such a price, that *that* Martin will live and come back, precisely how is the open question.

I have the feeling that *that* Martin, in some ways, is going to be much more in the possession of people outside of the United States, in Brazil, in Africa, in Asia, than in America, since *that* Martin is really a prophetic figure for the world more than he is for America. I think he is too much for America. He is too honest; he is too truthful; he is too loving for a culture that is fearful of the truth and is fearful of a genuine love especially of poor people. There will be voices in America that will try to hold on to that later Martin, but I think the kind of hysteria—let's use the wonderful word of Tennessee Williams—the hysteria of America doesn't allow it to really come to terms with the deep truth of its history, and in that sense *that* Martin is repressed. That's why all this notion of people walking around with the juxtaposition on the same shirt—Malcolm, Martin, Obama—is such a joke. And in people's minds, they really think all three are identical, and you say, "What? Wait a minute. Do you understand?" I mean, you got Obama, who is the friendly face of the American empire, with drone-dropped bombs killing innocent people, at home crushing the poor with policies that are pro–Wall Street and pro-oligarchy and pro-plutocracy. And you got Martin, who is with the poor folk who Obama is crushing, and Malcolm with the poor folk who Obama is crushing, especially the later Malcolm, who is a revolutionary even more so than Martin in some way. And you see all three of those and you can see the level of confusion and obfuscation that is taking place in America, which reinforces why the counter-revolution of the deeply conservative reactionary forces is triumphing.

CHB: But it's so easy because the media play into it. I read that you thought that the radical King in your own time, early as a young man at Harvard, was not yet the voice you listened to.[29] This would change in the next decade; that's what you said. And I wondered about that: Did it change in the eighties? Did you then read "Beyond Vietnam"? Did it resonate with the Left at that time?

CW: You know, I had already read the radical Martin and had great respect for the radical Martin, and as a Christian I have very deep ideological affinities with him in terms of religious sensibility. But what was lacking in Martin—and I continue to say it is lacking in Martin—was his refusal to identify or immerse himself in youth culture.

See, what Malcolm had was a style that resonated more with young people. Martin's style had difficulties, and even as a young person and as a young Christian, I could identify much more with Malcolm the way I could identify with Huey Newton,[30] Angela Davis,[31] and Stokely Carmichael.[32] It had something to do with church and the church leadership styles that Martin as a preacher tended to. And as a Southern preacher, too, a Black Southern preacher, his style was more distant from northern California rhythm and blues, funk orientation. Now, Malcolm himself was very conservative in some ways, especially as a member of the Nation of Islam, where they don't even have music in their rituals, you see, but you could just tell in his style that he was closer to the styles in youth culture. There was a certain swagger; there was a certain sincerity in keeping it real, which is what the funk is all about. So there were elements of James Brown, George Clinton, Bootsy Collins, Lakeside, Ohio Players. You could feel it in Malcolm, whereas in Martin, you couldn't feel that.

CHB: That's the same with the Du Bois we talked about. And it's again the upbringing. It would have been quite difficult for them to step beyond certain limits that are produced by a bourgeois upbringing and bourgeois values and the emphasis on turning children into "civilized" human beings.

CW: That's true, but part of it is choices. Habitus is fundamental, but there is still choice. You can think of figures who come out of this same context as Du Bois who fundamentally chose to identify with the blues the way Du Bois did not, see what I mean? Duke Ellington, bourgeois to the core, but that Negro genius that he was—you could see him identifying with Biggie and Tupac. He had that kind of capacious personality. Louis Armstrong—Negro genius that he was—of course, from the street, so he is a little different. You could see Louis sit down with Ice Cube and probably kicking and having a good time, you know what I mean, whereas with Du Bois that's not going to take place. You cannot see him sitting down with Billie Holiday; Billie Holiday would scare him to death. And I think that there is a sense in which George Clinton would scare Martin King to death: "George, what is all that hell, man? You know, I love you, but damn man, I don't understand, I don't understand." "Come on Martin, get into the groove!" That's not his style, and that's just something missing in Martin from my own point of view, just in terms of my own orientation. And it's not a major thing, but I do think that the appropriation of Martin by young people is ongoing here and around the world—because I mean youth culture has been Afro-Americanized around the globe now—so there is a sense in which any appropriation of Martin is going to be effected by the Afro-Americanization that is already taking place among young people in Asia, Africa, Europe, Central

America. He comes out of a different habitus that has its own specificity and distinctiveness. There is no doubt about that.

CHB: What about the space, the social space of the church today? You talked about the moral decline, and the church was always the institution that would provide a space for self-assertion, even in those much worse times such as slavery and militant Jim Crow in the South. What about young people and the church today? Is it only for the middle class, something you do on Sunday because it's proper to do? Or is there still real power in the churches?

CW: I was blessed to be at the Progressive Baptist Convention just a few weeks ago, which is the convention that Martin helped found when he was booted out of the National Baptist Convention in 1961, with Gardner Taylor,[33] who was the mentor of Martin King. He is now ninety-five years old. Brother Tavis Smiley and I were blessed to interview Reverend Taylor in front of the Progressive Baptist Convention, and it was something, because you look out, you see only about twenty-five hundred people there. Twenty years ago you would have seen ten thousand. That's the result of the decline of the denominations. So, two basic phenomena are taking place: First, the impact of market culture on the Black church is the decline of denominations, so you get the rise of nondenominational churches, so many of the members of Progressive Baptists joined the nondenominational churches. And the second phenomenon is the Pentacostalization of the nondenominational churches, you see. So that here you get Pentacostals, which is, of course, a denomination founded by Black Baptists, the fastest-growing denomination in the whole world, which places stress on the third person in the Trinity, on the Holy Ghost, the Holy Spirit and highly individualist salvation. Most Pentacostal churches shy away from direct political involvement or action. In addition, you get nondenominational churches growing. You end up with a towering figure like Bishop T. D. Jakes,[34] who is a spiritual genius, a great preacher, but doesn't have a whole lot of political courage. I could go on and on. Another towering figure is Bishop Glen Staples,[35] my dear brother, nondenominational and very much tied to working and poor people and politically active. Pentacostalism is still, in style, too funky for the well-to-do, the Black elites, you see, so that what happens is you get the breakdown of denominations, the Pentacostal styles becoming hegemonic.

But the prophetic element associated with the old denominations, like progressive Baptists, is lost. So that you have some prophetic folk, like Bishop Staples—and there are few like him—but for the most part, it really is a matter of spiritual stimulation and titillation that has market parallels and market stimulation and titillation, and these nondenominational churches really don't have the rich prophetic substance of courage, compassion, sacrifice, and risk. For example, there is the story that Wacquant and others tell about the $300 billion invested in the prison-industrial complex, the Marshall Plan for jails and prisons, so you get these escalating, exponentially increasing numbers of prisons, but most churches don't have prison ministers. So you get a sense how far removed they are from the suffering of the people. Now, the preachers probably have one or two Bentleys, some have Lamborghinis, but they don't have prison ministers, whereas the Progressive Baptist Convention in the 1950s, they are so attuned to the suffering of the people that wherever the people were being dominated, in whatever form they were dominated, they had a ministry that's somehow connected. And so in that sense, the market-driven religiosity of much of the Black church these days is counter to the prophetic sensibility of Martin—what Martin King was all about—and that's one of the major, major things missing in contemporary America. The two outstanding exceptions are my mentor, Reverend Herbert Daughtry, pastor of the House of the Lord Pentecostal Church, in Brooklyn, founder of the National Black United Front, an exemplary Black freedom fighter, and my dear brother Father Michael Pfleger, pastor at historic Saint Sabina, in Chicago, whose prophetic leadership is deeply grounded in King's witness and legacy.[36]

CHB: You associated the liberal Black church with social analysis, with an insight that goes with the preaching of how you can cope with these conditions, but you're saying that this element is basically lost these days?

CW: For the most part. I mean you get a J. Alfred Smith in Oakland, one of the great prophetic figures; Freddy Haynes or Carolyn Knight, major prophetic figures, or Reverend Dr. Bernard Richardson, Reverend Toby Sanders, Dr. Barbara King, or Reverend Dr. M. William Howard Jr., Reverend Dr. William Barber.[37] Of course, the great Vincent Harding—scholar, activist, teacher—is the reigning dean of King-like prophetic witness. So you have some exceptions, but generally speaking it's lost, and it's exacerbated in the age of Obama, because identification with Obama could easily become—in the eyes of Black leaders—an identification with the Black prophetic tradition. So that Obama displaces the Black prophetic tradition; people think they are doing something progressive and prophetic by supporting our Black president given the history of white supremacy in America, counter-hegemonic, countervailing and so forth, you see. And given the trauma of overcoming blatant legalized racism, Obama is counter-hegemonic, but it's overshadowed by his identification with the oligarchs, with his identification with the imperial killing machine and so forth. But that small sliver gives these Black leaders the sense of "I'm very progressive. I'm with the Black president. The right wing hate him, right wing want to kill him, right wing tell lies about him, but we are taking a stand," you see. And so it's very deceiving, very confusing, and very obfuscating in terms of any clear social analysis of the relations of domination and of power in American society.

CHB: So often the argument is "But isn't there progress? Not just that visual, symbolic progress, but the African American middle class is growing, after all, so what are you talking about?"

CW: Yes, it's true. And they could use that argument up until 2008, when the financial catastrophe took place owing to the greed of Wall Street bankers, when Black people lost 53 percent of their wealth.[38] So we are seeing the relative vanishing of the Black middle class, most of whom had wealth in their homes; large numbers lost their homes. The predatory lending that was connected to the market bubble that burst—those bad loans were for the most part given to Black and brown lower-middle-class people. They've lost their homes, and so there is a transformation taking place. For example, even in the churches, they used to preach prosperity gospel, but now with the lack of prosperity, the material basis of their theology is called into question.

CHB: Yes, I think, what you are talking about—the vanishing of the middle class—is a global development. But probably disproportionately so in the African American community, as always.

CW: Absolutely. In America, whites lost 16 percent wealth, while brown people lost 66 percent wealth. It was worse among Latinos than among Blacks, who lost 53 percent. On a global scale, you do have the middle class contracting with oligarchic and plutocratic power expanding. Now, for the seven past months,[39] 75 percent of corporate profits were based on layoffs, so corporations are actually able to make big money by cutting costs, which are primarily labor costs. And then, of course, they are sitting on $2.1 trillion that they are hoarding because they are scared that the next collapse is going to leave them dry. So that what happens is that the Black middle class loses—a Black *lumpenbourgeoisie* under the American bourgeoisie. We never really had a solid Black bourgeoisie, E. Franklin Frazier says in '57,[40] and he is absolutely right. Even given the unprecedented opportunity the last forty years, the Oprah Winfreys, the Michael Jordans, and so on, once you shave off the entertainers who make big money, we are still beneath the American middle class in terms of wealth. And right now the white household in America has twenty times more wealth than the Black: $113,000 for the average white family, Black is $5,000, Hispanic is $6,000.[41] And we are not even talking of the social neglect and economic abandonment of the poor, which is the kind of thing brother Tavis and I were accenting on the Poverty Tour. That has had no visibility since Martin was killed. Marian Wright Edelman has been heroic trying to make it visible, but she has had difficulty making it visible.[42] Part of Tavis's creative genius as a media figure is his ability to gain access to media sites to make things visible, so that even without a social movement you can go on a Poverty Tour and get the whole nation talking about poverty, from *Nightline* to CNN to C-SPAN to the *New York Times*, *Washington Post.* That's unprecedented in so many ways. But in the absence of a social movement, that's one of the best things you can do to try to shape the climate of opinion, try to have some impact on the public discourse in the country.

CHB: And that influence is stronger, more powerful than in King's days.

CW: Yes. That's true. Because King's social movement was an attempt to dramatize issues of injustice, and the Poverty Tour, which is what brother Tavis and I did, really is an attempt to dramatize the issue of poverty without a social movement. Now, I think that the aim of putting a smile on Martin's face in the grave is the highest criterion of a freedom fighter in America. And to put a smile on his face is to be willing to live and die and bear witness on behalf of those who are wrestling with all four of those issues: militarism, materialism, racism, and poverty. Now, I would include patriarchy and sexism—I would include homophobia as well—even though he didn't talk about them, so that when we are talking about racism, we are talking about a species of xenophobia. We could really just say xenophobia as a whole, so it includes anti-Semitism; it includes anti-Arab racism, anti-Muslim sensibility, and so on. But my hunch is that's probably the best we can do.

I think Sheldon Wolin is probably right with his notion of fugitive democracy,[43] where it is a matter of trying to generate and galvanize people to be organized and mobilized to bring power and pressure to bear, but know that the powers that be are going to either kill you, try to absorb you and incorporate you, or lie about you or try to undermine your movement by those weapons of mass distraction that we talked about before. It's very difficult to conceive of how the kind of revolution that Martin really wanted can take place given current arrangements. Now, it could just be a matter of my limited imagination, but the Frankfurt School and Wolin and the others just make more sense to me. And I think that's one reason why you have fewer persons who really want to put a smile on Martin's face, because the possibilities of actualizing what he was calling for tend to be so small, and most people don't want to fight for something that they don't think can be actualized or realized—especially in America—rather quickly.

CHB: It always impresses me that Noam Chomsky, an intellectual I appreciate very much, who is so marginalized—naturally—sharply analyzes the situation and sees the difficulties you were just talking about—of how change could come about—and yet always believes that people can do it. And I wonder how he sustains this belief, which seems to be based on some insight that it is possible.

CW: We just had him at Princeton, and I had a chance to speak to him and introduce him, and brother Noam, deep down he is a Cartesian, he really is. So he believes in not just the power of reason but the power of transparency and the power of clarity as themselves fundamentally just agents of change. Beckett, Chekhov, Schopenhauer, they are not part of his world. I think he has a limited grasp of the role of the nonrational, and so he easily pushes it aside, so he really believes that once people are exposed to the clear analysis that he has, somehow they will catch on.

CHB: That's what Du Bois believed.

CW: For a while, that's right. He really believed that it is ignorance standing in the way.

CHB: I think it's, on the one hand, rationality versus irrationality, but on the other hand, it's also about the interrelation of mind and body, because so much of how we look at the world, our perceptions, our orientations, are deeply ingrained in our bodies, and as embodied dispositions, they are persistent. Thus, according to Pierre Bourdieu, a change of habitus occurs only under certain conditions, mainly in moments of crisis.[44] So that is something that one has to address.

CW: You've got to come to terms with that. What happens is that the Cartesian element has its place because reason does have a role to play, but it can become a fetish; it can become an idol; it can become a form of false religiosity in order to sustain your optimism, and in some ways I think that's true for Noam. You know who I think is a better example is my dear brother Howard Zinn. I just wrote an introduction to his writings on race that was recently published.[45] Because Howard— like Noam—really believed in the power of reason, clarity, transparency, and analysis. But he also had a deep sensitivity to body, to nonrationality—or maybe nonrationality is not a good word—to trans-rationality—what culture is about—and so Howard had such a long view of things. Reminds me a little of Raymond Williams's wonderful book *The Long Revolution*,[46] which needs to be read and reread over and over again. And in that sense he is a little closer to reality in a way, whereas I think people like Wolin, they understand all the things that go into social transformation, and it's always messy, always.

CHB: What about King in that respect? What do you think?

CW: I think King always understood the mess, and I think once he hit those issues of class in Chicago and empire in Vietnam, the mess became more and more Beckett-like, which means all you can do is try to lay bare illuminating analysis and try to live a life committed to justice and love and truth. That's all you could do at that point. It's just a matter of integrity, because what you are up against is such a mess, in a very technical sense—which is a term which Beckett uses,[47] rather than

Being in Heidegger—and King understood that, he really did. And you wonder though—I mean, he died at thirty-nine—if he had lived to be sixty, what would Martin have done? That's still a question. Some say he would have been a professor in Union Theological Seminary. So he would have been an activist but would be teaching as well, because you have to be able to sustain yourself with something; you can't be an intense activist every week of your life the way he had done this from twenty-six to thirty-nine—thirteen years—you just can't do that, you know, especially if you had kids and grandkids and things. But you never know. I know Martin would have been fundamentally in solidarity with the struggles of poor people. I really do. And I think that he would have been a countervailing voice and a countervailing force against the Obama administration, and he would have spoken out very loudly. Now, he spoke out very loudly among Black politicians of his day, when he said that the US Congress was turning "the war on poverty into a war against the poor."[48] And when he supported Carl Stokes as mayor, and Stokes refused to invite Martin on the stage when he won,[49] Martin was very hurt. Martin was too radical. He had come out against Vietnam already. He was very hurt, and he would say over and over again, "These Black politicians kind of sell out just as quickly as any white politician. It's about the people!"

Now you see, Huey Newton and company, they loved that about Martin; even Amiri Baraka,[50] who Martin met before he died. Baraka was just telling me about that wonderful encounter that he and Martin had in '68 in March prior to the death in April, and they loved that about Martin, because they knew that his critique of Black bourgeois politicians was a powerful one. Though he supported these folks, they used him; they used his prowess, his charisma for their campaign, and then they win and they won't touch him with a ten-foot pole. Martin said: "What the hell is going on here?" They know what they do, you know. They know what they do. They got the big business community, the permanent government, to relate to and so forth.

I think if Martin had lived, he would have been critical of the later rule of Mandela as president of South Africa, given his complicity with the business class and given his willingness to in some ways downplay the plight of the poor of South Africa as he moved into the mainstream. You can see the same kind of Santaclausification, the same kind of complicity with the business elites in South Africa, the embrace by Bill Clinton, the embrace by Richard Stengel, the managing editor of *Time* magazine, so that any time now you talk about Mandela, Clinton and Stengel pop up rather than Sisulu and Slovo,[51] who were revolutionary comrades of the revolutionary Mandela, who spent twenty-seven and a half years in prison, you see. Martin would understand the ways that people's names are promoted and sustained by corporate money and elites who protect their names, but he would resist that kind of sanitizing, which is to say he would be critical of the way that he has been sanitized, too. In some ways it's probably an inevitable process, but even given its inevitability, it has to be criticized, because it is a shift away from the truth. And there's a distancing from the truth. He would still have great respect for Mandela, don't get me wrong, but he would be critical of that process. I think Mandela was critical of this process himself. He told me that when we met, when I gave that Mandela lecture and talked about the Santaclausification of Mandela himself in Africa. I think Martin would resonate with that. No doubt. There is no doubt that the great Nelson Mandela was the most courageous of men and most genuine of revolutionaries—yet as president of South Africa he ruled in a neoliberal manner.

Ella Baker, 1964

CHAPTER FOUR

The Heat of Democratic Existentialism

ELLA BAKER

Our project gained momentum, and so did the Occupy movement. The demonstration camp in New York City's Zuccotti Park triggered the vital question of all political movements—and especially grass-roots movements—how to organize and mobilize. No figure embodies more convincingly than Ella Baker the genius of grassroots organizing in the civil rights movement. Her deep commitment to democratic decision making turned her into an ideal choice for our next conversation, which took place in summer 2012, when the Occupy movement was at its height. With Ella Baker we opened up the field of the female voices within the Black prophetic tradition. The women, in contrast to their charismatic male companions, had not just been sanitized but, worse, marginalized.

CHRISTA BUSCHENDORF: In our three previous conversations we talked about Frederick Douglass, W. E. B. Du Bois, and Martin Luther King Jr. Even when we consider the tremendously rich tradition of African American intellectuals and activists, these were obvious choices. After all, all three were considered towering figures, if not the most towering intellectuals of their time, by their contemporaries as well as by posterity. To many, our choice to speak about Ella Baker will be much less evident, although she clearly belongs to the exclusive group of long-distance runners, i.e., freedom fighters who devote their whole lives to the struggle for freedom and justice. However, her life's work is more difficult both to access and to assess. First, as a highly skillful organizer, she often became an indispensible member of the organization for which she chose to work, but she never stood in the limelight of the movement. Second, while she held concise theories of social change and political action, she never put them down in writing. There is no memoir; there is no collection of essays. There are just speeches, a few newspaper articles, and interviews, but apart from that, we rely on biographers who consulted her papers and spoke to the people who knew her personally. Third, her very theory of political action is decidedly group-centered in that she firmly believed in a kind of grassroots organizing that would allow the poor and oppressed to get actively involved in the fighting. To Baker, the ideal activist was not the charismatic figure of the prophet who mobilizes the masses by mesmerizing speeches but an unassuming person who helps the suppressed to help themselves. As she put it in 1947, "The Negro must quit looking for a savior, and work to save himself."[1] And twenty years later, with regard to the Student Nonviolent Coordinating Committee, which she cofounded, she maintained, "One of the major emphases of SNCC, from the beginning, was that of working with indigenous people, not working for them, but trying to develop their capacity for leadership."[2]

If, then, Ella Baker may not be as obvious a choice as Douglass, Du Bois, and King, she nevertheless is, I think, a very obvious choice for you. So could you just start by giving us an assessment of why you cherish her personality and her work in the civil rights movement?

CORNEL WEST: I think in many ways Ella Baker is the most relevant of our historic figures when it comes to democratic forms of leadership, when it comes to a deep and abiding love for not just Black people in the abstract or poor people in the abstract, but a deep commitment to their capacities and their abilities to think critically, to organize themselves, and to think systemically, in terms of opposition to and transformation of a system. When we think of the Occupy movement   we do now live in the age of Occupy in this regard—and Ella Baker's fundamental commitment to what Romand Coles calls "receptivity"—Coles's work also was quite powerful in terms of Ella Baker's legacy[3]—learning to receive from the people, not just guide, not just counsel, not just push the people in a certain direction, but to receive from the people the kinds of insight that the people themselves have created and forged in light of a tradition of ordinary people generating insights and generating various visions. And so it's grassroots in the most fundamental sense of grassroots. And I don't think that even Douglass, in all of his glory, and Du Bois, in all of his intellectual genius, and King, in all of his rhetorical genius, have that kind of commitment to the grassroots, everyday, ordinary people's genius in this sense. And of course, there is a gender question as well: her powerful critique of patriarchal models of leadership, including especially messianic models of leadership, which ought to be a starting point for any serious talk about organizing and mobilizing and social change in the twenty-first century.

In addition, I was just in dialogue with my dear brother Bob Moses.[4] He spent a whole year at Princeton, and his office was right across the hall from mine. Of course, for him, Ella Baker is the grandest figure in radical democratic praxis, and he is very much a disciple of Ella Baker. He is quite explicit about that, very explicit that charismatic leadership, messianic leadership is something that he rejects across the board. But I think what comes through is that Ella Baker has a sensitivity to the existential dimension of organizing and mobilizing, and what I mean by that is that for her political change is not primarily politically motivated. This goes back to her early years in the Black Baptist women's missionary movement. When she talks about humility with the people, not even for the people but with the people, when she talks about service alongside the people, and when she talks about everyday people, everyday people's capacities becoming more and more manifest at the center of the movement, not something that is just used and manipulated by messianic leaders, but at the center of the movement, that's a kind of democratic existentialism of a sort that I see in her work—and I see in Bob Moses's. But you see it in very few people's works.

There are elements of this in some of the anarchists, and that's why I have a tremendous respect for anarchism, because anarchism has this deep suspicion of hierarchy, be it the state in the public sphere, corporations in the private sphere, or cultural institutions in civil society. We know Baker worked with George Schuyler, who called himself an anarchist in the 1930s. He ended up a reactionary right-wing brother, but he earlier called himself an anarchist.[5] We also know Bayard Rustin was an anarchist, called himself an anarchist quite explicitly.[6] We know that Dorothy Day called herself an anarchist, quite explicitly, till the day she died.[7] This is a great tradition I have great respect for, and I see it among my young brothers and sisters of all colors in the Occupy movement, even though I don't consider myself an anarchist. I do see similarities between Ella Baker's position and the council Communist tradition that called for Soviets without Bolsheviks, that called for workers' councils without a revolutionary vanguard party that served as managerial manipulators of the people in the councils, so that the self-organization of working people was the kind of radical organizing among everyday people without any managers, experts, or party members telling them what to do. And there is some overlap between Herman Gorter and Anton Pannekoek and some of the early council Communists that mean much to someone like myself coming out of a deep democratic tradition.[8] And so, ironically, Ella Baker, the very figure who one would think would be marginal vis-à-vis these male-type titans, ends up being the most relevant in light of our present dark times of political breakdown, economic decline, and cultural decay.

CHB: It is so interesting that the Occupy movement is definitely leaderless, tries to be leaderless and group-centered, which has great advantages. For one thing, you can't decapitate a movement easily by just killing one of its charismatic leaders. But more than that, as you just explained, it gives the group much more power, a power that it otherwise delegates to a representative. But even if we say today that this is why Ella Baker is more important, when we think back, what is your stance on the fact that after all we also needed a Martin Luther King Jr.? What, then, is to your mind the relation between those two forces, the charismatic leader-figure and the group-centered work that Ella Baker did?

CW: When Ella Baker says that the movement made Martin, Martin didn't make the movement, she is absolutely right, and so for me the greatness of Martin King has to do with the ways in which he *used* his charisma and *used* his rhetorical genius and *used* his courage and willingness to die alongside everyday people. The critique of Martin would be that the decision-making process in his organization was so top-down and so male-centered and hierarchical that one could have envisioned a larger and even more effective mass movement, especially when it came to issues of class, empire, gender, and sexual orientation. When he hit economic justice for janitors and the poor, and when he hit issues of American imperialism in Vietnam, he would not have been just dangling all by himself if there had been more political education and cultivation among the people in the organization and the community. And Ella Baker—who was shaped by the South, went to Shaw University in North Carolina, and then straight to New York City, where she runs the West Indian newspaper, and she is working with George Schuyler during his anarchist years, interacting with leftists, interacting with various progressives, but always rooted, always grounded—offered a deep democratic alternative to the model of the lone charismatic leader.

One of the things about Ella you might recall is that—and Bob Moses was telling me this, it was so striking—right in the middle of the movement, she pulled out to take care of her niece. And people said, "Wait a minute, this is something that you have been waiting for. This is the moment. The cameras are here." "I got my roots," you see, "my niece needs to be taken care of. She is, after all, by herself." And people would say, "Oh, but that's part of the gender question. She had to think of herself as a carer and nurturer." But, no, no, she puts things in perspective. Her caring for her niece in those years that her niece needed her was part and parcel of her calling as someone who is of service. But for Ella, her calling embraced both service to her family and service to the movement. For her, humility and service flow across the board, and so I think that her critique of the great Martin Luther King Jr. ought to be integral to any discussion about Martin Luther King Jr. She brings to her critique humility, service, and love; her own willingness to sacrifice. She's the kind of unassuming character who doesn't need the limelight at all in order to have a sense of herself. She doesn't need the camera. You know what happens is that these charismatic leaders become ontologically addicted to the camera. And it's a very sad thing to behold. You see it in Jesse Jackson, despite his rhetorical genius and great contributions to our struggles. We see it in Al Sharpton, despite his talent for adaptability and service. You saw it in the later years of Huey Newton, as great as he was in his early years. Angela Davis has resisted it. Bob Moses also resisted it. Stokely Carmichael—even given his greatness, incredible love for the people, and the deep influence of Ella Baker—was still much more tied to the charismatic model.[9] My dear brother the charismatic Reverend Dr. Jeremiah Wright—largely misunderstood and underappreciated—was demonized by the media and will, in the long run, be vindicated. But, like Ella, prophetic giant Dr. James Forbes Jr. defies these seductions.

CHB: One wonders, of course, whether there is not a natural relation between the possibility of becoming such a charismatic leader and a certain degree of narcissism, so it is an even greater accomplishment of those figures who do not develop in terms of egocentricity, and yet are great leaders. Baker often criticized the mostly male cofighters she had to put up with. As she recalled, they took it for granted that when there was a meeting she would take care of the people, so that they would have something to eat and drink, that the coffeemaker was running. Thus, there was always that double concern of hers. For she was not at all a person who was content with those everyday services to the movement; she had great foresight. In fact, this to me is another important feature of hers: the way she understood the whole process, namely, as something that would go on for a long time, because nothing would be accomplished in ten years or twenty years, but that nevertheless you would have to bring all your strength to it, even if you did not see much progress. She was looking ahead and willing even to pass on the baton to the next generation, to the next person who was there to serve, and that is one of her great strengths.

CW: Absolutely. There is a fundamental sense in which the age of Occupy is the age of Ella Baker. Even given the deep contributions of the legacies of Douglass and King—we could add Malcolm; we certainly would add Du Bois as well—for Ella Baker, you know, when you radically call into question the distinction between mental and manual labor, then that frees you up to engage in forms of activities in the movement that allow for a natural flow, from caring for the homeless, cooking food for the elderly, and reading Gramsci on what it means to be an organic intellectual all in the same afternoon, because these are all just functions of a freedom fighter, functions of an organic, catalytic figure, where the intellectual is not somehow either isolated or elevated and therefore distinct from the manual, tactile, touch, hands-on-activity.

You know, when I talked about Ella's democratic existentialism, it is relevant to me in terms of your point on narcissism and charismatic leaders, because anyone who is a long-distance freedom fighter has to have a tremendous sense of self-confidence, and the real challenge is how do you have this tremendous sense of self-confidence when you are being targeted by assassination attempts or threats; when you are rebuked, scorned, lied about, or misunderstood. You need self-confidence in order to keep going in a community and a network, but how do you hold on to self-confidence without sliding into self-indulgence? The only weapon against narcissism is a belief in self and a greater cause than the self that is severed from an obsession with self as some grand messianic gift to the world. And I think you could see elements of this in the other figures that we talked about: Douglass and King and Du Bois had unbelievable self-confidence, and at their best, they are Ella Baker–like; at their worst, they are narcissists. And of course, this is a struggle in the human soul in each and every one of us. But the major weapon against narcissism for me is a kind of spirituality or a spiritual strength that accents, on the one hand, gratitude—what it means to be part of a long tradition that has produced you and allowed you to have the self-confidence—because self-confidence doesn't drop down from the sky; it is cultivated over many, many years owing to earlier people, antecedent figures who had the same kind of self-confidence—so gratitude on the one hand, as a kind of democratic piety in that sense, if piety is understood as the debts you owe to those who came before tied to the tradition and community and legacy of struggle, and on the other hand, there is an indescribable joy in serving others. This joy in serving others is qualitatively different than pleasure in leading others.

CHB: And a third factor in combatting narcissism may be the belief in the cause, or do you take that for granted?

CW: That's true, the depth of your commitment to the cause. And that is, I think, very important, because when you really get at the complicated core or the mediated essence of Ella Baker, it really has so much to do with this kind of democratic gratitude of being in a tradition of struggle, of being an agent of change and transmitter to the younger generation, which allows you to make a Pascalian leap in belief in the capacities of everyday people, because it's a kind of leap of faith that you are having in their capacity to cultivate themselves. You

don't need messianic leadership; you don't need a revolutionary party; you don't need professionals and experts coming in
from the academy and telling you x, y, and z. You are in conversation with them, but they don't need to have an elevated
status. But it's that democratic gratitude on the one hand, and
it is that deep spirituality that actually I think was rooted initially in Baker's early Black Baptist experiences and the model
of her blessed mother, and then the depth of her belief, in the
cause, what she calls the cause of humanity.

CHB: Indeed, it wasn't just a particular cause, as important as the
civil rights movement she had actually worked for was to
her—she was in the NAACP for some twenty years. She said
explicitly that she worked for so many organizations and campaigns, more than thirty, I think, but in truth, she said, she
worked for a movement that is greater than all these particular struggles.[10]

CW: It would be wonderful if one were to meet members of a progressive organization and you asked them who do you work
for and they would say not the organization, whatever it is,
but I'm working for the freedom of human beings around the
world; I'm working for the cause; I'm working for justice, and
this organization is a means toward that end, this organization
is a vehicle or conduit through which my commitment to the
cause for humanity, the cause for social justice, the cause for
human dignity, beginning with poor and working people and
those Frantz Fanon called the wretched of the earth. She always kept that in mind. So even when it comes to the kind of
organizational chauvinism—organizations clash because they
are trying to gain access to a certain kind of turf on a terrain—she would look at that and say, "Oh, you are missing the
point." SCLC people wanted to know how she could make
that move from interim executive director of SCLC—before
Wyatt Tee Walker was to take it over in 1960—how she could
make that move so smoothly from SCLC to SNCC, when
the tension between SCLC and SNCC was so intense. She
is the only one who carries over and becomes a hero for the

young people. She's already an older person; the young people trusted her.

CHB: She never attempted to tell them to do it her way, but she
listened and engaged in what you would call, I assume, a Socratic dialogue.

CW: Oh, absolutely, a Socratic dialogue in the deepest sense. I'll
never forget Bob Moses recalling one of the meetings where it
was clear that SNCC was collapsing. It was right near the end,
very intense conversations, and Ella Baker was sitting there.
You could just see the internal pain, and more and more, the
young people were looking toward her to intervene to save and
rescue the organization. And she just sat there and listened,
and afterward people were saying like, "Damn, if Martin and
the others had been there, they would have come to our rescue. Can't you see this is the only way? We need this almost
Hobbesian sovereign, you know what I mean, to help impose
some order, so we can sustain an organization that we worked
so hard for. We don't understand your silence." And she said,
"It's up to you. It's up to you all. You all got to work it out. I
am just one voice." And of course, someone said, "We want
to hear that one voice!" Sometimes, you know—Bob Moses is
like this, too—sometimes you just wonder whether they could
be too reticent and too reluctant to speak. Their democratic
humility is never false, but their democratic receptivity could
be more balanced with bold democratic voicing.

CHB: She was convinced that if a movement cannot find a way from
within the group to go on, then it is no longer relevant. It
has to be replaced. It might have had its time, done its work.
And when she moved from SCLC to SNCC, it was in part, I
think, because she was frustrated, owing to what you talked
about earlier about hierarchy and the male chauvinism, which,
for example, never allowed her to have this post of executive
director fully. It was always interim. She showed that she could
do it, but she was a woman, so it was not acceptable to the
male-dominated group at that time. So she moved, because

she had more confidence in the radical thinking of the young, and she thought it was needed at that moment. Now, within SNCC, there were different developments, and I think at one point—it may have been earlier in their development than the moment you talked about—two groups within SNCC fought each other, and at that point she tried to reach a compromise with this idea: let's have two strains; let's have two subgroups that follow their agenda, and let's see how far this takes us. And it was accepted at the time, but that was probably already foreshadowing a conflict within the group, and she would have been the last one to fight for something that she thought, "Well, if it can't sustain itself, it is not worth fighting for. It has to be replaced. This is what a revolutionary process is about."

CW: And she understood it so very, very well. Again, that has something to do with the kind of revolutionary patience that she had which I am associating also with this radical democratic receptivity that Romand Coles has talked about with such insight. You know, we do have to pay tribute in so many ways to Joanne Grant and Barbara Ransby and Romand Coles and others who really have not just thought through and theorized but thrown their hearts and minds and souls into the radical democratic praxis of Ella Baker.[11] Because on the one hand, she seemed to be rather reluctant to write a book about what she was doing, or write a memoir about her life, all of those things, in some ways mitigating against her commitment to radical democratic praxis, and yet we know there was always a theoretical dimension to it,[12] because she was just so brilliant; she was so reflective, introspective, and spiritual all at the same time.

CHB: To come back to one of your points as to education and how it might work when you try to educate a group not by preaching, not by lecturing from top to bottom, but by engaging in a dialogue—it takes a long time to begin with.

CW: Absolutely. I think that the major limitation of Ella Baker's global historical work and witness is the tremendous clash between democratic time and market time. With the commodification of cultures around the world, most of us, if not all of us, live in market time, even if we are on the margins of the larger imperial system of our day. And market time is fast; it's quick; it's push-button; it's 24/7 cycles of media. Whereas democratic time, which has to do with the kind of organizing and mobilizing Baker was doing, requires a long revolution, in the language of the great Raymond Williams.[13] And it's a long memory, in the language of Mary Frances Berry and John Blassingame, who wrote that wonderful book together, *Long Memory*.[14] So, you get a long revolution, a long memory, a long struggle within democratic time; in market time: quick, quick, quick, quick, quick. And the charismatic leadership is very much tied to market time. It's fast, you see. You want to get the cameras to see those precious kids get mistreated in Birmingham, boom, flash. It's all around the world, quick, quick, quick. Congress has to do something; the president has responded, telephone calls. And Martin knew that he had to live in some way between times, right on the thin edge between democratic and market time. But that slow, bottom-up, democratic organizing that Ella talked about has always been associated with some of the best social movements.

For example, Saul Alinsky, who in some ways we associate these days with the Industrial Areas Foundation of my dear brother Ernesto Cortés[15]—they have been at this form of organizing in democratic time for thirty years, and you end up with some elected officials and local groups,[16] two elected city councilmen, and people say, "Damn, a whole generation and you got a union in place." And of course, they have done amazing things in terms of raising consciousness, because it's not just reflected in the electoral process. But from a market perspective, of course, you might say, "Eh, that's all you come up with in twenty-five years? When we got all these babies who die, we got all these struggles going on, and that's the best we can do?" And I think that's the challenge, maybe limitation is too strong a word, but it's a real challenge for the genius of Ella Baker.

CHB: And even more so today than in her time, because of the speed.

CW: Yes, hyper-capitalism, absolutely.

CHB: So the question is, how can change be brought about with the powers that be? Should we, like anarchists, work locally and change the system on the level of the local community and go on from there, and change it radically at a particular place and in a particular moment and thus make at least a small difference, rather than battling and struggling in market time and being shot dead or defeated? The question becomes the more urgent when we look at what we are fighting for and against right now and compare it to the past, when Ella Baker—just as you and many others still do in the present—talked about poverty and civil rights.

CW: But I wonder—here my own view becomes more manifest and pressing—when you look at it from the perspective of the powers that be, what do they find most threatening? That's always a measure, you see. And they are threatened by any serious challenge to their oligarchic power, to their profit-driven economic system and their cultural forms of distraction that keep the masses pacified. And I think that in the long run, they are more threatened by Ella Baker's mode of engagement; in the short run, they are more threatened by Martin King's mode of engagement, because for the FBI and the CIA and other repressive apparatuses in the nation-state in which we live, that patience and that receptivity, you can keep track of that more easily, and you can infiltrate it quicker,[17] whereas if the people who don't have revolutionary consciousness but do have a love for one leader, they see that leader shot down and mistreated, they are more likely to rebel. Now, that's not revolutionary action; that's rebellion.[18] And given the constraints of the system, in which electoral politics is so much dominated by big money and so forth, it's the rebellions that have played a fundamental role in getting concessions from the powers that be, more so than the long-term organizing that's quiet on the margins, hardly visible. When you have two hundred cities going up in flames, the powers that be have to concede something. They could go fascist and say, "No concessions at all," or they can be moderate and say, "We have to give a little bit. We have to be open for the expansion of the middle class. We have to bring in a relatively privileged people from the working class: women, Black folk, brown folk, red folk, or whatever." This middle class of color is a *lumpen-bourgeoisie* beneath the wealthier white bourgeoisie.

But I do think that—this is the Chekhov in me, of course[19]—I think that the cycles of domination and the cycles of death and the cycles of dogmatism are so deeply entrenched in human history, that more than likely the best we can do is to break the cycle. And even what we call revolution, when you think you really have broken the cycle in, say, the Soviet Union, Cuba, or what have you, the same cycle comes right back in new clothing. The men are heroic against the white supremacist powers, but look what they're doing to the women, and the straights are heroic, but look what they are doing to the gay brothers and lesbian sisters and bisexuals and transsexuals and so forth. Or the elderly seem to be heroic, but look how they are demeaning the youth—these different kinds of cycles. And, so, I am not suggesting that there are no breakthroughs or progress or betterment or amelioration, but Ella Baker is most relevant because she tells a fundamental truth about the need for democratic organizing. King becomes highly relevant in our time, less relevant than Ella in regard to democratic leadership. Ella Baker and Fannie Lou Hamer stand above Martin Luther King in their democratic existentialism; their democratic leadership and horizontal organization stand above his messianic leadership and hierarchical organization. All three have a love supreme for the people that is so visible, that cannot be denied. King's organizing fits well with market time and his murder generated massive outrage, and you end up with a real rupture in the cycle. It's not a change in the system, but it's a rupture in the cycle, and the powers that be have to make some concessions, you see. But deep democratic revolution requires the democratic existentialism of Ella Baker and Fannie Lou Hamer.

CHB: Back to the kind of organizing Baker practiced. I think one could distinguish even within her work the very patient, slow-pace education of groups and what follows from that and what she herself, I think, saw as the need for a more radical pushing of groups. That's why, to go back to that, she joined the youth and cofounded SNCC, because she hoped that, from that more radical group, less bourgeois, less concerned with respectability, and more radical in a broad sense, that something like a rupture might result, even out of a group. I think that was her hope. So she tries to do both, patient grass-roots organizing and speeding up the process through work with radical groups, which I think is particularly difficult. And one would have to ask oneself how far she got, but do you see the possibility of radicalizing groups, too, so that they work like charismatic leaders?

CW: Yes. You see, in my own view, that kind of crucial radicalizing of the group toward a more revolutionary consciousness becomes one of the essential elements in the rebellion. That is to say, when the rupture takes place and the system must just stop and respond rather than just keep going on and trying to deny the suffering of the people who are revolting. Now, whether in the end that generates the kind of system change that she wanted and I want, I don't know. But in my more Chekhovian thinking, I can see not so much a cycle but a spiralling, where these systems of domination and oligarchies reemerge and the hierarchies reemerge, the anti-democratic forms reemerge, and that revolutionary consciousness is this deep democratic consciousness suspicious of those hierarchies, suspicious of those oligarchies, and so on.

Here Clausewitz's philosophy of war[20] plays an important role for me—not in a moral sense but a crass political sense, in terms of just how cruel the struggle for power is and how gangster-like these thugs are who run things at the very, very top, who would kill anybody and do anything to reproduce their power. You see, you look at the number of times Martin went to jail, while Ella hardly ever went to jail—stark contrast! And when you talk about rupture, you're talking about a threefold moment of, first, hitting the streets—and Ella is already in the streets—and, second, being willing to go to jail, and, third, being willing to be killed. If you don't have those three elements, you don't have a movement. That is to say, you have to have people who are willing to take that kind of risk, and you need the blood of those martyrs to help fertilize the movement, which is not to view those martyrs as instruments, because they are still human beings, but that's the historical process. That's how bloody it is. It is just a fact. It can't be denied. When you juxtapose Ella Baker to Martin King, you see, one of the reasons why Martin's death generated the rebellions it did was because all three of those moments were satisfied and in a way in which they were not satisfied for Ella. Now, that's partly again a matter of both gender and theory. She called him the "Great One" and had her powerful critiques, but she never denied his deep love for the people, you see, just like she had that deep love for the people, as everybody who knew her, like Bernice Reagon, one of the great artists of the movement,[21] would say over and over again. But that's an interesting contrast when you think about it.

CHB: But I still wonder about certain aspects of that contrast. Now, Ella Baker could not have been the charismatic leader,[22] so the group did not feel represented by her. No one could have that identifying moment one had with King. So when you say this is threefold—you go to the street, you go to jail, and you get killed—she would not have gotten killed; it was not very likely. But does that really mean that revolt can only happen with the model of the charismatic leader? If we look again at the Occupy movement today, people go to the street; they are willing to go to jail; they are even willing to die. But there is no charismatic figure, and yet you have these three moments, or would you still make a distinction as to their effectiveness?

CW: That's an interesting question. You see, I think that when you satisfy all three of those moments in light of the Ella Baker model, I am not so sure that the death or deaths that take place could have the same galvanizing effect as the death of a highly charismatic, highly visible figure who touched the hearts, minds, and souls of people, you see. And because precious ordinary people are in a condition of catastrophe and wrestling with desperation, for them to break out of a mindset that is deferential to the powers that be, it is only a love that they have for someone they identified with, who was out there speaking on their behalf, that has the power to move them to rebellion.

CHB: It's very interesting, because both models work with the insight that it is not enough to understand a problem and then act politically; you need the emotional involvement. In the first model, we have the love toward a leader that you identify with and who acts for you. Now, Ella Baker would have said, "This is not my model, because it harms the potential activity of the group, of the masses, if they delegate. So I want the other model. What then is my means of arousing emotion? It is personal connections. People have to interconnect." And, again, you can say, and rightly so, it is so slow; it takes time to bring this process to a point that it becomes efficient. But to her it was the emotional binding of people that she would say is needed, but it works differently and, again, slower, not in market time.

CW: Exactly. I think, in the end, we have to say that there should be no discussion of Martin Luther King Jr. without Ella Baker, which is to say they are complementary. These two figures, voices, tendencies in the Black freedom movement, and particularly in the human freedom movement in general, they say something to young people these days in the age of Obama. See, Obama ends up being the worst example of messianic leadership, captured by a vicious system that is oligarchic domestically and imperialistic globally and uses the resonances of this precious freedom struggle as a way of legitimating himself in the eyes of both the Black people and the mainstream Americans, and acting as if as community organizer he has some connection to Ella Baker, which is absurd and ludicrous in light of him running this oligarchic system and being so proud of heading the killing machine of US imperial powers. So that when young people—who now find themselves in an even more desperate situation given the present crisis—think about the legacy of Martin King and the legacy of Ella Baker in the age of Obama, it compounds the misunderstandings and misconstructions, and sabotages the intellectual clarity and political will necessary to create the kind of change we need. To use jazz metaphors, what we need would be the expression and articulation of different tempos and different vibrations and different actions and different witnesses, so it's antiphonal; it's call-and-response, and in the call-and-response, there are Ella Baker–like voices tied to various kinds of deep democratic witnesses that have to do with everyday people organizing themselves. And then you've got the Martin-like voices that are charismatic, which are very much tied to a certain kind of messianic leadership, which must be called into question, which must be democratized, which must be de-patriarchalized. And yet they are part of this jazz combo.[23]

CHB: But it means we need to turn our attention to Ella Baker, because historically she has had—and understandably so, given the strong effect of charismatic leaders—she has had much less attention in the historical reception of the movement.

CW: Yes. Absolutely. And again, one of the ironies—I never met Ella Baker, but I recall taking my class down to the film *Fundi* when I was at Union Theological Seminary thirty years ago.[24] I was overwhelmed by it. Oh I was overwhelmed by it. It hit me so hard, because I just so much resonated with Ella. I could see Curtis Mayfield in her; I could see Bessie Smith in her; I could see the great gospel artist Shirley Caesar in her; I could see Aretha Franklin in her. And nothing moves me more than that level of artistic engagement with suffering and transfiguring it into vision and witness. I said to myself, "Ella Baker is one of the most charismatic figures I've seen on film, and yet she is fighting against charisma"; you know what I mean. So, what happens is, her critique of charisma goes hand in hand with an enactment of a kind of quiet, unassuming charisma, which swept me away.

Now, it could be that I am just tied to charisma in various forms, but I do think that you get ordinary people like Louis Armstrong; this brother is charismatic—and a genius—to the core. Now, with Ella Baker, you see it in the way she interacts. You look in her eyes and you get a sense of how she is reading people when she is silent that has its own kind of charisma, you know. Maybe it's a charisma to be deployed in democratic time in the service of the self-organization of everyday people. Martin's charisma is more usable in a market time, though it is just as genuine as Ella's charisma. I think, in the end, Ella's is probably closer to my own soul, but in terms of how you deal with this vicious system in which we find ourselves, you can see why Martin's love, which is continuous with Ella's love, becomes indispensable, and his death is nothing but an extension of his love. I mean, Martin's death is nothing but the love-ethic at work, just as Ella's long-distance struggles are extensions of a love-ethic at work, and both of them encountered that love-ethic in the Black family, initially in the Black church. And yet both, in the end, were scandalized by the Black church, which is to say they both end up on the margins of it, even as they are products of it. For brother Martin and sister Ella, it is a privilege to live and die for everyday people.

CHB: But for reasons that have nothing to do with their spirituality but rather with their outspoken political opinions in terms of how, for example, they use the word *socialism*.[25]

CW: That's right. Explicitly, publicly.

CHB: Yes, and the demand for the change of the system—they re-
semble each other very much in what they demand, certainly
the later King and, well, maybe even the early Baker,[26] but
certainly the later King.

CW: That's very true. Now, the speech that she gave in defense
of Puerto Rican independence in Madison Square Garden is
something that the film *Fundi* and other scholars have made
much of, and there she engages in explicit talk about colonialism, imperialism, some things that she had always talked about
but that now were more publicly projected. And to be publicly
associated with a Puerto Rican independence movement—of
the great Pedro Albizu Campos and Lolita Lebrón—that was
perceived to be an extension of the kind of terrorist attack on
the US Congress.[27] You know, for anybody, let alone a Black
woman, to be associated with that kind of movement, which
in the eyes of the public was nothing but crude terrorism, required a level of courage, which brings us back to that willingness to take a risk even in her own quiet—and in this case, not
so quiet—way, because she was quite eloquent in her speech
in front of thousands of people in Madison Square Garden.
Absolutely. Absolutely.

Malcolm X, 1964

CHAPTER FIVE

Revolutionary Fire

MALCOLM X

We agreed that a conversation about Malcolm X was a must, although he is undoubtedly the most controversial of the Black prophetic figures. Among too many white Americans he is often seen as a proponent of reversed racism, if not of hatred and violence. But even the Black community has been divided in assessing his status as a political leader. While the working poor respected his eloquence and honesty, and the "old" middle class was horrified, the "new" lower-middle class, especially students, greatly admired his rhetoric and sincerity. In part, the controversy is due to the continuous juxtaposition between Malcolm X and Martin Luther King Jr., a false opposition that is based on one-sided public images and that has led to a sanitized Martin and a demonized Malcolm, a gross mistake that overlooks what they share in common and how much they overlap.

In the fall of 2012, Occupy Wall Street was evicted from public spaces in a concerted action by law enforcement all over the United States, from New York City to Oakland. When we met in January 2013 for our dialogue on Malcolm X, it seemed to be the perfect time to discuss his revolutionary fire and its legacy among the younger generation.

CHRISTA BUSCHENDORF: You have repeatedly written about Malcolm X. In *Prophesy Deliverance!*, for example, you positioned Malcolm X as "the transitional figure who stands between King and the Black Marxists."[1] In your essay "Malcolm X and

Black Rage," you compared him with both his mentor Elijah Muhammad and Martin Luther King Jr., claiming that "Malcolm X articulated black rage in a manner unprecedented in American history. His style of communicating this rage bespoke a boiling urgency and an audacious sincerity." And you went on to state: "His profound commitment to affirm black humanity at any cost and his tremendous courage to accent the hypocrisy of American society made Malcolm X the prophet of black rage—then and now."[2] As to Malcolm X's cultural and political influence on yourself and Black fellow students at Harvard, you stressed in our dialogue on Martin King his attraction in terms of his style, his swagger, in contrast to the much revered, but to the youth less appealing, respectable King. And you pointed out that you would identify with Malcolm X's political vision rather than listening to the voice of the "Great Man who died for us,"[3] a viewpoint, as you add, that was to shift in the next decade. In fact, more recently you seem to have been highlighting the relevance of King. How then would you assess the impact of Malcolm X on African American political struggle and your own fight for justice and freedom today?

CORNEL WEST: Malcolm X is the great figure of revolutionary *parrhesia* in the Black prophetic tradition. The term *parrhesia* goes back to line 24A of Plato's *Apology*, where Socrates says, the cause of my unpopularity was my *parrhesia*, my fearless speech, my frank speech, my plain speech, my unintimidated speech. Malcolm is unique among the figures in the prophetic tradition to the degree to which he was willing to engage in unintimidated speech in public about white supremacy. We have had a number of Black figures who have done that in the Black context, but not in public the way Malcolm did. In that sense, he represents the standard. He reminds me of jazz musicians like Charles Mingus, who are always tied to the underdog, always looking at the world from below, but speaking so clearly.

Now what was he saying? Brother Malcolm begins where Marcus Garvey[4] left off, which is to say he represents a Black Nationalist tradition. But he is a revolutionary within that Black Nationalist tradition. And, like Garvey, he begins with the idea that the world has made being Black a crime—I intend to make it a virtue. White supremacy had told Black people that Black history is a curse, Black hope is a joke, and Black freedom is a pipe-dream, and you are locked in; you are trapped in a white-supremacist maze or labyrinth, and there is no way out. And Marcus Garvey, Elijah Muhammad, and the others came along and said: "The Negro is unafraid." So what Malcolm does is, he begins with this notion of the world making being Black a crime. He responds to this condition of being cursed and trapped by courageously exemplifying what it is and means to say: "I am unafraid. I will speak my mind." He is able to do so because of the love of Elijah Muhammad. Malcolm Little was a gangster, a street-gangster and hustler. And in the cell in Massachusetts,[5] he feels the love of the Honorable Elijah Muhammad—who is, of course, often viewed as a hater because he did believe that white people were devils, and he is wrong about that.[6] But Elijah Muhammad had a deep love of Black people, and he loved Malcolm Little into giving him the self-confidence to become Malcolm X.

Now, back to Garvey. Garvey also said that as long as Black people live in America, most of them will live lives of ruin and disaster, especially the poor and working class. Malcolm took that very seriously. When he looked at Black life in America, he saw wasted potential; he saw unrealized aims; he saw ruin and disaster. He saw forms of self-hatred and self-destruction running amok. So he is building on this Black Nationalist tradition that says, "America you have a weak will to justice when it comes to Black people and poor people. America, we have no disappointment in you because we have no expectations of you. You have no soul, you have no conscience when it comes to the plight of Black people, either enslaved, Jim Crowed, ghettoized, hated, despised, lynched, subjugated, whatever." This Black rage, viewed through the narrow lens of the American mainstream as Black revenge, sits at the center of Malcolm's soul. And there is just no one like him in terms of having the courage to risk life and limb to speak such painful—not just unsettling in the Socratic sense, but painful—truths about America, truths that are so difficult to come to terms with that they seem to be too much for the country. It's unbearable for the country to really look at all the rape, the violation, and the exploitation of Black people over four hundred years. It echoes Patrice Lumumba, when he told the king of the former Belgian Congo: "We shall never forget these scars, no matter how much reconciliation, no matter how much integration even, we shall never forget these scars."[7] That's Malcolm.

It reminds me of Faulkner when he says: "Memory believes before knowing remembers."[8] Memory of scars, memory of lynching, memory of being despised and spit on, rebuked and scorned—it's not a victim's mentality, as my right-wing brothers and sisters would put it, because there is and ought to be Jewish memory of pogroms, Jewish memory of Shoah and Holocaust; there is and ought to be Indigenous peoples' memory of dispossession of land and genocidal attack. It is that fundamental role of memory that Malcolm always invoked.[9] And to think that someone in a brief twelve-and-a-half years of his ministry could have had this kind of impact at the level of psyche and spirit is unique in modern history. Malcolm was a revolutionary prophet in speech and in spirit, and I think we need to hear him now as much as we need to hear Martin and Ella and Du Bois.

CHB: Malcolm X said that "the best thing that a person can be is sincere."[10] I think his sincerity is something that also made him so convincing to Blacks when they listened to him, because it was clear he would not put on a show, he would not engage in any sweet talk, but he would stand for what he presented to them.

CW: That's exactly right. The young hip-hop generation talks about "keeping it real." Malcolm was as real as it gets. James Brown talks about "make it funky." Malcolm would never de-odorize his discourse; it was always: "Bring in the funk, bring in the truth, bring in the reality." There is a fundamental sense in which Malcolm specialized in de-niggerizing Negroes. He took the nigger out of them. To niggerize a people is to make them afraid and ashamed and scared and intimidated, so that they are deferential to the powers that be. They scratch when it doesn't itch; they laugh when it ain't funny. They wear the mask, as Paul Laurence Dunbar wrote in his great poem.[11] And Malcolm came along and said, "No. I will take that nigger out of you. I'm gonna take it out of you." There is a wonderful motto on Elijah Muhammad's newspaper, founded by Malcolm X: "Islam dignifies." A niggerized people must be dignified. And if they are dignified in the right way and take that nigger out of themselves, they can stand up like human beings, with a steeliness in their backs and a heartiness in their hearts and a fortitude in their soul that allows them to think for themselves and work for themselves in the name of a self-respect and self-determination that was required if Black freedom was not to be a pipe dream, if Black history was not to be a curse, if Black hope was not to be a joke, and if being Black was not to be a crime.

CHB: It is an interesting strategy, if you think of the relation between the established who define you as an outsider and how difficult it is to get out of the range of the defining power. So what do you do? You reach out to another tradition, in Malcolm X's case, Islam, and that tradition gives you the possibility of a different self-definition in turn. But is there not at the same time a certain problem, if you then operate within a tradition that is not the common one within the Black community?

CW: Absolutely. Because you don't have any roots that resonate deeply in the culture of the people that you are speaking to. Islam did not have any deep roots in the history of Black people the way Christianity did. That's one of the reasons why Marcus Garvey always remained a Christian. His father, Marcus Sr., was very isolated but a great man; he always stood straight in Jamaica. His mother was Methodist. Garvey himself allowed for Muslims, atheists, different kinds of Christians to constitute his movement. But he had that deep Christian sensibility, whereas Malcolm, coming out of Elijah, went radically against the grain. He would identify with Christians like Nat Turner and John Brown and some of the great insurrectionists, or even the Deacons for Defense, who had their guns to defend themselves in North Carolina, with Robert Williams that influenced the Black Panther Party later on.[12] They were Christians coming out of the churches, but Malcolm, Elijah, they were starting something that was new in the States.

CHB: But not central.

CW: That's right. You know I have had wonderful dialogues with my dear brother Minister Louis Farrakhan, and I would push him on the issues of patriarchy and homophobia, anti-Semitism, and he always pushed me in his own powerful way.[13] But I used to tell him that the Nation of Islam could never become a mass movement among Black people because there is no music in their ritual. And music has really been the fundamental means by which Black people have been able to preserve sanity and dignity and, at our best, integrity. And to have no music in your ritual is an over-reaction against what Elijah Muhammad understood to be the naïve emotionalism of many Black churches. We should remember that Elijah Muhammad was Reverend Elijah Poole in the Baptist church before he was a Muslim, so he had his own Black Baptist roots, as it were. But he wanted to look outside to get a different vantage point. Christianity was, in the view of Elijah Muhammad and Malcolm X, a tool of the white man; it was an extension of white supremacy. You had the white Jesus looking like Michelangelo's uncle on the wall, rather than the Palestinian Jew that he was with a swarthy complexion and linked to Northern Africa as well as the Middle East. And they were right about that. Christianity had been whitewashed and Europeanized in a fundamental way, and there was no doubt that the white supremacy in the Christianity that the slaves appropriated was pervasive. Yet the prophetic tradition within the Christian context was able to listen, to resonate with much of what Malcolm X was talking about, even as we remained Christian. The theological genius of James Cone is the best example of the Christian response to Malcolm.[14]

CHB: I think, in terms of tactics, Malcolm X was so clever as to combine Muslim belief and Christian belief, in that in his speeches he would use Christian stories from the Bible, which were more familiar to his audience.

CW: Absolutely. And I think both the Honorable Elijah Muhammad and Malcolm X always looked at the world from below, echoes of the twenty-fifth chapter of Matthew: What you do for the least of these—the prisoner, the poor, the stranger, the widow, the fatherless, the motherless, the weak, the vulnerable—has lasting value. Even as Black Muslims, they could resonate with that theme, so they invoked Hebrew prophets, Isaiah, Amos; they invoked Jesus, emphasizing that sense of coming from below, looking at the world from below. One of my favorite formulations of Malcolm X is the epigraph in my chapter "The Crisis of Black Leadership" in *Race Matters*, where he tells the white mainstream: "You all say you respect me. If you can't respect the brother and sister on the block, the Black brother and sister on the block, then you don't really respect me."[15] And that's missing these days among most Black leaders. They think they are respected in some isolated, individualistic way as a Black person, and yet their second cousin is despised and held in contempt by the same white people or white establishment that respects them. And Malcolm says: "Wait a minute, this is a contradiction. Something wrong is going on here. Of course, we are individuals. We understand that. But the ways in which you separate me from my brother and sister on the block is just a way of viewing me as exceptional, incorporating me and still turning your eye or being indifferent toward my folk, my own family, community, slice of humanity." Malcolm would never, ever sell out to the powers that be. There would never be enough money, position, power, whatever that would allow him to violate his integrity and what I would call his magnanimity. And that's what makes Malcolm stand out these days, because everybody is up for sale, everything is up for sale. And if Malcolm were around and looked and saw all of these folk who have sold out he'd say: "I didn't know there was such a mass movement of house Negroes."

Who would have thought that the expansion of the Black middle class would lead toward a re-niggerization of Black professionals, because that is really what you have. You have Black professionals who have big money, a lot of prosperity, but are still scared, intimidated, have low self-respect, don't take a stand, don't want to tell the truth about the situation, let alone say, "If you don't respect the brother and sister on the block, the ones you send into prison, then you don't respect me." All they want is position, status, and cash. You see, Malcolm is too much of a challenge to them. That's another reason why we need him, because he shakes us, doesn't allow us to sell out in that way.

CHB: I'd like to come back to the point you make as to the importance of music. As far as I know, Malcolm X—at least during the phase when he was a member of the Nation of Islam— would not often refer to music or use musical metaphors, probably owing to the restrictions imposed by the leaders. And yet, one associates him in his appearance, in his rhetoric with music, with the tradition of jazz, especially.

CW: Malcolm was music in motion; he was Black music in motion; he was jazz in motion, and, of course, jazz has improvisation, swing, and the blues, as brother Wynton Marsalis says, those three fundamental elements. Malcolm could be improvisational; he could be so lyrical and so funny all at the same time, and in the next minute shift and be serious and push you against the wall. The way he spoke had a swing to it, had a rhythm to it; it was a call and response with the audience that you get with jazz musicians. And he was the blues. Blues is associated with catastrophe, and Malcolm would say over and over again: "You are not going to get something detached and disinterested from anybody who is sitting on the stove and the stove is burning their behind, no, they're going to holler out, they are going to respond deeply and viscerally."[16] He never forgot the Black folk on the stove. He never forgot the prison system: Black folk on the stove. Massive unemployment: Black folk on the stove. Indecent housing: Black folk on the stove. Inadequate healthcare: Black folk on the stove. And from the very beginning, from slavery to Jim Crow, so that the sense of catastrophe, the sense of emergency, the sense of urgency, the sense of needing to get it out, to cry out, to shout, somehow allowed that fire inside of his bones to be expressed with power and with vision. He never lost that. He never, ever lost that. The great Amiri Baraka has the same fire—literary genius, spiritual warrior, a Black revolutionary who never sold out. And that's so rare these days.

When you think about the legacy of Malcolm, you think, for example, of the great Reverend Walter Newton of Monroe, Louisiana, pastor of Bethel Baptist church.[17] He was full of fire. His son, Huey Newton, was full of fire, too. Yes, Huey was a preacher's kid. Walter was just like Malcolm's father, he was known to be always demonstrating, wouldn't allow his wife to work in the white households, would stand in front of the police telling them the truth. That's what Huey was exposed to when he was young. And Huey understood Malcolm's spirit. And so did the Black Panther Party, Bobby Seale,[18] Ericka Huggins,[19] and so many others. They understood Malcolm's spirit. The same is true of Amiri Baraka. Malcolm changed that brother's life from Le Roi Jones to Amiri Baraka.[20] There was something in Malcolm's sincerity, something in his integrity and his willingness to live and die that hit people so. He hit me hard too. Malcolm means the world to me, because he was someone with a deep love for people, in his case, especially, a love for Black people, and a willingness to speak the truth knowing that he would be crucified, knowing he would be demonized, knowing that he would be misunderstood, misconceived and yet continuing on in the Black context as well as the larger national and international context. And for someone to say I'm gonna bring the US government before the United Nations for the violation of human rights[21]—wow. Lord, Lord, that's my kind of brother!

CHB: I think, in a way, you break his message down to a core that would then also allow you to make the connection with the other figures, whereas in public discourse Malcolm X is usually separated from them owing to his demonization. In fact, the way you talked about why he is so important to you, you might even exchange the name and put in Martin Luther King, and there would be so many resonances, despite the differences with regard to certain issues.

CW: That's true. I think James Cone's great book on Martin and Malcolm is still the best juxtaposition we have.[22] He understands that the two go hand in hand. You can't talk about the one without the other. As for me, Malcolm has a revolutionary fire that Martin didn't have; Martin has a moral fire from the very beginning that Malcolm didn't get until later. Malcolm's love for Black people is so strong and so intense that early on it leads him to call white folk devils and give up on them, and I think he is wrong about that. Martin never did that, but Martin doesn't have the revolutionary fire that Malcolm had until the very end of his life. And by revolutionary fire I mean understanding the system under which we live, the capitalistic system, the imperial tentacles, the American empire, the disregard for life, the willingness to violate law, be it international law or domestic law. Malcolm understood that from very early on, and it hit Martin so hard that he does become a revolutionary in his own moral way later in his short life, whereas Malcolm had the revolutionary fire so early in life. It's just that he had to continually grow into his analysis of the system, when he embraces critiques of imperialism and capitalism, and he just tells the truth: "It looks like vultures to me."[23] He just lays it out.

Now, Malcolm wasn't talking that way in the 1950s, because he hadn't been exposed to it. But he never allows the analysis of the system to override or displace his understanding of the psyches, the souls, and the culture of Black people. You have to hold both at the same time, your analysis of the system—capitalism, imperialism, patriarchy, homophobia, these days, the ecological catastrophe owing to the capitalist domination—but at the same time, the need for an unleashing of the fire of the soul and an acknowledgment of the power of the spirit that fortifies us in order to fight. You can't be a warrior or a soldier without having your spirit intact, without having your sense of self-respect, self-regard, and self-esteem intact, and Malcolm always understood this fundamental truth.

CHB: The fact that he would keep the systemic analysis in the background was in part probably due to the restrictions of the Nation of Islam in terms of political engagement. He was not supposed—

CW: To be too politically involved. I hear what you are saying. The thing is, Elijah Muhammad did give Malcolm more freedom than he gave the other ministers, partly because Malcolm was just so charismatic, attracting so much attention. But at the same time, it's also true that Elijah Muhammad's own programs were not revolutionary programs at all—despite their powerful impact on many Black people, especially young Black men.

CHB: Malcolm stood out in that regard. But he becomes more politicized, consciously speaking about the system, about capitalism, later, after his break with Elijah Muhammad. What is interesting, though, in your talking about Malcolm is that you don't seem to rely on that break in your interpretation. As important as the change in Malcolm is—and I am sure you agree that it is—what you are saying is that there is a continuity that we must not overlook.

CW: I think that Malcolm X's break with Elijah Muhammad and
      the Nation of Islam was primarily driven by his deep love for
      Black people, and he did not see the Nation of Islam speak-
      ing to the suffering of Black people in the way that he would
      have liked. Now, we know there is a personal issue in terms
      of Elijah Muhammad's relations with women and so forth,
      but politically and ideologically, Malcolm was driven into a
      more radical direction because he could not accept some of
      the theology of the Nation of Islam, that part that was still
      waiting for the mother plane to arrive, waiting for the reign
      of the white man to come to an end, which was not princi-
      pally a matter of Black action but still divine action. So that
      even given Elijah Muhammad's critique of Christian pie-in-
      the-sky theology, he still had an otherworldly element in
      his Black Muslim theology. And Malcolm was just more and
      more talking about human action and collective agency and
      organization on the ground.
         I think it's impossible to understand the greatness of a
      Stokely Carmichael without understanding the impact of Mal-
      colm's talk about human agency and collective insurgency,[24]
      without any reference to any kind of otherworldly powers.
      By the time you get to the Black Panther movement, SNCC
      in its last stage, and then the League of Revolutionary Black
      Workers, Ken Cockrel, General Baker, Darryl Mitchell,[25] and
      others, you see Malcolm's legacy. Other legatees of Malcolm
      X today, like Mumia Abu-Jamal[26] and Assata Shakur,[27] grand
      figures that they are—most of them are in jail; they've been
      actually in jail for twenty, thirty years—were real warriors;
      those were the real soldiers, and the counterintelligence pro-
      gram of the FBI knew these were the ones to target.[28] Roger
      Wareham of the December 12 movement[29] went to jail for so
      many years; Elombe Brath, and H. Rap Brown[30]—these are
      the ones we don't really talk about because the system ran
      them down even though they are still holding on. And yet we
      need to take them very seriously.
         There are hundreds of political prisoners right now in
      America's jails who were so taken by Malcolm's spirit that they

became warriors, and the powers that be understood them as warriors. They knew that a lot of these other middle-class leaders were not warriors; they were professionals; they were careerists. But these warriors had callings, and they have paid an incalculable and immeasurable price in those cells. Many changed their names; some became Muslims; they had that same Malcolm X–like spirit. The grand artist and legendary educator Haki Madhubuti was deeply influenced by Malcolm X,[31] and Sonia Sanchez[32] and others on the female side. The great Toni Morrison, she has got a Malcolm X spirit in her sense of being an intellectual warrior, a kind of literary soldier, as it were, even given all of the white acceptance in the establishments of our day, and I think Toni Morrison would be the first to acknowledge the tremendous impact on her of Malcolm's revolutionary sincerity and his revolutionary love and his willingness to pay the ultimate price.

CHB: In regard to organization, Malcolm X was really not as important as others we have talked about in terms of organizing, although he did his own organizing once he was independent. He founded two organizations, the Muslim Mosque Incorporated and the Organization of Afro-American Unity. We have talked about these prophetic activists in terms of organic intellectuals, so in what sense does he fit into that Gramscian model?

CW: I think that Malcolm was indeed an organic intellectual, which is to say, he was a countervailing force and a counter-hegemonic voice against the powers that be. And by using all of the various linguistic tools that touch people's souls and hearts and minds and body simultaneously, his critiques and visions connected with the people. During his life his major weapons were his fierce intellect, undeniable sincerity, and oral power of presentation. After his death his autobiography emerges as another kind of intellectual weapon. There is a sense in which Malcolm actually lives in a very powerful way among large numbers of people through the autobiography, even more than for people who saw him speak physically.

CHB: So the organizing itself would not be necessarily part of the organic intellectual?

CW: For Gramsci, the war of position includes raising the consciousness of people and motivating them to fight for justice. Malcolm specializes much more in these activities than in building and sustaining organizational structures.

CHB: Malcolm X once said if you inspire the people, if you bring them to the political sense, you don't have to worry any longer; they become active themselves.[33] So that would explain why he thought he could, through his rhetorical power, lead the path to a revolutionary spirit in the people.

CW: I think that's true. In that sense he sounds like Ella Baker. I think if Malcolm were to choose between a Luxemburgist versus a Leninist conception of organization, where a Luxemburgist would put much more stress on the radical consciousness arising among the people themselves, and the people themselves creating their own organization—the so-called spontaneity thesis, or more spontaneous forms of organization—versus Lenin, where you get professional revolutionaries who then go out and bring the masses inside of a vanguard party, then Malcolm would be highly suspicious of a Leninist orientation. He would be much closer to a Luxemburgist one.

Just before he was shot, in New York in the Audubon Ballroom, Malcolm had planned on setting up his own mosque. He was a Sunni Muslim leader. When we think what it means to be a revolutionary Muslim in this day and age, when people are looking for ways in which Islam is compatible with democracy, compatible with progressive politics, compatible with revolutionary politics, Malcolm is a looming example of that. But he was going to be a Sunni Muslim clergyman with his own mosque, reaching out with his own organizations and programs for the poor. He would have relations with left wing-organizations, but he would not be a member of left-wing organizations. It's a fascinating development that could have taken place, that could have created a paradigmatic model of what it means to be a revolutionary Muslim in the way in which King at the end of his life becomes a revolutionary Christian, and both perspectives begin more and more to overlap. Their critiques of capitalism and imperialism led the FBI and the CIA to view them and their followers as the most fundamental and formidable threat to the status quo in the history of America. There would have been nothing like it, especially at a moment when so many of the white middle-class youth were responding against the draft, responding against the Vietnam War, upset deeply with Jim Crow in the South—all converging at the same time, Good God Almighty. You have such a fiery situation for social change; there is no doubt about it.

CHB: I think this is especially true for the US, because as we said in one of our other conversations, the Black Power movement had the difficulty of being too secular, not being able to stay in contact with Black masses who did not want to hear too secular a message.

CW: That's exactly right. But it's very interesting in our present moment, where there is a rising atheistic movement in the country. Now nearly 20 percent of Americans call themselves atheists,[34] and there are various atheistic clubs and atheistic groups in the Black community as well. Secularism is becoming more widespread, and it's a fascinating thing to see. Even as a Christian I think that a lot of this atheism is very healthy, because in many ways it is a rejection of the idolatry in the dominant churches; it's a rejection of the gods—small "g"—who are being worshipped in mainstream America and in mainstream Black America, and that kind of atheism is always healthy for prophetic religious people. It's healthy precisely because it allows people to freely think for themselves and engage in wholesale rejection of forms of idolatry, and, you see, the prophetic is predicated on critiques of idolatry. It is true that my atheistic brothers and sisters do not accept conceptions of God linked to love and justice as I do. But the atheistic movement itself can be one of the carriers of the prophetic tradition in its rejections of forms of idolatry that I find very healthy.

And we haven't had enough conversation about this in the country, let alone in Black America. You think of somebody like Bill Maher, my dear brother, who has played such an important role in giving me tremendous exposure around the country and the world in his TV shows, who is a proud atheist, a progressive atheist whose prophetic witness is undeniable. We could give many other examples in terms of popular culture; we have always had a number of prophetic atheists in the academy. If my only options for belief in God were the idols of our market culture, I would be an atheist too. But the Black prophetic tradition that produced me provides rich views of God that yield moral integrity, spiritual fortitude, and political determination.

CHB: I am so surprised that you maintain secularism is on the move, whereas from a European perspective, my hunch would be that religiosity is on the move again, that there has been a major backlash as to the secular force of enlightened humanism in the last ten, twenty years or so.

CW: Things have changed; the numbers are now turning in a very different direction. The new data that just came out in 2012 reported that 18 percent of the country call themselves atheists.[35] It's a major leap; it's the highest in the history of the country. Brother Robert Ingersoll[36] and brother Clarence Darrow,[37] two exemplary atheists back in the 1910s and '20s, are coming back now with tremendous force. I love their prophetic witness.

Much of the force of Malcolm's prophetic witness is his critique of idolatry in America. And again, that coincidence of critiques of idolatry from prophetic secular figures and critiques of idolatry from prophetic revolutionary Islamic figures like Malcolm or prophetic revolutionary Christian figures like the later King is fascinating. Du Bois is secular in so many deep ways, yet as we saw, he has a profound spirituality. Frederick Douglass began as a religious man and seems to have ended up agnostic. Ella came out of the church, but she was agnostic, too, I think.

CHB: Well, I think all these prophetic figures saw what Christianity could do to the suppressed, namely to suppress them even more. It was a tool, as you said before, of white supremacy. So there was always the ambivalence about the dangers of the church as an oppressive institution on the one hand, and on the other hand, the benefits of religion that might carry you on in your struggle.

CW: That's exactly right. And although we are unable to actually do a longer reflection on the great James Baldwin, we should not overlook the sublime fact that he exemplifies the prophetic tradition in a literary form and a political form on a very high level. When he left the church, as he says in order to preach the gospel,[38] he was agnostic from fourteen years old until he died. So he had the church in his heart and in his soul in terms of love, love, love, because he is on the love train; he is a love supreme kind of brother, like the one and only John Coltrane. But Baldwin is secular in terms of any cognitive commitments to God; he is agnostic to the core.

CHB: I'd like to come to another issue that plays such a great role with all the activists, namely their stance vis-à-vis self-defense, the question as to whether to fight with military weapons or not. We have the position of nonviolence of Martin Luther King; we have Ella Baker's pacifism; and we have the notion of self-defense in the case of Malcolm, which has always been exaggerated as militancy. Where do you stand on that?

CW: Martin thought that there was something distinctive about the Negro, that we had certain peculiar spiritual gifts that allow us to withstand suffering and pain and respond by opting for a nonviolent strategy. It's almost a kind of implicit moral superiority that we had accumulated over time that didn't allow us to engage in that kind of gangster-like activity, whereas with Malcolm, you know, Malcolm would say over and over again: "I am the man you think you are. What do you think you would do after four hundred years of slavery and Jim Crow and lynching? Do you think you would respond nonviolently? What is your history like? Let's look at how you have responded when you are oppressed. George Washington—revolutionary guerrilla fighter!"[39] Malcolm was just so direct. One could easily imagine his response to Johnny Carson if he'd been on *The Tonight Show* and had been asked, "Well, what do you think about the Negro problem? What does the Negro really want?"—"Well, brother Johnny, what do *you* really want? Do you want your children to live in a safe neighborhood, do you want a job with a living wage, do you want decent health care, do you want respect for yourself and your community? There is no Negro problem. We want what you want. We are the people you think you are. If you are in our situation, what do you think you would want? And how would you go about getting it?" As has been reported, Richard Nixon says in his files: "If I was a Black man I would be head of the Black Panther Party. If I was a Black man I wouldn't put up with all this violation and exploitation. I'm Richard Nixon." And all Malcolm would say is: "Listen to the Man." You see what I mean. There is that line in Du Bois where he says that if in fact the slave insurrectionists were whites struggling against Black supremacy, they would be heroes in every corner of the European world.[40] So Malcolm was saying explicitly: "Be honest, y'all."

So when it comes to self-defense, it's a matter of "by any means necessary," as he said in the great Oxford Union Debate.[41] "Oh, my God, does that mean you pick up the gun?" "Do *you* have a history of picking up the gun? Did *you* drop the bombs on Nagasaki and Hiroshima? Whose history are we talking about? We are human beings, man. We just like you in that sense." Now Martin would come back and say, "Malcolm, you are scaring them, brother. Oh, you got them so upset. They get so scared; they gonna be harder on us now than ever." And Malcolm would say: "I'm not talking about strategy; I'm talking about the truth at this point. But Martin, we got to be honest, the community you are leading—even given your spiritual and moral ideals and vision—that's how they really think. Most of them are just scared. They are scared to the core, and as long as they stay scared, they don't even follow you in any serious way." So you can imagine the juxtaposition there.

If there was an imaginary meeting between Malcolm and Martin it would go as follows: Malcolm would say: "Brother Martin, Garvey and others have told us that the vast majority, the masses of Black people, will never be treated with dignity. They will always live lives of ruin and disaster tied to the prison system in the hoods and the projects. There might be spaces for the middle classes, but there will never be for the masses." And Martin would say: "No, I can't believe that. I just can't. We've got to redeem the soul of America." Malcolm would say: "There is no soul, Martin." "That can't be true, Malcolm." But then Martin would come back to Malcolm and say: "So what you gonna do after you tell your truths? You gonna follow Elijah and create a Black state in the Southern United States that has the same chance as a snowball in hell?" Malcolm would come back and say: "But the chance of your integration full-scale is a snowball in hell too! It's gonna be a truncated integration. It's gonna be assimilation; it's gonna be the bourgeoisification of Black people. Some may go all the way up to the White House, but even when they get to the White House, they still going to have the crack houses; they still gonna have the prison-industrial complex, and if he doesn't say a mumbling word about the new Jim Crow, that's going to get worse and worse, and unemployment will be getting worse and worse. So even with a Black person in the White House, Garvey is still right." You see.

And then Martin and Malcolm would look at each other with tears flowing down their faces because both of them love Black folk so, and they bend over and say: "Let's sing a song. Let us sing a song." You know what I mean. Maybe a little George Clinton, maybe a little Stevie Wonder. We need some

Aretha Franklin here; we need some Billie Holiday and some Sarah Vaughan and some Curtis Mayfield. "Sing a song, Martin!" And Martin would say: "We gonna go crazy." "No, we just gonna keep on pushin'." Because it ain't a question of what is at the moment credible; it's a matter of what has integrity, of what is true, what is right, and what is worthy of those who struggled and died for us and for the precious children. That's what brings Martin and Malcolm together.

That's what we need so much more now in our situation, because when you actually look at what some of the revolutionary solutions are, they seem to be so far-fetched, and usually when people see that, they say: "Let me go back to my careerism; let me go back to my individualism; let me go back to my hedonism; let me go back to my narcissism." And Martin and Malcolm, with tears flowing as they both, in their sacrificial and magnificently loving ways, say: "No, just because the solutions are far-fetched, it doesn't mean you sell your soul for a mess of pottage. That's not the conclusion. This is not only about being successful. This is fundamentally about being faithful to the freedom struggle that has brought us as far as it has."

CHB: And Ella Baker would be right there and say: "The revolutionary process takes a long, long time, and we have to have the patience to maintain it, to keep it going."

CW: That's exactly right, that revolutionary patience. Eldridge Cleaver wrote a piece years ago in a magazine on revolutionary patience. He was still a revolutionary at that time; he hadn't become a right-wing Republican. But it's a very difficult and very powerful notion of revolutionary patience, of keeping your integrity even when the rest of the world seems to want to sell everything and everybody, or buy everything and everybody.

CHB: And claiming that the problem has gone, after all.

CW: That's the denial that goes hand in hand with the careerism.

CHB: I would like to address the question of nationalism at this point, because you have been such a critic of nationalism. How does that affect your appreciation of Malcolm X?

CW: Because I am such a critic of all forms of nationalism, be they Italian, German, Ethiopian, Japanese, American, or Black nationalism, I appreciate the progressive revolutionary versions of all of those nationalisms.[42] That's why somebody like Walt Whitman still means much to me, although he is very much a nationalist. And Malcolm is a nationalist; he really is a Black Nationalist, though he represents a very revolutionary and progressive wing of it. I think nationalism is the dominant form of idolatry of modernity, and therefore internationalism and universalism for me has to be always at the center of how I think about the world and how I analyze the world. But we do come in specific human bodies, communities, nations; and therefore we do have to talk about gender and color and race, class and nation. Malcolm's internationalism is something that, especially at the end of his life, becomes highly attractive and, in the end, indispensable for any serious talk about social change. The same is true with Martin, especially at the very end. Martin actually shifts from being a US patriot to becoming a serious revolutionary internationalist.

But I have to be honest that Malcolm's revolutionary Black Nationalism is something that cannot be overlooked. Think of Manning Marable's powerful biography[43]—Manning was my very dear brother; I loved him very deeply, respected him dearly—I think that the fervor and the fire of Malcolm's revolutionary Black Nationalism doesn't come fully through in the text. I think that the book Herb Boyd and Amiri Baraka and others published in response to Marable's book is a very important dialogue.[44] They make that point—and they are on to a very important insight there—that you can't view Malcolm through the categories of mainstream leftist analysis. Malcolm as Social Democrat—that does not capture his fervor and his fire. That's why I started this interview with Garvey, because Garvey was not a revolutionary Black Nationalist the way Malcolm was. But there is no Malcolm X without Marcus Garvey. There is no Malcolm X without Elijah Muhammad. It's inconceivable. It's impossible given his own personal pilgrimage, his own individual trajectory into becoming the great prophetic revolutionary figure that he was, and therefore we really have to wrestle with this issue of nationalism. How could it be that this Black Nationalist tradition dishes out such remarkable revolutionary fervor and insight?

CHB: I think this is true of all our prophetic figures: they are more complex than we sometimes can deal with. We have to look at the various aspects, because it's also true that Malcolm X did have notions of socialism, certainly of anti-capitalism. To come back to nationalism, I think what it achieves is it transcends the individualism once you have group thinking, a we-identity, a we-consciousness that makes you stronger. From your point of view, it is unfortunate when this we-identity is a national one, is a patriotic one. But then again, many of these intellectuals start with a patriotic sense of we-identity, which incorporates a civil rights struggle, and then move on to a fight for human rights. And there is a clear pattern of this shift, certainly in Du Bois; in King, too; and especially in Malcolm X. We can't stop at civil rights; we have to move on to human rights, and then the struggle becomes international, and that's another kind of we-identity. It is no longer limiting because it turns into a freedom to unite and identify with ideals that could be shared by all.

CW: Shared by all, the species. And it even—as our animal rights brothers and sisters would say—includes all sentient beings. But because nation-states have been the shells into which most of the democratic possibilities have to filter, you have to deal with nationalisms and nation-states; there is no doubt about that. It's just that you have to be able to have a we-consciousness that transcends nationalisms, and that is why the transnationalism and internationalism of the progressives and revolutionaries is so fundamental. I used to sit at the feet of Harry Haywood, who wrote a great autobiography called

Black Bolshevik.[45] He was probably the most famous Black Communist in the twentieth century. He was the first to put forward the Black-nation thesis in the Soviet Union in the 1920s. And here he was, tied to an internationalist movement, Communist movement, that still was trying to get them to see that Black people constituted a nation that required its own self-determination and its own freedom and liberation. So, somehow, he is wrestling with the we-consciousness of Black people as a Black nation and the we-consciousness of being a Communist, which is the human race as a whole. And Harry Haywood and others who come after, such as the Communist Labor Party, led by Nelson Perry, was very important for the Black-nation thesis in the 1970s, which built on Haywood's early work. We need to go back to some of those discussions given the interdependence and the international struggles today. I used to argue with brother Haywood, and I was very young and he was an old man, but we would go at it. I said that I believed in Black peoplehood, but not Black nationhood; that we were a distinct people who had created ourselves over against the emergence of a US nation-state that didn't want to treat us with dignity and oftentimes didn't want us here other than to exploit our labor. That means we are so tied into the emergence of the US nation-state and we are often tied to the nationalism, tied into the patriotism as well as tied into the chauvinism, because every nationalism that I know has been patriarchal, class-ridden, homophobic, and usually xenophobic, so that you have to be profoundly suspicious of all forms of nationalism. Yet nationalism is the very terrain upon which you must work.

And I think part of the problem of the Black prophetic tradition is that some of us are so eager to become flag-wavers that we don't want to bear the cross of internationalism that highlights the struggles of poor peoples here in our nation and all around the world. And that's a fundamental question: Are you going to be a flag-waver or a cross-bearer? I use the cross here in a metaphoric sense, not just in a Christian sense. Malcolm was a cross-bearer rather than a flag-waver. In our day, the age of Obama, most Black leaders are flag-wavers; they don't want to be cross-bearers at all. That's the last thing they want to be. They want the acceptance of the US nation-state; they want the acceptance of the US mainstream. So they are silent on drones; they are silent on the centrality of the new Jim Crow in terms of Black life; they are silent on the trade union movement being crushed; they are silent on the Wall Street criminality. And this is the challenge of the Black prophetic tradition at its best, with Malcolm the exemplary revolutionary wing. Not every member of the Black prophetic tradition is a revolutionary like Malcolm. He's a very special kind of brother. He really is. There is no Black prophetic tradition without the Malcolms and others, but he is very distinct in this regard. But at the same time, if we don't come to terms with this challenge, then we end up being just these deferential flag-wavers, thinking that somehow we are keeping alive the Black prophetic tradition. This self-deception must be shattered—in each and every generation.

CHB: What do you think about the legacy of Malcolm X? For a long time there was no strong legacy, but it picked up again in the nineties, when, as critics would claim, he entered popular culture. What becomes of him in being appropriated by popular culture? Is it really a genuine Malcolm, in your sense, that is evolving there, or is it just an icon that is about memory, maybe even nostalgia about a dead man, rather than evoking a revolutionary struggle?

CW: On the one hand, the centrality of memory of the revolutionary wing of the Black prophetic tradition—Malcolm is a grand example of that—the memory of him and the others is very important. That's why, in a certain sense, I thank Spike Lee, Denzel Washington, and the others who forced us to talk about Malcolm.[46] Now, in a highly commodified country, Malcolm will become commodified.[47] In a country obsessed with patriotism, they will designate a stamp for him. That's the last thing he wanted. "I want a free people. I don't want a stamp."

CHB: As to the stamp, to me it exemplifies the demonized Malcolm. The photograph chosen is quite unbecoming, showing a strained, almost sinister facial expression that is highlighted by the unnatural twist of his eyes. This image enforces the marginalization from the point of view of the mainstream.

CW: The fact that the establishment authorizes the stamp with that image is part of the paradox; that's part of the contradiction. But to keep alive the memory, even when you have the stereotype, you have the occasion to call it into question and therefore constitute a continuation of the conversation, because to wipe him completely out of memory, that's the sad thing. You go to a group of young people—Let's say I would go to Newark and talk and write on the board "Malcolm X," they would say: "Malcolm the tenth, who was he?" That's to wipe out his memory, you see what I mean. Whereas when you say "Malcolm X," "Yeah, didn't brother Spike make a movie about that Negro"—they wouldn't say "Negro"; they use the n-word—"make a movie about that nigger? Yeah, I don't know too much about him, but Spike was getting it on, Spike was getting it on." At least you have a hook to say, "Well, let's see who Spike was talking about." Now, granted, you get the critiques of Spike's film from brother Amiri Baraka, brother Maulana Karenga, and the others.[48] And that's wonderful, because they are veteran revolutionaries themselves, and they want to preserve the integrity of the memory of Malcolm. And Spike is the younger generation, and Spike is not a revolutionary. He is a courageous and gifted artist and a towering figure in a deeply racist Hollywood trying to make movies about Black people as full-fledged human beings. And he is close to Obama, too. He has his critique of Obama, I think, but he is very close to Obama, raised big money for Obama. But I do thank Spike for having the courage to take Malcolm's greatness on. And no one can do full justice to Malcolm in a film, book, or interview. It's just a fact. Even James Baldwin's script, which, I am sure, was powerful—I never read it—but he couldn't do justice to Malcolm, no way.[49] And even, for example, the New Black

Panthers—and of course, you know Bobby Seale and the others have criticized them and in some ways condemned them: "This is not a continuation of what we were doing; they are too anti-white; they are too xenophobic"—and brother Bobby Seale has got some very good points to make, but I still have a certain love for the New Black Panther Party. They can learn; they can grow; but they have a certain fearlessness like Malcolm. Why? Because they talk about his courage, and you can be courageous and still xenophobic—you need to call it xenophobia—but they are at least willing to stand up and at least keep certain organizations going, and they can mature the way Malcolm himself matured.

In our time, the spirit of Malcolm X is most clearly expressed in the revolutionary politics of *Black Agenda Report*, led by my dear brother Glen Ford and brother Bruce Dixon and sister Nellie Bailey, sister Margaret Kimberley, brother Anthony Monteiro, and sister Leutisha Stills.[50] I also discern his spirit in the courageous work of my dear brother Carl Dix of the Revolutionary Communist Party, led by brother Bob Avakian,[51] as well as the prophetic witness of Chris Hedges, Glenn Greenwald, and Larry Hamm.[52] Needless to say, the lives and work of the great Harry Belafonte and renowned James Cone still speak loudly.[53] The dramatic art of brother Wren Troy Brown's great Ebony Repertory Theatre is a sign of hope, as are the scholarly works of Robin D. G. Kelley, Imani Perry, Katie Geneva Cannon, Emilie Townes, Matthew Briones, Andre Willis, Michael Hanchard, Leonard Harris, Eddie Glaude, Gerald Horne, Farah Jasmine Griffin, Lucius Outlaw, and others. And the musical artistry of Dead Prez, KRS-One, Immortal Technique, Brother Ali, Jasiri X, Javon Jackson, Ravi Coltrane, Rah Digga, Mos Def, E-40, Erykah Badu, Jill Scott, India.Arie, the Last Poets, James Mtume, Lupe Fiasco, and others keep the memory of Malcolm X's legacy alive. But the issue of memory in a commodified society is always difficult; it's very hard, and that's part of our challenge. Malcolm's revolutionary *parrhesia*—that unintimidated, fearless, frank, plain speech and putting your body on the line—is the core of our challenge. This kind of prophetic witness can never fully and thoroughly be crushed. Even when you kill the body, the words still linger in the air, and it touches people. People take it and run and do with it what they will, and that's part of breaking that cycle of hatred and domination that we talked about in relation to Ella Baker. But you and I know it is impossible to even think about the Black prophetic tradition without making Malcolm X a central figure in it, regardless of what the mainstream thought then, thinks now, or will think in the future.

Ida B. Wells, 1893

CHAPTER SIX

Prophetic Fire

IDA B. WELLS

We wanted to end our conversation on a high note full of the prophetic fire we started with. Thus in January 2013, we met on two
consecutive days to discuss first Malcolm X and then Ida B. Wells.
As far apart as they are in time and as different as they are in social
background, they share an uncompromising radical spirit that is expressed in fearless speech. Yet such boldness is the more extraordinary in a woman, let alone a woman in the nineteenth century. As a
female voice in the Black prophetic tradition, Wells, like Ella Baker,
has often been a victim of public amnesia. We want to honor her
outstanding example of prophetic witness by giving her the last word.

CHRISTA BUSCHENDORF: With Ida B. Wells, we go back to the
    nineteenth century, where we started. Historically speaking,
    she stands between Frederick Douglass and W. E. B. Du Bois,
    and she knew both men personally. Wells was the pioneering
    figure in the anti-lynching campaigns of her day, and the way
    in which she courageously and undauntedly took up a difficult
    and dangerous struggle against prejudices about the "beastly
    nature" of the Black man, certainly renders her a worthy can-
    didate in our series of long-distance freedom fighters in the
    Black prophetic tradition. Like Du Bois, she was shaped by
    Victorian America, and her bourgeois background means that
    evaluating her from today's point of view is difficult. We have

to contextualize her, and so we will try to get at her core by doing just that. So could you start by assessing Ida B. Wells's importance in the tradition of the Black struggle for freedom?

CORNEL WEST: Ida B. Wells is not only unique, but she is the exemplary figure full of prophetic fire in the face of American terrorism, which is American Jim Crow and Jane Crow, when lynching occurred every two and a half days for over fifty years in America. And this is very important, because Black people in the New World, in the Diaspora, Brazil, Jamaica, Barbados, were all enslaved, but no group of Black people were Jim Crowed other than US Negroes. And what I mean by Jim Crow is not just terrorized, not just stigmatized, not just traumatized, but, what we talked about before, niggerized. Black people were first reaching citizenship after the most barbaric of all civil wars in modern times—750,000 dead, we are told now.[1] Black people are made slaves, then citizens, then are remade into subjects who are subjected to an American terrorist order—despite Black resistance. They are no longer slaves in the old sense, yet not citizens, but sub-citizens, namely subjects, namely Negroes, namely niggers who are wrestling with this terror.

Why is this important? Because, I would argue, Jim Crow in some ways is as important as slavery in understanding the mentality, understanding the institutions, and understanding the destiny of Black folk. A lot of people want to jump from slavery into the civil rights movement. But, no, right when the American social order was providing opportunities for white immigrants all around the world between 1881— Let's begin with the pogroms that escalate in Russia at the time with the death of the tsar[2] and the waves of white immigrants who come to the United States and who begin to gain access to some of the opportunities afforded here—that is precisely the time in which Jim Crow emerged. It consolidates in the 1890s, along with the American imperial order in the Philippines and Cuba, Guam, and other territories. So you get six million people of color outside the United States, and you get

the terrorized, traumatized, stigmatized order, which is a Jim
Crow order, in the United States. That's the context for Ida.

Why is she so unique? Well, the textbook version of Black
history is the following. You get W. E. B. Du Bois versus
Booker T. Washington: The nice little deodorized discourse
of Booker T., who is tied to the white elites, who has access to
tremendous amounts of money, who has his own political machine, moving in to take over Black newspapers and pulling
Black civic organizations under his control while refusing to
say a mumbling word publicly about lynching, which was the
raw face of American terrorism against Black people. Then
you get Du Bois, who did want to talk about civil rights, who
did want to talk about political rights, but in no way targeted
the lynching face of American terrorism the way Ida B. Wells
did. Ida B. Wells, in so many ways, teaches us something that
we rarely want to acknowledge: that the Black freedom movement has always been an anti-terrorist movement, that Black
people in America had a choice between creating a Black
al-Qaeda or a movement like Ida B. Wells's, which was going
to call into question the bestiality and barbarity and brutality
of Jim Crow and American terrorism and lynching, but would
do it in the name of something that provided a higher moral
ground and a higher spiritual ground given her Christian
faith, not opting for a Black al-Qaeda that says, "You terrorize
us; we terrorize you. You kill our children; we kill your children." No, not an eye for an eye, a tooth for a tooth, where we
end up both blind and toothless. She said: "We want a higher
moral ground, but I'm going to hit this issue head-on."

And that is in so many ways relevant today, because we
live in an age in which people are talking about terrorism,
about terror, all the time. Here we have much to learn from
an Ida B. Wells, who was born a slave, orphaned young—both
her parents die of yellow fever in Hollis Springs, Mississippi.
She makes her way with two of her sisters to Memphis, is
run out of Memphis, even as she begins to emerge as a prophetic voice in *Free Speech and Headlight*, a newspaper that she
begins to edit, and then with the lynching of three men in

Memphis, brother Tom and brother Calvin and brother Will, on March 9, 1892,[3] the white elite puts a bounty on her head, because she wants to tell the truth—like Malcolm X, *parrhesia* again, the fearless speech. Thank God for T. Thomas Fortune, who welcomed her to New York and invited her to write for his newspaper, the *New York Age*.[4] And this was where she published the two classics, *Southern Horrors*, in 1892, and *A Red Record*, in 1895.

And it is important to use the language of American terrorism, because we live in an age where, when people think of terrorism, they usually think of a very small group of Islamic brothers and sisters, whereas, of course, terrorism has been integral to the emergence and the sustenance of the American democratic experiment, beginning with indigenous peoples and slavery. But after the Civil War, we get a new form of terrorism—crimes against humanity—that sits at the center of American life, and Ida B. Wells forces us to come to terms with that.

CHB: Maybe we should mention the interim of Reconstruction, because right after the Civil War the situation was improving in terms of political power of Blacks. And what Ida B. Wells reveals then—in contrast to the understanding of most people, including Black people, including Douglass—what she reveals is that it is in reaction to the very success of Black people, their rising on the social ladder, their becoming respectable, learned, and a political power, too, that terrorism sets in. And she saw through the story that was fabricated at the time that this was all about Black men wanting white women; she saw that it was a pretext; that, in fact, what this was all about was a reaction to a change of the hierarchical order, and, of course, especially in the South, where white people did not want Black people to rise. And I think that is the truth she told in all fearlessness, a truth that was very important even for Blacks to understand.[5]

CW: I think that's very true. Actually, I would go to 1876 and 1877 with the so-called Compromise, which is a capitulation that allowed for the withdrawal of the military troops in the South, which would allow for states' rights to become predominant, which would allow for white supremacists powers to take over so that the Ku Klux Klan and the White Citizens' Councils would move into positions of power culturally, economically, and politically, and so Black folk would be subject to that kind of terror. The troop withdrawal allowed for an emerging reconciliation between the former foes, the Confederacy and the Union. Now the South and the North are able to view themselves more and more as a family, and they are unified by the scapegoat, they are unified by these Black folk who are sacrificed with the withdrawal of the troops.

It had much to do, of course, with the fact that other issues were emerging, issues of depression, issues of international relations, and they were just tired of dealing with the so-called race question; they were tired of dealing with the legacy of white supremacy. So that even great figures like William Lloyd Garrison—for whom I have tremendous respect, who gave his time, energy, and life to abolish slavery—do not engage in the kind of follow-through to deal with the vicious legacy of white supremacy after the Civil War. Now that slavery is over, the notion is "Thank God, it's all done; the business is over."

Now, let me tell a story. I was at West Point the other day and was talking to a number of students and professors there. The biggest picture in the library they have at West Point is of Robert E. Lee, who was superintendent of West Point when he was part of the Union army, but was only a colonel in the Union army. He became a general in the Confederate army. And the painting they have of him is in Confederate attire, with a Black slave bowing in the right corner. So Lee is a general in the army of rebels and traitors against West Point. They were telling me that the reconciliation on the military front began when the soldiers from the South joined the soldiers in the North in the Spanish-American War, so that the imperial front becomes a space for them of coming together. Then, by the end of the Spanish-American War, lo and behold, West Point embraces the memory of Robert E. Lee.

Then, in 1971, President Nixon tries to force them to have a monument to Confederate troops and Confederate soldiers. Nixon appoints Alexander Haig to establish the monument. There was Black opposition—they had just admitted Black soldiers to West Point in the sixties—the Black cadets strongly rejected the idea; there was tremendous disarray, and West Point gave up on the idea. So you see, this tribute to the legacy of white supremacy remains integral to West Point, past and present.

So on the imperial front, after Reconstruction, the white Southerners and the white Northerners were able to come together, subordinate the peoples of color in Hawaii, in Guam, in the Philippines, in Puerto Rico, and domestically subordinate the Black folk, so that, lo and behold, the Confederate and the Union view themselves as part of a cantankerous family not really at odds over whether the Union ought to exist or not, but a cantankerous family whose members have more in common than what separates them. And there is a united front against Black folk internally and brown folk externally, and to me this is really important, because Ida B. Wells is willing to speak courageously and sacrificially and candidly about the brutality of American terrorism at home and acknowledge the terrorism abroad.[6]

Unlike Booker T. Washington, Ida B. Wells publicly denounced lynching. Du Bois is not really hit by the issue until he sees the knuckles of lynching victim Sam Hose on display in Atlanta, gives up his detached, disinterested, scientific orientation and becomes a political activist—now this is seven years after Ida B. Wells has a bounty on her head!

CHB: True. But it needed that confrontation, and he reacts to the experience, whereas Ida B. Wells has that experience earlier; she is in the South. And in the Memphis lynching, one of the three victims, Tom Moss, was one of her close friends; she was godmother to his daughter. So I think it is about the immediate confrontation, and when Du Bois is confronted, it changes his life just as much as it changed her life.

CW: That's true. But you know, Du Bois is in Nashville in the 1880s as a student at Fisk University and then teaches those two summers there in a small town in Tennessee, so he must have heard about the lynching and the terror.

CHB: In his autobiography he writes about that very different kind of— He would not call it terror but a kind of discrimination of Blacks in the South that he was not used to. But as far as I remember, he does mention lynching, but it is the lynching of Sam Hose that, as he puts it, "startled me to my feet."[7]

CW: Exactly. But there is something about—and I love it—sister Ida B. Wells's rebellious spirit. As a youth, she had a deep suspicion of authority.[8] She reminds me of Malcolm, and Malcolm reminds me of her in terms of this willingness to be candid and honest about any sources of pain and suffering, and you speak to it directly regardless of the price, regardless of what burden goes along with it, or whatever cost you have to pay.

CHB: The first time she was so courageous was when her parents had just died and the community decided to distribute the children, her five younger siblings, to be adopted by other families, and as a young girl of sixteen, she says: "No. No way. You can't do that. Give me a job instead, and I will take care of my brothers and sisters." It was unheard of for so young a woman to be the independent head of a family, and it was highly suspicious, and she got the reaction of the community in the form of really vicious slander: when Dr. Gray, a white physician, returned the savings her dying father had entrusted to him, and when the community noticed the transaction taking place in the town square, she is immediately suspected of prostituting herself. So we see early in life the bravery of a young woman who would take the responsibility for her family, which was something that did not fit into the Victorian model of womanhood, and thus people resented it and consequently suspected her of a transgression of quite a different type. That is the first moment when you see her courage.

CW: So true. Then we get her Rosa Parks–like act of protest on the railroad train. That's still very early in her life. She refuses to give up her seat in the first-class ladies' coach and is removed by force. She takes it to the court; she wins; the case goes to a higher court; she loses; she must pay fees, but she takes a stand. You are so right about this willingness of this young, militant, uncompromising, bold, and fearless woman.

CHB: And she sacrifices, because she can't finish school, and when later she attends a graduation ceremony at her former school, she is in tears because she was not able to graduate. That was the price she had to pay. She makes up for it with her own tireless efforts to learn and to read, but it is a price she has to pay for speaking out and for taking care of her family.[9]

CW: And as a teacher taking care of the family, she discovered that she was being paid thirty dollars a month and the white teachers are being paid more than twice that much. She could already see the deeply racist practices there. And we should note, of course, her summers at Fisk University. Like Du Bois, she did spend time at Fisk University. But it also shows she has a tremendous drive for studying and love of learning, not just for knowledge in the abstract but also the very process of coming to know, the very process of being committed to exploring, a sense of intellectual adventure, trying to be culturally cultivated in a variety of different ways by means of voracious reading, conversation, dialogue.

CHB: As a young woman teaching, she reaches out to young men. In part, of course, she is looking for a partner; that was natural at her age. But sometimes what she wants is a companion to talk with and to be inspired by, someone who is an intellectual, and she loves these discussions but has the problem of decorum, because she is admonished that this is not done. You need a chaperone, all these rules of etiquette against which she often rebels.[10] Another point, though, in terms of learning and aspiring to more learning: she is never allowed to teach above the fourth grade, and at one point she realizes that this is unsatisfactory—and here her activist side comes to the fore. She wants to be more influential by becoming a journalist and discovers that this is her true vocation. She writes: "It was through journalism that I found the real me."[11]

CW: You know, Ida B. Wells was the first Black correspondent to a major white newspaper, the *Daily Inter-Ocean* in Chicago, when she was on her tour in Britain, forming the British Anti-Lynching Society—not because Britain had a lynching problem. Britain was deeply racist, but they never had a Jim Crow system. Yet progressive British whites were deeply concerned about the lynching taking place in America. And Ida went there in the 1890s twice and helped form that society and wrote various articles back to that Chicago newspaper. But as a journalist, she had a vocation to tell the truth at an observational level. It reminds me in some ways of the great text of Theodore Weld and Angelina Grimké, *American Slavery As It Is*,[12] which became a best seller in 1839. And it was observational; it was like William Cobbett[13] in England or Harriet Martineau,[14] where you observe and picture for your audience in a dramatic fashion the suffering and the misery of your fellow human beings, in this case of Blacks vis-à-vis a white audience. And what Ida B. Wells does as a journalist is not just report in a regular way, but she presents these dramatic portraits with statistics, with empirical data, but also stories. Ida was saying: "Let me tell you about these seventeen lynchings, where the myth was to protect white womanhood's purity and so forth. No, there was a fear of economic competition. No, there was a sense of arbitrary targeting of these Black men that had nothing to do whatsoever with white sisters." So you are right about the journalistic vocation and the calling. And, my God, journalism is about dead in America today, given that most journalists are extensions of the powers that be, but in those days there was prophetic witness, and Ida B. Wells was one of the great pioneers of this prophetic journalism.

CHB: Yes, she was what today we would call an investigative journalist, because she often travelled to the places where the lynching had happened and she investigated what was going on there. And then she found out what you just said about the pretext of lynching and the truth. But sometimes she was too radical even for her time. In May 1892, in the context of the Memphis lynching, she warned her white male fellow citizens that they should not go too far:

> Eight Negroes lynched since last issue of the *Free Speech*. Three were charged with killing white men and five with raping white women. Nobody in this section believes the old thread-bare lie that Negro men assault white women. If Southern white men are not careful they will over-reach themselves and a conclusion will be reached which will be very damaging to the moral reputation of their women.[15]

But here, as in so many other cases, when she was really radical, she had to cope with the consequences, and the consequences were severe, because, in this case, with her insinuation of consensual relationships between white women and Black men, she had enraged the white elite of Memphis, who in reaction formed a "committee" of leading citizens who completely demolished the printing office of the *Free Speech*.[16] But often she was even too provocative for her journalist colleagues, so even at a time when, as you pointed out, journalism was more substantial, she went over the top sometimes.

CW: Yes, when you think of the history of American journalism, people often evoke Upton Sinclair and even Jack London and other muckrakers who were investigating various forms of social injustice and social misery. But Ida B. Wells was there ten, fifteen years before. *The Jungle* was published by 1906,[17] while Ida B. Wells was already there in 1892. As to her radicality, it shows in her statement about the Winchester rifle: that ought to have a place of honor in every Black household.[18] Now that's going to get our dear sister into a whole lot of trouble. She sounded like Deacons for Defense, Robert Williams down in North Carolina, the Black Panther Party, Huey Newton, which is about self-defense: arm yourself and make sure you police the police, so the police do not kill you.[19]

CHB: And, again, it was the incident of the lynching in Memphis, when she herself bought a revolver and said, "Well, if I'm attacked, I won't die like a dog, but I will see to it that someone else—"

CW: "—Goes before me."[20] Now, you would not hear that out of a Booker T. Washington or W. E. B. Du Bois, maybe a William Monroe Trotter.[21] I could hear William Trotter saying something like that, actually. But when you are so far ahead of your time, full of so much prophetic fire as Ida B. Wells—and then, when she marries Ferdinand Barnett, Ida B. Wells-Barnett— the level of loneliness is intense. You feel all by yourself, isolated, misunderstood, and misperceived. We see this over and over again in our prophetic figures. This is something she probably exemplifies more so than any of the figures that we have examined.

CHB: And in part because she is a woman, and you expect less of that kind of blazing spirit of hers, that militancy, in a woman.[22] As I said before, she did not succumb to the image of the Victorian woman, although she grew out of an education that was very strict, teaching her to adhere to that very model, and you see the impact of that education in her early years,[23] before she renounced that ideal, and said, "To hell with it, I am here to do something for others." For example, when her case against the railroad was overthrown, she said she was very disappointed because with her trial she had wanted to achieve something for her people.[24] The responsibility she feels as an activist is her focus now, and she is less occupied with respectability and proper behavior. At the same time, she always has to defend herself, because she is so often attacked for being a woman who is—

CW: Independent and free-thinking. Now, of course, in that case against the railroad, her lawyer is bought off by the railroad. They pay a bribe to him, and he actually succumbs, you know. This Negro, he is selling his soul, while she is fighting for justice. So she has to get a white lawyer who has more integrity in order to fight her case, and yet at the same time she doesn't give up on the Negro; she just recognizes how cowardly some of these bourgeois Negroes can be. When we think of two classic texts by Evelyn Higginbotham and Kevin Gaines on the politics of respectability and the difficulty of women, especially in a Victorian period in which respectability has such weight and gravity,[25] we see an obsession with gaining access to status and stature, with a sense of decorum and tact. Ida B. Wells is able to show that bourgeois respectability is usually a form not just of moral blindness and political cowardice, but it is also a form of conformity that hides and conceals some of the more vicious realities going on in that day. Picture this: Ida B. Wells is focusing on the barbarity of American terrorism while the mainstream is preoccupied with the politics of respectability. Most female citizens of the time are trying to prove to the male normative gaze that they are worthy of being treated in a certain kind of way. All the burden is on them: "You have to show yourself worthy for us to be accepting of you." And Ida B. Wells shatters that, so that the cost that she has to pay at that time is enormous, and yet she comes back to us as, in some ways, a contemporary, for we take for granted the emptiness of these forms of respectability she attempted to shatter at tremendous personal cost.

CHB: To come back to her loneliness, she was active in so very many organizations, it's incredible, but they were bourgeois organizations, Christian organizations, that is, all middle-class organizations, and working within those groups, her base was the middle class. Especially later on, when she lived in Chicago, she was often lonely because she went too far for the middle-class sensibilities, and the sensibilities of middle-class women in particular, and she was not ready to compromise. In fact, she often scolded herself for her temper and told herself that she would have to be more reticent, and when she failed and refused to compromise, she ended up being marginalized within an organization that in some cases she had founded herself.

CW: Over and over again. I think there was a kind of a myth of Ida B. Wells-Barnett that she was difficult to get along with, when, in fact, she would advocate the truth.[26] You can go right down the row: Her critique of Booker T. Washington about his reticence to say a word about American terrorism,[27] and he comes at her very intensely: "Oh she is ridiculous."[28] Her critique of W. E. B. Du Bois, who did take her name off of the list at the founding of the NAACP, and she comes at him, too. Her mistreatment by Black women in the Black club movement that she had helped initiate; there was an Ida B. Wells Club in Chicago, and she didn't get enough respect from them. Mary Church Terrell[29] and Margaret Washington, the wife of Booker T. Washington, both became presidents in the Black club movement organization that Ida B. Wells-Barnett created, while she herself was never, ever a national president. But also her willingness to take on powerful white sisters, like Mary Ovington in the NAACP. They clashed, and Wells was explicit about her critique of Ovington's paternalism, her racist and sexist arrogance toward her.[30] The same would be true with the famous case of Frances Willard. When Willard is in England, Wells attacks her: "Well, you are talking about woman's rights in America, and you are pushing it here in England, you haven't said a mumbling word about lynching." "Well, maybe I have." "Well, where is it then?" Willard got caught, she was exposed, and Ida was quite explicit about that.[31] But we have that kind of willingness with Wells to tell the truth, Black men, white men, white women, Black women. Other than Ferdinand and the kids and the Sunday school class she so loved and taught for ten years,[32] there is not a whole lot left. Jane Addams[33] was a friend, of course, but Wells had a critique of Jane Addams, too. So you would want to say: "Ida, this is Socratic and prophetic all the way down. How does one cope with this loneliness?" She reminds me of

my dear sister, comrade, and coauthor bell hooks[34] for all of
her courage, consistency, and compassion.

CHB: And yet Wells is so untiring in her activities. There is always
so much she is doing at the same time, so that she is active
instead of becoming discouraged or even depressed.

CW: That's a good point: she is forever going at it. Even though,
you know, there are moments in *Crusade for Justice*, her great
classic autobiography, that bring tears to your eyes, when she
feels as if she was often abandoned by her own people[35] and
never really appreciated by the movements that she helped
initiate and create. She was willing to stand alone—her view
was, "I don't mind being the lonely Negro who stands up for
truth"—and yet I also get a sense that she did yearn and long
for some kind—not just of comradeship but an appreciation
of the depth of her sacrifice and the breadth of her contribution to the movement.

CHB: There is something else linked to that, namely, that so many
times her emphasis is on the unity of Black people, or rather
the lack of it. In her autobiography, she quotes extensively
from a provocative address W. T. Stead delivered at Bethel
AME Church in Chicago in 1894, in which he exclaimed:
"You people have not been lynched enough! You haven't been
lynched enough to drive you together! [. . .] Any ten-year-old
child knows that a dozen persons fighting as one can make
better headway against ten times its number than if each
were fighting singlehanded and alone."[36] Wells-Barnett herself makes that point often, and like Stead, gets angry that it
seems to be impossible for Blacks to show the cohesion that is
needed for effective political fight. Unity, coherence in political struggle was of great importance to her, and she was often
disappointed that she couldn't make herself understood to her
co-fighters.[37]

CW: I think that one of the loneliest roads to travel is to be a
de-niggerized Black person among a niggerized people. She
sees the great potential of Black people, but she also sees the

fear, the insecurity, the inferiority complexes, the cowardliness, the conformity, the complacency, the apathy, the inertia among the people. I guess she felt what the great Harriet Tubman is known to have felt when she went into the belly of the slavocracy beast so many times: "I rescued many slaves, but I could have saved a thousand more if the slaves knew they were slaves." Mentally, psychically, spiritually, they were still tied to the master, and the decolonizing of the mind, heart, and soul had to go hand-in-hand with an attempt to break from the institution of slavery, and I think this is something Ida B. Wells was wrestling with during the phase of American terrorism and Jim Crow. She was dealing especially with middle-class Negroes, because you are right that so much of her world was still circumscribed by a middle-class world. I think she had a deep love for poor Black people, but she was not a part of the organizations of poor Black people. Now as a Baptist, she was a member of the largest denomination of Black people as a whole, with large numbers of poor Black people. The best friend I have ever had—my dear brother James Melvin Washington—wrote the great book on Black Baptists called *Frustrated Fellowship*.[38] Sister Ida was deeply frustrated with Black Baptists who were often stratified by class in local churches. This class division made it difficult for Ida B. Wells to be able to fully be what she would have liked to be, which was a freedom fighter grounded in the organizations of Black people across the board, poor, working class, rural, urban, whatever.

CHB: But although she was not based in the poor people's organizations or activities, she would always work for them, and she went to their neighborhoods, and then, again, she was disappointed by the ladies in the clubs with whom she wanted to work in those neighborhoods, because they would say: "Oh no, we won't go there."[39] She was ready to do just that and to be on the spot for the poor people to try to improve their situation. But it is really a question whether it was feasible for her as a member of the middle class to do what Ella Baker later did. I wonder was it feasible, historically? It's something that we should not hold against her, because she might have risked losing what she needed to engage in a successful fight, namely being grounded in the middle class on whose support and money she depended.

CW: Scholars like sister Hazel Carby and Angela Davis[40] and others have made the points—and rightfully so—that you already have a focus on the workplace in terms of the kind of violation and rapes of Black women in the white household, given the role of the white men with Black women working as domestic maids. And the women's club movement was focused on the workplace in a way in which Du Bois and Washington were not. In the case of Ida B. Wells, you get the focus on the workplace and the lynching, and then, of course, you also have the focus on prophetic civic institutions that generate a certain kind of prophetic civic consciousness.

ChB: She also emphasizes women's suffrage.

CW: And women's rights, absolutely. But when you think of Black women grounded in and attuned to poor people's struggles, as, for example, in the arts, as the emergence of the great blues singers Ma Rainey and Bessie Smith—and the first wave of the blues singers were primarily women before the men take over—and most of these talented sisters came from poor communities. There is no doubt that Ida B. Wells is one of the great crusaders for justice during the period of American terrorism in its raw form in the face of Black people. One can't think of any greater figure, and yet when it comes to issues of poverty, race, and gender, we think of Fannie Lou Hamer; we think of Ella Baker; we think of Victoria Garvin;[41] we think of subsequent freedom fighters, who hit those issues—legendary Angela Davis, now, Michelle Alexander come to mind. So that it is not in any way to put down the great Ida to acknowledge her middle-class context. But it is about how we appropriate, critically engage a giant like Ida B. Wells so that we can learn, and so that we can build on not just her great example but on her witness that connects us to the example of so many others at the time. But in terms of political affiliation—unlike Du Bois, King, Baker, and Malcolm X—she did not side with socialism, let alone Marxism. Yet throughout her life she stayed committed to the plight of working-class Blacks.[42]

CHB: There is very little about African American culture in her autobiography. It is very focused on the political situation.

CW: And you know that culture plays an important role, because she is in the church every Sunday.

CHB: Right, and that is, of course, an issue. One of the many battles she fights is the integration of the YMCA and YWCA.[43] And she makes a very interesting point, namely—and I admire her sharp, analytical mind—she is discussing the crime rates in Chicago on a panel, and the statistics show crime rates among Black people are high. Now, the usual explanation is essentialism, naturalization, they are what they are. But she contradicts the common rationalization by pointing out that all the organizations of uplift that serve the white population are closed to Blacks:

> The statistics which we have heard here tonight do not mean, as it appears to mean, that the Negro race is the most criminal of the various race groups in Chicago. It does mean that ours is the most neglected group. All other races in the city are welcomed into the settlements, YMCA's, YWCA's, gymnasiums and every other movement for uplift if only their skins are white. [. . .] Only one social center welcomes the Negro, and that is the saloon. Ought we to wonder at the harvest we have heard enumerated tonight?[44]

CW: It's a social-historical explanation.

CHB: Exactly, and that is her strength in terms of her intellect, in terms of the kind of analysis she undertakes, systemic analysis, which was her forte when she revealed what was behind the lynching, because that's a sociological argument as well. And she is avant-garde here, too.

CW: It's amazing.

CHB: In *A Red Record*, for example, she explicitly refers to sociology:

> The student of American sociology will find the year 1894 marked by a pronounced awakening of the public conscience to a system of anarchy and outlawry which had grown during a series of ten years to be so common, that scenes of unusual brutality failed to have any visible effect upon the humane sentiments of the people of our land.[45]

So she talks about sociology when this is still a new discipline, and not only that, but she understands sociological thinking, and she does so when she talks about lynching and then later on when she talks about institutions of uplift in the city. She was ahead of her time.

CW: Way ahead of her time, light-years ahead of her time. That is so true. Now, when you think, though, the same figure would work with Frederick Douglass and write with Frederick Douglass in a pamphlet in protest against the World's Fair in Chicago in 1893,[46] but also would work with Du Bois,[47] as well as with Garvey,[48] it's very interesting, and especially with the great preacher in Chicago, Reverend Junius Caesar Austin Sr. He worked with Garvey, with A. Philip Randolph; he was pastor at the Pilgrim Baptist Church; he was called the "Dancing Preacher"—no one like him. He had Mahalia Jackson in the choir; he had Thomas A. Dorsey, considered the father of Black gospel music, playing the piano, with the Dancing Preacher preaching every Sunday in Chicago. Now, that's culture; it's religious culture, but that's culture, and it would be fascinating to know what Wells actually thought about those cultural dimensions you were talking about. Now, of course, Chicago was also the great center for the blues, probably the greatest center for American blues other than the Mississippi

Delta, for so many Mississippi folk went straight up to Chicago. But she doesn't tell us too much about that more secular form of Black culture,[49] but we know it had tremendous impact on her in a variety of different ways. But what a life, what scope and what depth, bringing together so much of the best of the Black prophetic tradition in terms of being willing to bear witness and lay bare the truth, speak out with courage, keep somehow a love flowing, even given the kinds of betrayals by Black men and white men, and Black women and white women. It is an extraordinary life!

CHB: I would like to raise the question that we addressed with regard to all our figures, namely, how she fits the category of an organic intellectual.

CW: I would argue that Ida B. Wells-Barnett is the most courageous Black organic intellectual in the history of the country, because when you look at what she faces: lynching, American terrorism, especially with vigilante activity of citizens condoned by the nation-state—and when the powers that be are able to use the repressive apparatus of the nation-state to come at you, you have to wait to get to Martin King to get another courageous intellectual like that, or Huey Newton. Imagine the raw power of the American racist imperial state coming down on you in that way—allowing its citizens to kill at whim, blow up homes, and so forth—and she remains as strong as ever, with her Winchester rifle and the Holy Ghost. It's hard to think of a more courageous organic intellectual. Garvey as an organic intellectual and leader—he goes to prison, he is wrongly incarcerated, and so forth, but I don't think he ever has to deal with the raw violence coming at him like Ida. I don't think Malcolm had this raw repressive apparatus of the nation-state coming at him in that way. We know that it was targeting him, but not in that way. It's not until we get to King and Huey Newton that organic intellectuals are targeted by raw state power like that faced by Ida B. Wells-Barnett. And we must keep in mind, she is a Black woman organic intellectual being targeted.

CHB: I mentioned her immensely broad activities in various organizations and the projects she takes care of. For example,
she founds the first Black kindergarten in Chicago, and she
also creates a social center with a reading room. This is in
the Chicago phase, when she is still active in national issues
like the anti-lynching campaign, woman's suffrage, and so on,
but at the same time concentrates very much on local politics
and projects focusing on helping the people in her hometown.
And I am wondering whether you see a parallel to the development of the Occupy movement, which started as a movement in the streets and now has shifted. Occupy still exists,
but it exists in other forms, often local activities, for example,
supporting people to prevent them from being evicted from
their homes, activities like that.

CW: She certainly is so multicontextual in her radical activism.
She is a radical reformist moving from a variety of different
organizations all connected with a commitment to justice,
but it's rare to see someone involved on so many different
terrains and spheres and fronts and still with a family, with
children, with a husband, brother Ferdinand, who is a highly
distinguished citizen and freedom fighter in his own right.
I do think that the Occupy movement could learn from the
kind of decentralization, the kind of differentiated forms of
activism that she engaged in herself while still trying to keep
that prophetic fire burning. I think you are absolutely right
about that. We said that the age of Occupy is the age of Ella
Baker; we could argue that the age of Occupy is Ella Baker in
a deep sense in terms of organizing and Ida B. Wells-Barnett
in terms of the multicontextual. Today, of course, it's ecological, anti-corporate, critiques of globalization, of the oligarchs
and plutocrats who rule around the world, but it's still a general principle of multicontextual activism that we see enacted
in Ida B. Wells-Barnett.

     If Ida is to be judged by the great leaders of her time, when
you think of Booker T. Washington and W. E. B. Du Bois,
and T. Thomas Fortune and Mary Church Terrell, and Mary

McLeod Bethune,[50] these are towering figures in their own right, but she would certainly be the most militant, the most outspoken, and, in many ways, the most courageous. Well, we don't want to overlook George Washington Woodbey, the Black Socialist preacher who ran with Eugene Debs in 1908 as vice president.[51] He was militant; he was uncompromising; and he was already connected to critiques of capitalism and imperialism and so forth. He was pastor at San Diego Mt. Zion Baptist Church for decades, a great towering figure who also deserves to be part of this great pantheon. But in the end, I think, we have to come back to sister Ida. We must learn from her in terms of moral integrity, spiritual fortitude, and political determination.

Last Words on the Black Prophetic Tradition in the Age of Obama

The great irony of our time is that in the age of Obama the grand Black prophetic tradition is weak and feeble. Obama's Black face of the American empire has made it more difficult for Black courageous and radical voices to bring critique to bear on the US empire. On the empirical or lived level of Black experience, Black people have suffered more in this age than in the recent past. Empirical indices of infant mortality rates, mass incarceration rates, mass unemployment, and dramatic declines in household wealth reveal this sad reality. How do we account for this irony? It goes far beyond the individual figure of President Obama himself, though he is complicit; he is a symptom, not a primary cause. Although he is a symbol for some of either a postracial condition or incredible Black progress, his presidency conceals the escalating levels of social misery in poor and Black America.

The leading causes of the decline of the Black prophetic tradition are threefold. First, there is the shift of Black leadership from the voices of social movements like those in this book to those of elected officials in the mainstream political system. This shift produces voices that are rarely if ever critical of this system. How could we expect the Black caretakers and gatekeepers of the system to be critical of it? This shift is part of a larger structural transformation in the history of mid-twentieth-century capitalism in which neoliberal elites marginalize social movements and prophetic voices in the name of consolidating a rising oligarchy at the top, leaving a devastated working class in the middle, and desperate poor people whose labor is no longer necessary for the system at the bottom.

Second, this neoliberal shift produces a culture of raw ambition and instant success that is seductive to most potential leaders and intellectuals, thereby incorporating them into the neoliberal regime. This culture of superficial spectacle and hyper-visible celebrities highlights the legitimacy of an unjust system that prides itself on upward mobility of the downtrodden. Yet, the truth is that we live in a country that has the least upward mobility of any other modern nation![1]

Third, the US neoliberal regime contains a vicious repressive apparatus that targets those strong and sacrificial leaders, activists, and prophetic intellectuals who are easily discredited, delegitimated, or even assassinated, including through character assassination. Character assassination becomes systemic and chronic, and it is preferable to literal assassination because dead martyrs tend to command the attention of the sleepwalking masses and thereby elevate the threat to the status quo.

The central role of mass media, especially a corporate media beholden to the US neoliberal regime, is to keep public discourse narrow and deodorized. By "narrow" I mean confining the conversation to conservative Republican and neoliberal Democrats who shut out prophetic voices or radical visions. This fundamental power to define the political terrain and categories attempts to render prophetic voices invisible. The discourse is deodorized because the issues that prophetic voices highlight, such as mass incarceration, wealth inequality, and war crimes such as imperial drones murdering innocent people, are ignored.

The age of Obama was predicated on three pillars: Wall Street crimes in the financial catastrophe of 2008; imperial crimes in the form of the USA PATRIOT Act and National Defense Authorization Act, which give the president sweeping and arbitrary power that resembles a police or neofascist state; and social crimes principally manifest in a criminal justice system that is in itself criminal (where torturers, wire tappers, and Wall Street violators of the law go free yet poor criminals, such as drug offenders, go to prison). This kind of clear and direct language is rare in political discourse precisely because we are accustomed to be so polite in the face of crimes against humanity. The role of the Black prophetic tradition has always been to shatter the narrow and deodorized discourse in the name of the funky humanity and precious individuality of poor people. How rarely this takes place today! The profound failings of President Obama can be seen in his Wall Street government, his indifference to the new Jim Crow (or prison-industrial complex) and his expansion of imperial criminality in terms of the vast increase of the number of drones since the Bush years. In other words, the Obama presidency has been primarily a Wall Street presidency, drone presidency, mass surveillance presidency unwilling to concretely target the new Jim Crow, massive unemployment, and other forms of poor and Black social misery. His major effort to focus on poor Black men was charity and philanthropy—not justice or public policy.

The state of Black America in the age of Obama has been one of desperation, confusion, and capitulation. The desperation is rooted in the escalating suffering on every front. The confusion arises from a conflation of symbol and substance. The capitulation rests on an obsessive need to protect the first Black president against all forms of criticism. Black desperation is part of a broader desperation among poor and working people during the age of Obama. The bailout of Wall Street by the Obama administration, rather than the bailout of homeowners, hurt millions of working people. The refusal of the Obama administration to place a priority on jobs with a living wage reinforced massive unemployment, and the sheer invisibility of poor people's plight in public policy has produced more social despair among weak and vulnerable citizens. The unprecedented historical symbolism of the first Black president has misled many if not most Black people to downplay his substantial neoliberal policies and elevate his (and his family's) brilliant and charismatic presence. Needless to say, the presence of his brilliant and charismatic wife, Michelle—a descendent of enslaved and Jim-Crowed people, unlike himself— even more deeply legitimates his symbolic status, a status that easily substitutes for substantial achievement. The cowardly capitulation of Black leadership to Obama's neoliberal policies in the name of the Black prophetic tradition is pathetic. The role of the NAACP, National Urban League, and Black corporate media pundits, who so quickly became Obama apologists, constitutes a fundamental betrayal of the Black prophetic tradition. The very idea of Black prophetic voices as an extension of a neoliberal and imperial US regime is a violation of what the Black prophetic tradition has been and is. This violation enrages me when I think of the blood, sweat, and tears of the people who created and sustained this precious tradition. The righteous indignation of the Black prophetic tradition targets not only the oppressive system that dominates us but also the fraudulent figures who pose and posture as prophetic ones while the suffering of the people is hidden and concealed. To sell one's soul for a mess of Obama pottage is to trash the priceless Black prophetic tradition. Is it not hypocritical to raise one's voice when the pharaoh is white but have no critical word to say when the pharaoh is Black? If the boot is on our neck, does it make any difference what color the foot is in the boot? Moral integrity, political consistency, and systemic analysis sit at the center of the Black prophetic tradition.

Since the rise of the neoliberal regime, the Black struggle for freedom has been cast or reduced to an interest group, one among other such groups in American politics. Even the motto of the Black Congressional Caucus, the apex of Black elected officials, is "We have no permanent friends or permanent enemies—only permanent interests." How morally empty and ethically deficient this motto is— no reference to moral principles, ethical standards, or grand visions of justice for all; just permanent interests, like the Business Roundtable for Wall Street oligarchs, the American Israel Public Affairs Committee (AIPAC) for the security of Israel, or the National Rifle Association for gun ownership. The Black prophetic tradition indeed includes interests but goes far beyond such narrow calculations and stresses a moral high ground of fairness and justice for all. The Black prophetic tradition surely begins on the chocolate side of town, but like the blues and jazz, it has a universal message for all human beings concerned about justice and freedom.

It is no accident that the "permanent interests" of the Black Congressional Caucus so quickly became Black middle class interests given the neoliberal regime to which they were accommodating. To be a highly successful Black professional or politician is too often to be well adjusted to injustice and well adapted to indifference toward poor people, including Black poor people. The Black prophetic tradition is fundamentally committed to the priority of poor and working people, thus pitting it against the neoliberal regime, capitalist system, and imperial policies of the US government. The Black prophetic tradition has never been confined to the interests and situations of Black people. It is rooted in principles and visions that embrace these interests and confront the situations, but its message is for the country and world. The Black prophetic tradition has been the leaven in the American democratic loaf. When the Black prophetic tradition is strong, poor and working people of all colors benefit. When the Black prophetic tradition is weak, poor and working class people are overlooked. On the international level, when the Black prophetic tradition is vital and vibrant, anti-imperial critiques are intense, and the plight of the wretched of the earth is elevated. What does it profit a people for a symbolic figure to gain presidential power if we turn our backs from the suffering of poor and working people, and thereby lose our souls? The Black prophetic tradition has tried to redeem the soul of our fragile democratic experiment. Is it redeemable?

—CW

Introduction: Why We Need to Talk About Black Prophetic Fire

1. Cornel West, "Pragmatism and the Tragic," in West, *Prophetic Thought in Postmodern Times*, vol. 1, *Beyond Eurocentrism and Multiculturalism* (Monroe, ME: Common Courage Press, 1993), 45; cf. Cornel West, "Pragmatism and the Sense of the Tragic," in West, *Keeping Faith: Philosophy and Race in America* (New York: Routledge, 1993), 114.

2. West, "Pragmatism and the Tragic," 32.

3. Cornel West, *Race Matters* (New York: Vintage, 1994), 147.

4. James Baldwin, "Down at the Cross," in *The Fire Next Time* (New York: Vintage, 1992), 26; cf. Pierre Bourdieu, *Pascalian Meditations* (Stanford, CA: Stanford University Press, 2000), 170.

Chapter One: It's a Beautiful Thing to Be on Fire

1. "The Meaning of July Fourth for the Negro," speech at Rochester, New York, July 5, 1852, in *Frederick Douglass: Selected Speeches and Writings*, ed. Philip S. Foner (Chicago: Lawrence Hill Books, 1999), 188–206 (hereafter cited as *Selected Speeches*). One of Douglass's most powerful orations, it is best known in its abbreviated version published by Douglass himself, with other extracts from his speeches, under the title "What to the Slave Is the Fourth of July?" in an appendix to his autobiography *My Bondage and My Freedom* in Frederick Douglass, *Autobiographies*, ed. Henry Louis Gates Jr. (1855; New York: Library of America, 1994), 431–35.

2. Angela Davis's first lecture as an assistant professor of philosophy at the University of California at Los Angeles was on Frederick Douglass. "Angela said for a people in slavery 'the first condition of freedom is an open act

of resistance—physical resistance, violent resistance.'" Howard Moore Jr., "Angela—Symbol in Resistance," in *If They Come in the Morning: Voices of Resistance*, ed. Angela Y. Davis et al. (New York: Third Press, 1971), 191–92. See also chap. 3, n. 31.

3. Toward the end of his life, Douglass gave two speeches against the "frequent and increasing resort to lynch law in our Southern States." "Lynch Law in the South" was published in the renowned *North American Review* (July 1892); reprinted in *Selected Speeches*, 746. According to the editor, "[A]ll the fire of his early years returned as Douglass struck out hard against the defenders of lynching" (*Selected Speeches*, 746). Provoked by the outcry it caused, Douglass extended his attack in his last major address, "Why Is the Negro Lynched?" published in a pamphlet entitled *The Lesson of the Hour* (1894); reprinted in *Selected Speeches*, 750–76.

4. "Oration in Memory of Abraham Lincoln, delivered at the unveiling of the Freedmen's Monument in Memory of Abraham Lincoln, in Lincoln Park, Washington, D.C., April 14, 1876," in *Selected Speeches*, 616–24. The sculptor Thomas Ball had designed the statue that Douglass criticized later for presenting "the Negro on his knees when a more manly attitude would have been indicative of freedom" (615). Yet Douglass failed to come up to his own standards expressed in his 1852 oration (see above, n. 1), when he had demanded: "We have to do with the past only as we can make it useful to the present and to the future" (193).

5. Owing to a result of a highly contested election, the nineteenth president of the United States, Rutherford B. Hayes, was inaugurated in early March 1877 as a result of the so-called "Compromise of 1877," which allowed the Republicans to claim the presidency in exchange for ending the implementation of Reconstruction in the Southern states. Immediately afterwards, Hayes appointed Douglass United States Marshal of the District of Columbia, and despite substantial opposition, Douglass was confirmed by the Senate on March 17, 1877. According to Douglass, one of the reasons against his appointment was that "a colored man at the *Executive Mansion* in white kid gloves" should perform the ceremony "of introducing the aristocratic citizens of the republic to the President of the United States" (*Life and Times of Frederick Douglass Written By Himself*, in *Autobiographies*, 856). Although Douglass had protested the diminishing Republican commitment to Reconstruction during the election campaign, he was silent when the newly elected president decided to withdraw federal troops from the South.

6. "Yeah, brother, you find me in a crack house before you find me in the White House." Jeff Sharlet, "The Supreme Love and Revolutionary Funk of Dr. Cornel West, Philosopher of the Blues," *Rolling Stone*, May 28, 2009.

7. Michael Lind, *The Next American Nation: The New Nationalism and the Fourth American Revolution* (New York: Free Press, 1995).

8. Herman Melville juxtaposes the illusion of individual autonomy with the reality of social interdependence, when, in chap. 108 of *Moby-Dick*, he has Ahab, the epitome of human hubris, complain about his dependence on the carpenter who is in the process of crafting an artificial leg for him: "Here I am, proud as a Greek god, and yet standing debtor to this blockhead for a bone to stand on! Cursed be that mortal inter-indebtedness which will not do away with ledgers." *Moby-Dick or The Whale* (Evanston: Northwestern University Press/Newberry Library, 1988), 471–72.

9. The two prominent Abolitionists authorize, as it were, Douglass's narrative; see William Lloyd Garrison's preface and a letter by Wendell Phillips to Douglass in *Narrative of the Life of Frederick Douglass, an American Slave. Written by Himself* (1845), in Douglass, *Autobiographies*, 3–10, 11–13.

10. Cornel West with David Ritz, *Brother West: Living and Loving Out Loud* (Carlsbad, CA: Smiley Books, 2009).

11. Douglass, *Narrative*, in *Autobiographies*, 33.

12. Douglass, *My Bondage and My Freedom* (1855), in *Autobiographies*, 169.

13. Douglass, *Life and Times* (1881; rev. 1893), in *Autobiographies*, 492.

14. For an extended argument, see Christa Buschendorf, "'Properly Speaking There Are in the World No Such Men as Self-Made Men': Frederick Douglass's Exceptional Position in the Field of Slavery," in *Intellectual Authority and Literary Culture in the US, 1790–1900*, ed. Günter Leypoldt (Heidelberg: Winter Verlag, 2013), 159–84.

15. Douglass, *Narrative*, in *Autobiographies*, 97.

16. Ludwig Andreas Feuerbach, *The Essence of Christianity* (1841), trans. from the second German edition by Marian Evans (London: Chapman, 1854; New York: Blanchard, 1855). Based on a fundamental critique of Hegelian idealism, Feuerbach interpreted religion anthropologically, claiming that God is a mere projection of human beings that reflects their desire for self-transcendence.

17. In 1860, Douglass read Feuerbach's *Essence of Christianity* with his German friend Ottilie Assing, who seems to have tried to convert Douglass to agnosticism and in a letter to Feuerbach (1871) claimed, "Douglass has become your enthusiastic admirer." See Maria Diedrich, *Love Across the Color Lines: Ottilie Assing and Frederick Douglass* (New York: Hill and Wang, 1999), 227–29. See also the allusion to Feuerbach in a letter by Assing to Douglass (Jan. 6, 1879), in which she encouraged him to write a sequel to his second autobiography that "would furnish an abundance of [. . .] highly interesting material, and of all things your conversion to free thinking, how through your

own courage and strength, with Feuerbach tendering a helping hand to you as it were, you broke the chains of a second bondage." *Radical Passion: Ottilie Assing's Reports from America and Letters to Frederick Douglass*, ed., trans., and introduced by Christoph Lohmann (New York: Peter Lang, 1999), 351. Douglass, however, preferred not to mention Feuerbach in *Life and Times*.

18. In Douglass's 1846 report of his visit to the Scottish town of Ayr, the birthplace of "the brilliant genius," he describes the social position of the poet in terms reminiscent of his own recent experiences: "Burns lived in the midst of a bigoted and besotted clergy—a pious but corrupt generation—a proud, ambitious, and contemptuous aristocracy, who, esteemed a little more than a man, and looked upon the plowman, such as was the noble Burns, as being little better than a brute." Philip S. Foner, *The Life and Writings of Frederick Douglass*, vol. 1., *Early Years, 1817–1849* (New York: International Publishers, 1950), 153. The eighteenth-century poet was a stern critic of false claims of authority, a passionate spokesperson for the working poor, and a resolute defender of the dignity of the common man. Not surprisingly, "Douglass had a special fondness for the highland singer shared by many American Negroes." Arna Bontemps, *Free At Last: The Life of Frederick Douglass* (New York: Dodd, Mead, 1971), 127. Almost fifty years after his tour through Scotland, Douglass connected the suppression of independent thinking in his former life as a slave with Burns's poem "Man Was Made to Mourn": "Obedience was the duty of the slave. I in my innocence once told my old master that I thought a certain way of doing some work I had in hand the best way to do it. He promptly demanded, 'Who gave you a right to think?' I might have answered in the language of Robert Burns, 'Were I designed your lordling's slave, / By Nature's law designed, / Why was an independent thought / E'er placed in my mind?' But I had not then read Robert Burns. Burns had high ideas of the dignity of simple manhood." "The Blessing of Liberty and Education" (1894), in *The Frederick Douglass Papers*, series 1, *Speeches, Debates, and Interviews*, vol. 5, *1881–95*, ed. John W. Blassingame and John R. McKivigan (New Haven, CT: Yale University Press, 1992), 565.

19. "Hereditary bondmen, know ye not / Who would be free, themselves must strike the blow?" Douglass quotes the famous couplet from Lord Byron's *Childe Harold's Pilgrimage*, canto ii, stanza 76, at the end of chap. 17 of *My Bondage and My Freedom*, in which he describes the long victorious battle with the notorious slave breaker Covey, a victory that Douglass considered the turning point in his life as a slave (*Autobiographies*, 287). Douglass's library contained both *The Works of Robert Burns* (1837) and *The Works of Lord Byron* (New York: Blake, 1840). See William L. Petrie and Douglas E. Stover, eds.,

Bibliography of the Frederick Douglass Library at Cedar Hill (Fort Washington, MD. Silesia Companies, 1995).

20. John T. Grayson is still at Mt. Holyoke, where he conducts research on the women in Douglass's life.

21. *Autobiographies*, 431, 432.

22. See Christa Buschendorf, "The Shaping of We-Group Identities in the African American Community," in *The Imaginary and Its Worlds: American Studies after the Transnational Turn*, ed. Laura Bieger et al. (Hanover, NH: Dartmouth College Press/University Press of New England, 2013), 84–106.

23. Here and elsewhere in our dialogue, West refers to the title of what has become the classic of anticolonialism by the trained psychiatrist, Marxian revolutionary humanist, and activist Frantz Fanon: *The Wretched of the Earth* (1961), trans. Constance Farrington, preface by Jean-Paul Sartre (New York: Grove Press, 1963); new edition, trans. Richard Philcox, foreword by Homi K. Bhaba (New York: Grove Press, 2004). For Fanon's influence on the Black Power movement, see David Macey's acclaimed biography, *Frantz Fanon* (2000; London: Verso, 2012), 23.

24. "Inasmuch as ye have done it to the least of these my brethren, ye have done it unto me." Matthew 25: 40.

25. In reflecting upon critiques of optimism, West mentions major French and German eighteenth-century Enlightenment thinkers. Voltaire's most famous work, *Candide, or Optimism* (1759), is a satire on philosophic optimism represented by the protagonist's mentor Pangloss. In *Rameau's Nephew* (written between 1760 and 1774), Denis Diderot criticizes contemporary French society in the form of a highly satirical philosophic dialogue. The major philosopher of German idealism, Immanuel Kant, postulated man's exercise of rationality and self-determination (*What Is Enlightenment?* 1784), but in his philosophy of religion he saw a propensity of human beings toward radical evil (*Religion within the Boundaries of Mere Reason*, 1793). The playwright and critic Gotthold Ephraim Lessing put his ideal of brotherly love and religious tolerance into his drama *Nathan the Wise* (1779); in his various contributions to contemporary theological controversies he was known for his position of critical questioning.

26. John Stauffer, "Frederick Douglass's Self-Fashioning and the Making of a Representative American Man," in *The Cambridge Companion to the African American Slave Narrative*, ed. Audrey Fisch (Cambridge, UK: Cambridge University Press, 2007), 210.

27. "An organic intellectual, in contrast to traditional intellectuals who often remain comfortably nested in the academy, attempts to be entrenched

in and affiliated with organizations, associations, and, possibly, movements of grass-roots folk." Cornel West, *The American Evasion of Philosophy: A Genealogy of Pragmatism* (Madison: University of Wisconsin Press, 1989), 234. The conception of the "organic intellectual" stems from the Italian thinker in the Marxist tradition, Antonio Gramsci, who discusses it in his essay "The Intellectual Selections from the Prison Notebooks." See Gramsci, *Selections from the Prison Notebooks*, trans. and ed. Quintin Hoare and Geoffrey Nowell Smith (New York: International Publishers, 1971), 5–23. West has appropriated Gramsci's core concept of hegemony ("the set of formal ideas and beliefs and informal modes of behavior, habits, manners, sensibilities, and outlooks that support and sanction the existing order") and his view of "organic intellectuals as leaders and thinkers directly tied into a particular cultural group primarily by means of institutional affiliations" to the Black prophetic tradition as early as *Prophesy Deliverance! An Afro-American Revolutionary Christianity* (Philadelphia: Westminster Press, 1982; Louisville, KY: Westminster John Knox Press, 2002; anniversary ed. with a new preface by the author), 119, 121. In his book on American pragmatism, West explains why his own concept of prophetic pragmatism "is inspired by the example of Antonio Gramsci [. . .] the major twentieth-century philosopher of praxis, power, and provocation" whose "work is historically specific, theoretically engaging, and politically activistic in an exemplary manner" (*American Evasion of Philosophy*, 231).

28. The English journalist William Cobbett (1763–1835) investigated the difficult living conditions of the English rural population on the basis of first-hand observations published under the title *Rural Rides* in 1830.

29. There seems to be no evidence that Douglass read the liberal political journalist and literary critic William Hazlitt (1778–1830), who is considered one of the greatest essayists in the English language.

30. Douglass possessed several volumes of the works of John Ruskin, who was not only the major art historian of the Victorian era but also an early critic of modern industrial capitalism whose utopian vision of human society was to inspire many Socialists. It is interesting to note that Douglass owned not only studies in art history, e.g., *Lectures on Architecture*, but also three famous Ruskin lectures, "Work," "War," and "Traffic," collected in *The Crown of Wild Olive* (New York, n.d. [1866]); see *Bibliography of the Douglass Library*, s.v. Ruskin.

31. An avid disciple of Ruskin, the prolific writer of poetry and fiction and staunch Socialist William Morris applied Ruskin's concept of the revival of craftsmanship to the art of textile design and in 1861 founded a decorative arts firm together with the artists Edward Burne-Jones, Dante Gabriel

Rossetti, and others. But as with Hazlitt, there is no evidence of Douglass's reception of Morris.

32. The Scottish philosopher, historian, and essayist Thomas Carlyle published *Sartor Resartus* in 1831, followed by *The French Revolution* (1837) and *On Heroes and Hero Worship and the Heroic in History* (1841). For Carlyle's 1849 "Occasional Discourse on the Nigger Question," see *Collected Works*, vol. 11, *Critical and Miscellaneous Essays: Collected and Republished in Six Volumes*, vol. VI (London: Chapman and Hall, 1870), 169–210.

33. James McCune Smith, "Introduction," in Douglass, *My Bondage*, in *Autobiographies*, 132.

34. On Douglass's reading of Emerson, see Stauffer, "Frederick Douglass's Self-Fashioning," 205. In addition, there are references to Emerson in Douglass's published papers. In his early years in the North he regularly attended popular lectures, and among the lecturers he heard was Emerson; see *Frederick Douglass Papers*, vol. 1: *1841-46*, xxiii; and in a manuscript (ca. 1865), he "discusses Emerson's comments on producers and poets" (*Frederick Douglass Papers*, series 1, vol. 3: *1855-63*, 620).

35. Gay Wilson Allen, *Waldo Emerson: A Biography* (New York: Viking Press, 1981).

36. Lawrence Buell, *Emerson* (Cambridge, MA: Belknap Press of Harvard University Press, 2003). Referring to Emerson's address on British emancipation, Buell states: "Never before had he so firmly associated himself in public with any social reform movement, on the same platform with noted activists like Frederick Douglass" (251). Buell also presents evidence from Emerson's papers that Douglass knew Emerson's *Representative Men*: soon after its publication, on February 5, 1850, Douglass had written Emerson to ask for a copy (368, n. 14).

37. *Frederick Douglass and Herman Melville: Essays in Relation*, ed. Robert S. Levine and Samuel Otter (Chapel Hill: University of North Carolina Press, 2008).

38. See Sterling Stuckey's article "Cheer and Gloom: Douglass and Melville on Slave Dance and Music," in ibid.: "Melville's evocation of the music described by Douglass is so faithful to its tragic joy-sorrow quality that, as we shall see, blues form and feeling shape and suffuse his writing style at critical junctures in the novel" (71).

39. See also William V. Spanos, *The Legacy of Edward W. Said* (Urbana: University of Illinois Press, 2009).

40. William V. Spanos, *Herman Melville and the American Calling: Fiction After Moby-Dick, 1851–1857* (Albany: State University of New York Press,

2008); and William V. Spanos, *The Errant Art of Moby-Dick: The Canon, the Cold War, and the Struggle for American Studies* (Durham, NC: Duke University Press, 1995). Meanwhile Spanos has published the third volume "in a trilogy whose essential aim is to retrieve Herman Melville's subversion of the myth of American exceptionalism": *The Exceptionalist State and the State of Exception: Herman Melville's* Billy Budd, Sailor (Baltimore: Johns Hopkins University Press, 2011), xi.

41. In the last and programmatic chapter of *The American Evasion of Philosophy*, "Prophetic Pragmatism," West explains that he defines his conception of pragmatism as "prophetic" because "it harks back to the Jewish and Christian tradition of prophets who brought urgent and compassionate critique to bear on the evils of their day. The mark of the prophet is to speak the truth in love with courage—come what may" (233).

42. Robert S. Levine, *Dislocating Race and Nation: Episodes in Nineteenth-Century Literary Nationalism* (Chapel Hill: University of North Carolina Press, 2008).

43. Charles Sumner served as US senator from Massachusetts from 1851 to 1874. A staunch and eloquent spokesman for the abolition of slavery and a harsh critic of Lincoln's moderate politics toward "slave power," he remained a strong advocate for civil and voting rights for the freedmen after the Civil War. One of Sumner's colleagues and friends was the German American Carl Schurz, who, as a student, had fought in the German Revolution of 1848, and after his emigration to the United States in 1852 brought his belief in democratic principles to the fight for the emancipation of slaves. Schurz served as a brigadier general in the Union army, held political posts under Presidents Lincoln and Hayes, and became the first German American to be elected to the US Senate (Missouri), in 1869.

44. See Levine, *Dislocating Race and Nation*, 209.

45. For Collins's remark, "Give us the facts, we will take care of the philosophy," see Douglass, *My Bondage*, in *Autobiographies*, 367.

46. See John Stauffer, *Giants: The Parallel Lives of Frederick Douglass and Abraham Lincoln* (New York: Twelve, 2008), 87–88.

47. The novel *The Autobiography of an Ex-Colored Man* was published anonymously in 1912 because Johnson was afraid it might harm his reputation as a diplomat; it appeared under his name in 1927 (by Knopf) with an introduction by Carl Van Vechten. James Weldon Johnson, *Along This Way: The Autobiography of James Weldon Johnson* (New York: Viking Press, 1933).

48. This was prior to Obama's retreat on green issues such as the Keystone Pipeline.

49. Frederick Douglass, "West India Emancipation," speech delivered at Canandaigua, NY, August 3, 1857, in *Selected Speeches*, 367. In this speech Douglass again quotes Byron: "Who would be free, themselves must strike the blow" (366); see also above n. 19.

50. "I had reached the point, at which I was *not afraid to die*." In Douglass, *My Bondage*, in *Autobiographies*, 286. Douglass cites Patrick Henry in connection with his first attempt at escape and points out that "incomparably more sublime" is "the same sentiment, when *practically* asserted by men accustomed to the lash and chain—men whose sensibilities must have become more or less deadened by their bondage" (312).

51. Douglas A. Blackmon, *Slavery by Another Name: The Re-Enslavement of Black Americans from the Civil War to World War II* (New York: Random House, 2008).

52. Leon F. Litwack, *Trouble in Mind: Black Southerners in the Age of Jim Crow* (New York: Knopf, 1998). See also Isabel Wilkerson, *The Warmth of Other Suns: The Epic Story of America's Great Migration* (New York: Random House, 2010).

53. W. E. B. Du Bois, *Dusk of Dawn: An Essay Towards an Autobiography of a Race Concept* (1940), in *The Oxford W. E. B. Du Bois*, ed. Henry Louis Gates Jr. (New York: Oxford University Press, 2007). The nineteen-volume edition of Du Bois's works is dedicated to Cornel West.

54. "The anti-slavery platform had performed its work, and my voice was no longer needed. [. . .] A man in the situation in which I found myself has not only to divest himself of the old, which is never easily done, but to adjust himself to the new, which is still more difficult. [. . .] But what should I do, was the question. I had a few thousand dollars [. . .] saved from the sale of 'My Bondage and My Freedom,' and the proceeds of my lectures at home and abroad, and with this sum I thought [. . .] [to] purchase a little farm and settle myself down to earn an honest living by tilling the soil." Douglass, *My Bondage*, in *Autobiographies*, 811, 812.

Chapter Two: The Black Flame

1. This conversation was recorded in the summer of 2010 and was first published under the title "'A Figure of Our Times': An Interview with Cornel West on W. E. B. Du Bois," in the *Du Bois Review* 10, no. 1 (2013): 261–78.

2. Cornel West, "W. E. B. Du Bois: The Jamesian Organic Intellectual," in West, *American Evasion of Philosophy*, 138–50.

3. Cornel West, "Black Strivings in a Twilight Civilization," in *The Future of the Race*, ed. Henry Louis Gates Jr. and Cornel West (New York: Vintage,

1997), 53–112, 180–96, 55; reprinted in *The Cornel West Reader* (New York: Civitas, 1999), 87–118, 571–79.

4. Ibid., 55.

5. West alludes to the main work of the eminent eighteenth-century British historian Edward Gibbon, *The History of the Decline and Fall of the Roman Empire*, in six volumes (1776–88).

6. In *Dusk of Dawn*, Du Bois carefully registers his intellectual development from both conformity with the Puritan work ethic ("My general attitude toward property and income was that all who were willing to work could easily earn a living; that those who had property had earned it and deserved it and could use it as they wished; that poverty was the shadow of crime and connoted lack of thrift and shiftlessness. These were the current patterns of economic thought of the town of my boyhood" [9]) and consent to the ideology of the "White man's burden" ("French, English and Germans pushed on in Africa, but I did not question the interpretation which pictured this as the advance of civilization and the benevolent tutelage of barbarians" [21]) to insights into the international scope of the problem of labor and property, which he first gained during his studies at the University of Berlin in 1892–1894, when he "began to see the race problem in America, the problem of the peoples of Africa and Asia, and the political development in Europe as one [23]."

7. *The Negro* covers African history and cultures and contains one chapter each on the slave trade and on "The Negro in the United States" (New York: Holt, 1915). Cf. Du Bois on the sequence of his writings on Africa in the foreword to *The World and Africa: An Inquiry into the Part Which Africa Has Played in World History* (1946; Oxford, UK: Oxford University Press, 2007): "Twice before I have essayed to write on the history of Africa: once in 1915 when the editors of the Home University Library asked me to attempt such a work. The result was the little volume called *The Negro*. [. . .] Naturally I wished to enlarge upon this earlier work after World War I and at the beginning of what I thought was a new era. So I wrote *Black Folk: Then and Now* (1939), with some new material and a more logical arrangement. But it happened that I was writing at the end of an age which marked the final catastrophe of the old era of European world dominance. [. . .] I deemed it, therefore, not only fitting but necessary in 1946 to essay again not so much a history of the Negroid peoples as a statement of their integral role in human history from prehistoric to modern times" (xxxi). By 1946, Du Bois views the history of European colonialism from a Marxian perspective: "I have also made bold to repeat the testimony of Karl Marx, whom I regard as the greatest of modern philosophers, and I have not been deterred by the witch-hunting which always follows mention of his name" (xxxii).

8. Studies on Du Bois as "sociological pioneer" have increased considerably in the past decade. On Du Bois's exclusion from the canon of sociology in the past and the increasing recognition of his work in the social sciences, see the introduction to *The Social Theory of W. E. B. Du Bois*, ed. Phil Zuckerman (Thousand Oaks, CA: Sage, 2004). See also Robert A. Wortham's numerous publications on Du Bois's sociology, especially on the sociology of religion: "Du Bois and the Sociology of Religion: Rediscovering a Founding Figure," *Sociological Inquiry* 75, no. 4 (2005): 433–52; "W. E. B. Du Bois, the Black Church, and the Sociological Study of Religion," *Sociological Spectrum* 29:2 (2009), 144–72; "W. E. B. Du Bois and the Scientific Study of Society: 1897–1914," in *W. E. B. Du Bois and the Sociological Imagination: A Reader, 1897–1914*, ed. Robert A. Wortham (Waco, TX: Baylor University Press, 2009), 1–20. For the neglect of Du Bois within the discipline of sociology on the one hand, and his achievements in the fields of urban and rural sociology, the sociology of race, gender, religion, as well as education and crime on the other hand, see *W. E. B. Du Bois*, ed. Reiland Rabaka (Farnham, UK: Ashgate, 2010). Drawing upon Michel Foucault's theories, Rabaka has written extensively on Du Bois; most relevant with regard to Du Bois's innovative transdisciplinary method is his monograph *Against Epistemic Apartheid: W. E. B. Du Bois and the Disciplinary Decadence of Sociology* (Boulder, CO: Lexington Books, 2010). For a broader approach that situates Du Bois and other Black sociologists in the field of US-American sociology, see the seminal study by Pierre Saint-Arnaud, *African American Pioneers of Sociology: A Critical History*, trans. Peter Feldstein (Toronto: University Press, 2009 [French original, 2003]. Saint-Arnaud summarizes Du Bois's significance as follows: "[G]iven the enormous scope of the task Du Bois had assigned himself—that of rehistoricizing the Negro 'problem,' which the Anglo-American paradigm viewed through an ahistorical lens—he had to *invent* sociohistorical analysis as such. He had to revolutionize his field in order to make room for black sociology" (143).

9. To be more precise, no review of *The Philadelphia Negro: A Social Study* (Boston: Ginn & Co., 1899) appeared in the *American Journal of Sociology*, at the time the only American journal in that field; moreover, as Saint-Arnaud puts it, "As for the possibility that Du Bois might actually publish a paper in the *Journal*, it was completely out of the question" (*African American Pioneers*, 155). Cf. Du Bois's comment on the academic neglect of the Atlanta University studies on the social condition of African Americans he and his team of social scientists undertook between 1896 and 1914: "Our reports were widely read and commented upon. On the other hand, so far as the American world of science and letters was concerned, we never 'belonged'; we remained unrecognized in learned societies and academic groups. We rated merely as Negroes studying

Negroes, and after all, what had Negroes to do with America or science?" *Autobiography of W. E. B. Du Bois: A Soliloquy on Viewing My Life from the Last Decade of Its First Century* (New York: International Publishers, 1968), 145.

10. Du Bois, *Dusk of Dawn*, 67.

11. See Du Bois: "Once in a while through all of us there flashes some clairvoyance, some clear idea, of what America really is. We who are dark can see America in a way that white Americans can not." "Criteria of Negro Art," *Crisis* 32 (October 1926): 290.

12. "A Klee painting named 'Angelus Novus' shows an angel looking as though he is about to move away from something he is fixedly contemplating. His eyes are staring, his mouth is open, his wings are spread. This is how one pictures the angel of history. His face is turned towards the past. Where we perceive a chain of events, he sees one single catastrophe which keeps piling wreckage upon wreckage and hurls it in front of his feet. The angel would like to stay, awaken the dead, and make whole what has been smashed. But a storm is blowing from Paradise; it has got caught in his wings with such violence that the angel can no longer close them. This storm irresistibly propels him into the future to which his back is turned, while the pile of debris before him grows skyward. This storm is what we call progress." Walter Benjamin, "Theses on the Philosophy of History" (1940), in *Illuminations*, ed. Hannah Arendt, trans. Harry Zohn (New York: Harcourt, Brace & World, 1968), 257–58.

13. "I did not understand at all, nor had my history courses led me to understand, anything of current European intrigue, of the expansion of European power into Africa, of the Industrial Revolution built on slave trade and now turning into Colonial Imperialism; of the fierce rivalry among white nations for controlling the profits from colonial raw material and labor—of all this I had no clear conception. I was blithely European and imperialist in outlook; democratic as democracy was conceived in America" (Du Bois, *Dusk of Dawn*, 16–17).

14. See Du Bois on his earlier faith in the power of enlightenment: "The Negro Problem was in my mind a matter of systematic investigation and intelligent understanding. The world was thinking wrong about race, because it did not know. The ultimate evil was stupidity. The cure for it was knowledge based on scientific investigation" (*Dusk of Dawn*, 30). By 1940, Du Bois had developed a more differentiated view: "Admitting widespread ignorance concerning the guilt of American whites for the plight of the Negroes; and the undoubted existence of sheer malevolence, the present attitude of the whites is much more the result of inherited customs and of those irrational and partly subconscious actions of men which control so large a proportion of their deeds. Attitudes and habits thus built up cannot be changed by sudden assault"

(ibid., 98). In hindsight, Du Bois himself names the theoretical munitions that allowed him to transform his position. "My long-term remedy was Truth. carefully gathered scientific proof that neither color nor race determined the limits of a man's capacity or desert. I was not at the time [in 1906] sufficiently Freudian to understand how little human action is based on reason; nor did I know Karl Marx well enough to appreciate the economic foundations of human history" (ibid., 145).

15. See Du Bois's concept of "the negro co-operative movement" (*Dusk of Dawn*, 106–9).

16. Loïc Wacquant, *Punishing the Poor: The Neoliberal Government of Social Insecurity* (Durham, NC: Duke University Press, 2009).

17. Du Bois stresses that in the South he "had accepted and embraced eagerly the companionship of those of my own color" (*Dusk of Dawn*, 17). He describes his first encounter with "the frenzy of a Negro revival in the untouched backwoods of the South" in the beginning of chap. X of *The Souls of Black Folk* (1903; New York: Modern Library, 2003), 190–91.

18. See Du Bois's self-characterization in *Dusk of Dawn*: "In general thought and conduct I became quite thoroughly New England. [. . .] I had the social heritage not only of a New England clan but Dutch taciturnity. This was later reinforced and strengthened by inner withdrawals in the face of real and imagined discriminations. [. . .] The Negroes in the South, when I came to know them, could never understand why I did not naturally greet everyone I passed on the street or slap my friends in the back" (9).

19. The book ends with a credo, as it were, a praise of "tragicomic hope" that "is wedded to a long and rich tradition of humanist pursuits of wisdom, justice, and freedom from Amos through Socrates to Ellison. The high-modern moments in this tradition—Shakespeare, Beethoven, Chekhov, Coltrane—enact and embody a creative weaving of the Socratic, prophetic, and tragicomic elements into profound interpretations of what it means to be human. These three elements constitute the most sturdy democratic armor available to us in our fight against corrupt elite power." Cornel West, *Democracy Matters: Winning the Fight Against Imperialism* (New York: Penguin, 2004), 217.

20. The essay referred to is entitled "Of Beauty and Death." It juxtaposes the enjoyment of beauty in nature with the painful experience of social death under Jim Crow in a dialogue with a female friend, "who is pale and positive," and accuses the first-person narrator, a persona of Du Bois, of being "too sensitive." *Darkwater: Voices from Within the Veil* (1920; New York: Washington Square Press, 2004), 171.

21. "The Souls of White Folk." It is interesting to note that in this essay, Du Bois anticipates the negative reaction of white readers to his collection of

essays, fiction, and poetry: "My word is to them mere bitterness and my soul, pessimism" (Du Bois, *Darkwater*, 21). As David Levering Lewis points out in his "Introduction," in "many of the mainstream American newspapers and periodicals the standard reproach was similar: *Darkwater* was tragically infected with its author's bitterness" (xvi).

22. Ibid., 35–36.

23. As Du Bois stated in the manifesto "Krigwa [= Crisis Guild of Writers and Artists] Little Theatre Movement," "a real Negro theatre" should be "About us, By us, For us, and Near us," *Crisis* 32 (July 1926): 135. "I believed that the pageant, with masses of costumed colored folk and a dramatic theme carried out chiefly by movement, dancing and music, could be made effective. [. . .] I wrote and staged an historic pageant of the history of the Negro race, calling it 'The Star of Ethiopia.' Before a total attendance of thirty thousand persons, we played it on the floor of an armory with three hundred fifty actors" (*Dusk of Dawn*, 136). After this first performance in New York in 1913, the pageant was reproduced in Washington in 1915 and in Philadelphia in 1916. It should be pointed out that Du Bois clearly understood that the genre was doomed to fail due to the competition from technically advanced media: "But alas, neither poetry nor pageants pay dividends, and in my case, they scarcely paid expenses. My pageant died with an expiring gasp in Los Angeles in 1925. But it died not solely for lack of support; rather from the tremendous and expanding vogue of the motion picture and the power of the radio and loud speaker. We had no capital to move into this field and indeed in face of monopoly, who has. Yet, my final pageant took place significantly in Hollywood Bowl, and was still a beautiful thing" (137). On the popularity of the pageant in America as a genre of political struggle in general and Du Bois's pageant in particular, see Soyica Diggs Colbert's interpretation of *The Star of Ethiopia* in her informative study *The African American Theatrical Body: Reception, Performance, and the Stage* (New York: Cambridge University Press, 2011), 48–90.

24. See "The Talented Tenth Memorial Address" (delivered at the Nineteenth Grand Boulé Conclave, Sigma Pi Phi, 1948); reprinted in Gates and West, *Future of the Race*, 159–77. In his attempt "to re-examine and restate the thesis of the Talented Tenth" (159), Du Bois concedes that he erroneously "assumed that with knowledge, sacrifice would automatically follow. In my youth and idealism, I did not realize that selfishness is even more natural than sacrifice" (161). Conceptually, the major shift is from individual to "group-leadership," or the "Guiding Hundredth," which then "calls for leadership through special organization" (168, 177).

25. See Shirley Graham Du Bois's portrait of her husband in *His Day Is Marching On: A Memoir of W. E. B. Du Bois* (New York: Lippincott, 1971),

which not only conveys Du Bois's superior intellect, stalwart courage, and prophetic vision but also his sharp wit and (oftentimes mischievous) humor. On her own political activism, which has all too often been neglected, see Gerald Horne and Margaret Stevens, "Shirley Graham Du Bois: Portrait of the Black Woman Artist as a Revolutionary," in *Want to Start a Revolution? Radical Women in the Black Freedom Struggle*, ed. Dayo F. Gore et al. (New York: New York University Press, 2009), 95–114.

26. "It is difficult to let others see the full psychological meaning of caste segregation. It is as though one, looking out from a dark cave in a side of an impending mountain, sees the world passing and speaks to it; speaks courteously and persuasively, showing them how these entombed souls are hindered in their natural movement, expression, and development. [. . .] It gradually penetrates the minds of the prisoners that the people passing do not hear; that some thick sheet of invisible but horribly tangible plate glass is between them and the world. They get excited; they talk louder; they gesticulate. [. . .] They may scream and hurl themselves against the barriers, hardly realizing in their bewilderment that they are screaming in a vacuum unheard and that their antics may actually seem funny to those outside looking in" (Du Bois, *Dusk of Dawn*, 66).

27. Ibid., 67.

28. In *The American Evasion of Philosophy*, West calls *Black Reconstruction* the "most significant product of Du Bois' encounter with Marxist thought" (146) and gives an example of Du Bois's "graphic and hyperbolic language": "America thus stepped forward in the first blossoming of the modern age and added to the Art of Beauty [. . .] and to Freedom of Belief [. . .] a vision of democratic self-government. [. . .] It was the Supreme Adventure, in the last Great Battle of the West, for that human freedom which would release the human spirit from lower lust for mere meat, and set it free to dream and sing. And then some unjust god leaned, laughing, over the ramparts of heaven and dropped a black man in the midst. It transformed the world. It turned democracy back to Roman Imperialism and Fascism; it restored caste and oligarchy; it replaced freedom with slavery and withdrew the name of humanity from the vast majority of human beings." Du Bois, *Black Reconstruction in America: An Essay Toward a History of the Part Which Black Folk Played in the Attempt to Reconstruct Democracy in America, 1860–1880* (New York: Harcourt, Brace, 1935), 29–30; cf. West, *American Evasion of Philosophy*, 147.

29. John A. Hobson (1858–1940) was an English economist and prolific writer best known for his critique of imperialism as a consequence of modern capitalism.

30. See West: "The last pillar of Du Bois's project is his American optimism. Like most intellectuals of the New World, he was preoccupied with

progress. [. . .] Du Bois tended to assume that U.S. expansionism was a sign of probable American progress. In this sense, in his early and middle years, he was not only a progressivist but also a kind of American exceptionalist. [. . .] Du Bois never fully grasped the deeply pessimistic view of American democracy behind the Garvey movement" ("Black Strivings," 71–72). In a footnote to this passage West highlights the importance of two essays by Du Bois, one of which he mentions above: "Du Bois confronts this pessimism most strikingly in two of the most insightful and angry essays in his corpus—'The White World,' in *Dusk of Dawn* (1940), and 'The Souls of White Folk,' in *Darkwater* (1920)" (West, "Black Strivings," 187n27).

31. "I just cannot take any more of this country's treatment. We leave for Ghana October 5 and I set no date for return. [. . .] Chin up, and fight on, but realize that American Negroes can't win." Du Bois quoted in Gerald Horne, *Black and Red: W. E. B. Du Bois and the Afro-American Response to the Cold War, 1944–1963* (Albany: State University of New York Press, 1986), 345; see also, West, *American Evasion of Philosophy*, 149.

32. For an extended argument regarding the similarities between "the Russian sense of the tragic and the Central European Jewish sense of the absurd and the black intellectual response to the African-American predicament," and Du Bois's neglect of this connection, see West, "Black Strivings," 76–79, 184n14, 187–90n29.

33. See chap. 1, n. 23.

34. For the passage we refer to, see chap. VI of *The Souls of Black Folk* entitled "Of the Training of Black Men": "I sit with Shakespeare and he winces not. Across the color line I move arm in arm with Balzac and Dumas [. . .] I summon Aristotle and Aurelius and what soul I will, and they come all graciously with no scorn or condescension" (109–10).

35. See West, "Black Strivings," 190–91n30.

36. On the influence of German and European culture and manners in general on his education, see the chap. "Europe 1892 to 1894" in Du Bois, *Autobiography*.

37. Du Bois wrote a very positive review of Wright's 1941 photo-history *12 Million Black Voices: A Folk History of the Negro in the United States* (photo direction Edwin Rosskam); he was more skeptical of Wright's autobiography *Black Boy* (1945), which he considered "as a work of art patently and terribly overdrawn" (see reviews nos. 104 and 115 in *Book Reviews by W. E. B. Du Bois*, ed. Herbert Aptheker (Millwood, NY: KTO Press, 1977), and he was highly critical of Wright's book *Black Power: A Record of Reactions in a Land of Pathos* (New York: Harper, 1954): "Naturally I did not like Richard Wright's book.

Some of his descriptions were splendid but his logic is lousy. He starts out to save Africa from Communism and then makes an attack on British capitalism which is devastating. How he reconciles these two attitudes I cannot see." Letter to George Padmore, December 10, 1954, in *The Correspondence of W. E. B. Du Bois*, vol. III, *Selections, 1944–1963*, ed. Herbert Aptheker (Amherst: University of Massachusetts Press, 1954), 375.

38. Edward J. Blum, *W. E. B. Du Bois: American Prophet* (Philadelphia: University of Philadelphia Press, 2007).

39. "The Revelation of Saint Orgne, the Damned," commencement address, 1938, Fisk University; reprinted in *W. E. B. Du Bois Speaks: Speeches and Addresses, 1920–1963*, ed. Philip S. Foner (New York: Pathfinder, 1970), 111.

40. Ibid.

41. Nikos Kazantzakis (1883–1957) is best known for his novels *Zorba the Greek* (1946; trans. 1952), *The Greek Passion* (1948; trans. 1954), *The Last Temptation of Christ* (1951; trans. 1960), and *Saint Francis* (1954; trans. 1962). He also wrote the play *Buddha* (1941–1943; trans. 1983) and the epic poem *The Odyssey: A Modern Sequel* (1938; trans. 1958). In 1928, while Kazantzakis worked at the first version of the *Buddha*, a verse tragedy he later destroyed, he also developed ideas for a screenplay on Lenin that he hoped to turn into a film; see *The Selected Letters of Nikos Kazantzakis*, ed. Peter Bien (Princeton, NJ: Princeton University Press, 2012). Another link between Du Bois and Kazantzakis is their interest in the Bolshevik Revolution and the Russian experiment in Communism, which led them both to travel to Russia in the 1920s. In 1927, Kazantzakis was a guest of the Soviet government for the celebrations of the tenth anniversary of the revolution, and in his letters from Moscow, he praised "the atmosphere [. . .] filled with spirit, every race has come to worship at the red Bethlehem" (*Selected Letters*, 278). See also his travel book *Russia: A Chronicle of Three Journeys in the Aftermath of the Revolution*, trans. Michael Antonakes and Thanasis Maskaleris (Berkeley, CA: Creative Arts Book, 1989). Cf. Du Bois's summary of his impressions of Russia during his trip in 1928: "Yet, there lay an unforgettable spirit upon the land" (*Dusk of Dawn*, 143); see also chap. IV, "The Soviet Union," *Autobiography*, 16–25.

42. Just forty days before he was assassinated, Martin Luther King Jr. spoke at an event marking the hundredth anniversary of Du Bois's birth, at Carnegie Hall in New York City, "Honoring Dr. Du Bois," in *Black Titan: W. E. B. Du Bois*, ed. John Henrik Clarke et al. (Boston: Beacon Press, 1970), 176–83.

43. Ibid., 181–82, 183.

Chapter Three: Moral Fire

1. The first and slightly different version of this chapter appeared as "We Need Martin More Than Ever" in *Amerikastudien/American Studies* 56, no. 3 (2011): 449–67. A shortened version was published in the German political journal *Die Gazette* (Summer 2013), translated into German by Marlon Lieber.

2. Cornel West, "Prophetic Christian as Organic Intellectual: Martin Luther King, Jr.," in *The Cornel West Reader*, 426; first published in Cornel West, *Prophetic Fragments: Illuminations of the Crisis in American Religion and Culture* (1988; Grand Rapids, MI: Eerdmans Publishing, 1993), 3–12.

3. Quoted in James Cone, "'Let Suffering Speak': The Vocation of a Black Intellectual," in *Cornel West: A Critical Reader*, ed. George Yancy (Malden, MA: Blackwell, 2001), 108.

4. Cornel West, "Introduction: The Crisis in Contemporary American Religion," *Prophetic Fragments*, ix-xi; reprinted in *The Cornel West Reader*, 338.

5. Martin Luther King Jr., "The Good Samaritan," sermon at Ebenezer Baptist Church, Atlanta, August 28, 1966; quoted in David J. Garrow, *Bearing the Cross: Martin Luther King, Jr., and the Southern Christian Leadership Conference* (New York: Vintage, 1988), 524.

6. "Let us march on poverty, until no American parent has to skip a meal so that their children may march on poverty, until no starved man walks the streets of our cities and towns in search of jobs that do not exist." Martin Luther King Jr., "Our God Is Marching On!" speech, Montgomery, AL, March 1965, in *I Have a Dream: Writings and Speeches That Changed the World*, ed. James M. Washington (New York: Harper, 1992), 123.

7. See Tavis Smiley and Cornel West, *The Rich and the Rest of Us: A Poverty Manifesto* (New York: Smiley Books, 2012).

8. Abraham Joshua Heschel, descended from a highly distinguished family of Polish Hasidic rabbis, was able to escape to London shortly before the German invasion of Poland, from where he emigrated to the United States in 1940. One of the leading Jewish theologians of the twentieth century and an advocate of interreligious dialogue, Heschel—on the basis of his study of Hebrew prophets and what in his University of Berlin doctoral dissertation he called "prophetic consciousness" (*Die Prophetie*, 1936)—insisted on combining religious commitment with social activism. He supported the civil rights movement, e.g., by taking part in the Selma-Montgomery march, and he spoke out against the Vietnam War (see, for instance, a publication on behalf of the interfaith group Clergy and Laymen Concerned About Vietnam, Robert McAfee Brown, Abraham J. Heschel, and Michael Novak, *Vietnam: Crisis of Conscience* (New York: Association Press, 1967). Heschel was one of

the speakers at New York's Riverside Church on April 4, 1965, when King gave his controversial speech "Beyond Vietnam," also known as "A Time to Break Silence." As Heschel wrote in 1972: "Would not our prophets be standing with those who protest against the war in Vietnam, the decay of our cities?" See Michael A. Chester, *Divine Pathos and Human Being: The Theology of Abraham Joshua Heschel* (London: Mitchell, 2005), 195.

9. Michelle Alexander, *The New Jim Crow: Mass Incarceration in the Age of Colorblindness*, foreword by Cornel West (New York: New Press, 2010).

10. Loïc Wacquant, *Punishing the Poor: The Neoliberal Government of Social Insecurity* (Durham, NC: Duke University Press, 2009).

11. Though Coretta King chose not to reveal this in her autobiography, she did mention that "Martin had, of course, read Karl Marx, who, he said, had convinced him that neither Marxism nor traditional capitalism held the whole truth, but each a partial truth." Coretta Scott King, *My Life with Martin Luther King, Jr.* (London: Hodder and Stoughton, 1970), 71. Cf. King's statement about their first date: "I never will forget, the first discussion we had was about the question of racial and economic injustice and the question of peace." *The Autobiography of Martin Luther King, Jr.*, ed. Clayborne Carson (New York: Warner, 1998), 35. King's autobiography contains an extended passage on Marxism, in which King criticizes the "materialistic interpretation of history," the "ethical relativism," and the "political totalitarianism" of the "Communist writings" of Marx and Lenin on the one hand, yet acknowledges that Marx had made him "ever more conscious [. . .] about the gulf between superfluous wealth and abject poverty" on the other hand (*Autobiography*, 21). As early as 1952, King, in a letter to his wife, addressed the failure of the capitalist system: "So today capitalism has out-lived its usefulness. It has brought about a system that takes necessities from the masses to give luxuries to the classes" (ibid., 36). By 1967 King did not hesitate to publicly question the capitalist economy, for example, when, in his last Southern Christian Leadership Conference (SCLC) presidential address, he spoke about "restructuring the whole of American society" and declared "that one day we must come to see that an edifice which produces beggars needs restructuring" and that "you begin to ask the question, 'Who owns the oil?'" In summary, he claimed, "When I say question the whole society, it means ultimately coming to see that the problem of racism, the problem of economic exploitation, and the problem of war are all tied together." "Where Do We Go From Here?" in *A Testament of Hope: The Essential Writings and Speeches of Martin Luther King, Jr.*, ed. James M. Melvin Washington (San Francisco: HarperCollins, 1991), 250. For a thorough and differentiated assessment of King's adoption of ideas of Marxism and democratic socialism, see Adam Fairclough, "Was Martin Luther King a

Marxist?," *History Workshop Journal* 15 (Spring 1983): 117–25; reprinted in *Martin Luther King, Jr.: Civil Rights Leader, Theologian, Orator*, vol. 2, ed. David J. Garrow (Brooklyn, NY: Carlson, 1989), 301–9.

12. Like King, Norman Thomas was very much influenced by Walter Rauschenbusch, a leading voice of the Social Gospel movement. And, like King, Thomas believed in nonviolent activism in the tradition of Gandhi and spoke out fervently against US militarism. Apart from Rauschenbusch's Christian concept of socialism, it was the extreme poverty and utter despondency of the working class of all colors, which Thomas witnessed as a social worker in lower Manhattan and later as a pastor of the East Harlem Church and which turned him toward a socialist critique of capitalism. In the chapter "The Negro," in his study *Human Exploitation in the United States* (New York: Frederick A. Stokes, 1934), 258–83, he discusses at length the interrelation between Black economic exploitation in the twentieth century and "the plantation psychology"; in emphasizing in particular the economic and psychological factors of lynching, he draws upon the case studies in Arthur Raper's *The Tragedy of Lynching* (Chapel Hill: University of North Carolina Press, 1933). He supported major civil rights campaigns, and though physical frailty prevented him from joining the Selma marches in 1965, he was one of the speakers at the March on Washington in August 1963. In 1965, King wrote an article about Thomas entitled "The Bravest Man I Ever Met," *Pageant* 20 (June 1965), in which he praised him for his undaunted commitment to the cause of justice and equality. For further details on Thomas's fight for racial justice and his relations with King, see Harry Fleischman, *Norman Thomas: A Biography: 1884–1968*, with a new chapter, "The Final Years" (New York: Norton, 1969), 323–24; and Raymond F. Gregory, *Norman Thomas: The Great Dissenter* (New York: Algora, 2008), 250–51, 271–72. West is an honorary chairman of the Democratic Socialists of America, the institutional heir of Norman Thomas's legacy.

13. Walter R. Chivers taught sociology at Morehouse College from 1925 to 1968. For his impact on other Black sociologists, his devotion to teaching, and his activism based on his early experiences as a social worker, see Charles V. Willie, "Walter R. Chivers—An Advocate of Situation Sociology," *Phylon* 43, no. 3 (1982): 242–48. John H. Stanfield, who considers King "a public sociologist par excellence," puts great emphasis on the Morehouse curriculum, with its stress "on thinking sociologically to promote the public good of racial justice," and maintains that Chivers, "who was the chief black community researcher for Arthur Raper's (1933) *The Tragedy of Lynching*" (see above, n. 12) "had a profound influence on King." Stanfield, s.v. King, *The Blackwell*

Encyclopedia of Sociology, vol. 5, ed. George Ritzer (Oxford, UK: Blackwell, 2007), 2465 67.

14. The Student Nonviolent Coordinating Committee (SNCC), an essential organizational force in the sit-ins, freedom rides, and voter-registration activities, turned more radical in the mid-1960s and under its new chairman, Stokely Carmichael (Kwame Ture), propagated "Black Power." A seminal text that presented "a political framework and ideology" of this revolutionary faction of the movement was *Black Power: The Politics of Liberation in America*, by Stokely Carmichael and Charles V. Hamilton (New York: Random House, 1967), vi; an enlarged edition with a new afterword by both authors critically discussing their concepts appeared in 1992. It clearly stated the necessity for a grassroots model: "The power must be that of a community" (ibid., 46). On SNCC's concept of Black Power, see also Stokely Carmichael, "What We Want," *New York Review of Books*, September 1966; reprinted as "Power and Racism" in *Stokely Speaks: From Black Power to Pan-Africanism* (1971; Chicago: Chicago Review Press, 2007), 17–30. For confrontations between Carmichael and King, see Garrow, *Bearing the Cross*, 481–85; for King's critique of Black Power politics, see the chap. "Black Power" in Martin Luther King Jr., *Where Do We Go from Here: Chaos or Community?* (1967; Boston: Beacon Press, 2010), 23–69.

15. Both Stanley David Levison, a Jewish businessman and member of the Communist Party who had been introduced to King by Bayard Taylor Rustin in the mid-1950s, and Rustin himself were close advisors to King. The FBI's supposition that Levison was a Communist agent prompted the wiretapping of Levison and King, and led Robert Kennedy to exert great pressure on King. See Taylor Branch, *Parting the Waters: America in the King Years, 1954–63* (New York: Simon & Schuster, 1988), 516–18, 835–38. Rustin, a Quaker, champion of nonviolent struggle, and one of the most important organizers of the movement, withdrew from the front line when his homosexual orientation was used to compromise King. Thus, *Brother Outsider* (Nancy Kates and Bennett Singer, dir. [California Newsreel, 2002]) is an appropriate title for a documentary on Rustin's life. For a study that analyzes Rustin's marginal position from the perspective of relational sociology, see Nicole Hirschfelder's PhD dissertation, "Oppression as Process: A Figurational Analysis of the Case of Bayard Rustin," University of Tübingen, 2012.

16. Per a May 22, 1967, Harris poll.

17. Carl T. Rowan was a highly successful and influential journalist in the 1960s. His syndicated columns were published in more than a hundred American and international newspapers, and in addition, he had contracts as a

weekly radio and TV commentator. In 1964 and 1965, he was director of the US Information Agency and, thus, became the first black man to be present in meetings of the National Security Council. In a *Reader's Digest* article published in September 1967, Rowan distanced himself from King, whose civil rights activism he had formerly covered very favorably ("Martin Luther King's Tragic Decision"). It is interesting to note that in a speech given February 14, 1965, Malcolm X, speaking about tokenism, mentioned Rowan: "Tokenism benefits only a few. It never benefits the masses. [. . .] So that the problem for the masses has gone absolutely unsolved. The only ones for whom it has been solved are people like [. . .] Carl Rowan, who was put over the USIA, and is very skillfully trying to make Africans think that the problem of black men in this country is all solved." *Malcolm X Speaks: Selected Speeches and Statements*, ed. George Breitman (New York: Pathfinder, 1990), 174.

18. Roy Wilkins, executive secretary of the National Association for the Advancement of Colored People in the 1960s, was an impassioned spokesman for the civil rights movement, yet a staunch critic of militant voices. His friend Whitney Moore Young Jr., who firmly believed in operating within the system, became famous for his successful work as executive director of the National Urban League.

19. The Southern Christian Leadership Conference (SCLC) was founded in early 1957 as an organization that endorsed forms of nonviolent protest. King became its first president, and Ella Baker was its first and—in the beginning—only staff member.

20. On the fear of these and other prominent African Americans that King's radical criticism of the Vietnam War might harm the civil rights movement, see Henry E. Darby and Margaret N. Rowley, "King on Vietnam and Beyond," *Phylon* 47, no. 1 (1986): 49–50.

21. Sacvan Bercovitch, *The American Jeremiad* (Madison: University of Wisconsin Press, 1978).

22. On Clarence B. Jones and the plan to put the United States on trial at the UN, see also below, chap. 5, n. 21.

23. There has been an increase in the last decade in scholarly attention toward Black Greek-letter organizations. For an account of the origins and legacy of the Alphas, see Stefan Bradley, "The First and Finest: The Founders of Alpha Phi Alpha Fraternity," *Black Greek-Letter Organizations in the Twenty-First Century*, ed. Gregory S. Parks (Lexington: University Press of Kentucky, 2008), 19–39.

24. Fred Hampton, leader of the Chicago chapter of the Black Panther Party, was twenty-one years old when he was assassinated in a Chicago police raid in December 1969; Bobby Hutton, treasurer of the Black Panther Party,

was not yet eighteen when, on April 6, 1968, he was shot dead by Oakland police.

25. Fannie Lou Hamer began her work in the civil rights movement as a voter registration activist, and although she experienced severe physical abuse by law enforcement officers, she refused to be intimidated and remained committed to the struggle for civil rights, e.g., as a candidate of the Mississippi Freedom Democratic Party for Congress in 1965. Like King, she would call America "a sick place," and like Malcolm X, she insisted on fighting not just for civil rights but for human rights; see, for example, her speeches "America Is a Sick Place, and Man Is on the Critical List" (May 27, 1970) and "Nobody's Free Until Everybody's Free" (July 10, 1971), in *The Speeches of Fannie Lou Hamer: To Tell It Like It Is*, ed. Maegan Parker Brooks and Davis W. Houck (Jackson: University Press of Mississippi, 2011).

26. Tavis Smiley's well-known PBS television special called *Beyond Vietnam* is the best treatment of this historic speech. For the speech, see "A Time to Break Silence," in *Testament of Hope*, 231–44.

27. Cf. the seminal volume of essays by Vincent Harding, *Martin Luther King: The Inconvenient Hero* (Maryknoll, NY: Orbis, 2008, rev. ed.), in which he challenges the "amnesia" vis-à-vis the national hero and quotes the poem "Now That He Is Safely Dead," by Carl Wendell Himes Jr., who, as early as 1977, wrote: "Dead men make / such convenient heroes: They / cannot rise / to challenge the images / we would fashion from their lives" (3).

28. "Eugene Debs was one of the greatest trade unionists as well as the leader of the US Socialist Party. His crusade against vast wealth inequality was legendary, yet despite his own antiracist views, he could not convince his organization to integrate with peoples of color" (West, *Democracy Matters*, 53). Like Debs, Jim Larkin was a Socialist and a trade union leader who, during his stay in the United States, became a speaker for the Socialist Party of America and supported Debs's presidential campaign. A famous legend has it that he once "unbuttoned his shirt to reveal a cross, and told his largely atheist [New York] audience: 'There is no antagonism between the Cross and socialism. [. . .] I stand by the Cross and I stand by Karl Marx.'" See Emmet O'Connor, "James Larkin in the United States, 1914–1923," *Journal of Contemporary History* 37, no. 2 (2002): 185.

29. "At that time [in the early seventies], MLK was a grand example of integrity and sacrifice but, in sharp contrast to Malcolm X, not a distinct voice with a credible politics in our Harvard conversations. [. . .] King was for us the Great Man who died for us—but not yet the voice we had to listen to, learn from and build on. This would change in the next decade." Cornel West, "Introduction: The Making of an American Democratic Socialist of African

Descent," in West, *The Ethical Dimensions of Marxist Thought* (New York: Monthly Review, 1991), xv–xxxiv; reprinted in *The Cornel West Reader*, 6–7.

30. In 1966, Huey P. Newton cofounded the Black Panther Party, which he and his combatant Bobby Seale conceptualized under the influence of Malcolm X and on the basis of writings by revolutionaries such as Mao Zedong, Frantz Fanon, and Che Guevara. Though the Black Panthers established armed self-defense patrols that often led to violent confrontations with the police, they also ran social programs, e.g., the children's breakfast program and free clinics.

31. Angela Y. Davis has been a radical activist since her youth, an associate of the Black Panther Party and a member of the Communist Party of the United States. For her early years of activism, her trial and acquittal of the charge of first-degree murder in the early 1970s, which had turned her into an internationally known and supported political prisoner, see Angela Davis, *An Autobiography* (New York: Random House, 1974). In her latest book, *The Meaning of Freedom*, a collection of unpublished speeches, she emphasizes the interconnectedness of the issues of power, race, gender, class, and mass incarceration, arguing for, among other things, the abolition of the prison-industrial complex. *The Meaning of Freedom*, foreword by Robin D. G. Kelley (San Francisco: City Lights Books, 2012). See also above chap. 1, n. 2.

32. For Stokely Carmichael, see above, n. 14.

33. Dr. Gardner C. Taylor, recognized for his elegant rhetorical style, is yet another prominent example of spiritual leadership and social activism.

34. Thomas Dexter Jakes maintains the television ministry of the Dallas-based Potter's House, which he founded in 1996.

35. Glen A. Staples is pastor of the Temple of Praise in Washington, DC.

36. "Under the dynamic leadership of Rev. Herbert Daughtry, the National Black United Front (composed of black Christians, Marxists, nationalists, and left-liberals) has established itself as the leading voice of progressive black America. Far beyond liberalism and indifferent to social democracy, this Christian headed-group is staunchly anti-US imperialist and vaguely pro-Socialist with a black nationalist twist. With the founding of the African Peoples' Christian Organization in March 1983, Rev. Daughtry has extended his vision by supplementing the National Black United Front with an exclusively Christian organization, especially for those prophetic black Christians demoralized and debilitated by the secular ideological battles in NBUF: Rev. Daughtry continues to head both organizations" (West, *Prophetic Fragments*, 71). Daughtry's most well-known book is *No Monopoly on Suffering* (Trenton, NJ: Africa World Press, 1997), with an introduction by Cornel West. The

well-respected Father Pfleger is the John Brown of contemporary America—a white leader profoundly committed to Black freedom. West has preached annually in his church for fifteen years. See Robert McClory, *Radical Disciple: Father Pfleger, St. Sabina Church, and the Fight for Social Justice* (Chicago: Chicago Review Press, 2010).

37. J. Alfred Smith Sr., pastor emeritus of Allen Temple Baptist Church, in Oakland, clearly reveals his commitment to the tradition of prophetic Christianity in the title of his 2004 autobiography: *On the Jericho Road: A Memoir of Racial Justice, Social Action, and Prophetic Ministry*, with Harry Louis Williams II (Downers Grove, IL: InterVarsity Press, 2004). Frederick Douglas Haynes III is senior pastor at Friendship-West Baptist Church, Dallas. Rev. Dr. Carolyn Ann Knight studied under Cornel West at Union Theological Seminary, where she received a master's of divinity and a master's of sacred theology; she earned a doctor of ministry from United Theological Seminary in Dayton, Ohio. She founded "Can Do" Ministries, devoted to the spiritual and intellectual advancement of youth, and she was professor of preaching at Interdenominational Theological Center in Atlanta for many years. She is one of the great preachers of her generation. Rev. Dr. Bernard Richardson is the dean of Howard University's historic Andrew Rankin Memorial Chapel and professor at Howard University's Divinity School. West has preached in this chapel annually for the past twenty years. Rev. Toby Sanders is pastor of the Beloved Community, former president of the Trenton Board of Education, and "dean" of the New Jersey STEP prison/college program (directed by Margaret Atkins), in which West teaches philosophy with 140 brothers/students in Rahway. Rev. Dr. Barbara King is the founder/minister of the Hillside Chapel and Truth Center in Atlanta. Rev. Dr. M. William Howard Jr. is the pastor of Bethany Baptist Church in Newark, New Jersey, and was the first Black president of the National Council of Churches. Rev. Dr. William Barber is one of the grand King-like figures in our time.

38. For statistics on housing and wealth distribution quoted in this passage and the next, see the Pew Research Center analysis based on 2009 government data: Rakesh Kochhar et al., *Twenty to One: Wealth Gaps Rise to Record Highs Between Whites, Blacks, Hispanics* (Washington, DC: Pew Research Social and Demographic Trends, July 26, 2011), http://www.pewsocialtrends.org/2011/07/26/wealth-gaps-rise-to-record-highs-between-whites-blacks-hispanics.

39. West refers to the period between December 2010 and August 2011.

40. E. Franklin Frazier, *Black Bourgeoisie* (Glencoe, IL: Free Press, 1957).

41. Kochhar, *Twenty to One*. For soaring corporate profits based largely on layoffs, see, for example, Floyd Norris, "As Corporate Profits Rise, Workers'

Income Declines," *New York Times*, August 5, 2011. The figure of $2.1 trillion is based on Federal Reserve statistics released in 2011 and discussed widely, e.g., by Jacob Goldstein on National Public Radio, September 20, 2011.

42. Marian Wright Edelman, a civil rights attorney, graduate of Yale University Law School, the first African American woman admitted to the Mississippi Bar, and promoter of the Poor People's Campaign, is best known for her indefatigable work on behalf of poor children, e.g., with the Children's Defense Fund.

43. Wolin defines democracy as a "project concerned with the political potentialities of ordinary citizens, that is, with their possibilities for becoming political beings through the self-discovery of common concerns and of modes of action for realizing them." Consequently, democracy "seems destined to be a moment rather than a form." Sheldon S. Wolin, "Fugitive Democracy," *Constellations* 1, no. 1 (1994): 11, 19.

44. Though Bourdieu argues that "there is an inertia [. . .] of habitus" (*Pascalian Meditations*, 160), he also emphasizes that habitus can be "practically transformed" and even "*controlled*" through awakening consciousness and socioanalysis." Pierre Bourdieu, *In Other Words: Essays Towards a Reflexive Sociology*, trans. Matthew Adamson (Cambridge, UK: Polity, 1994), 116.

45. *Howard Zinn on Race*, introduction by Cornel West (New York: Seven Stories Press, 2011).

46. Raymond Williams, *The Long Revolution* (London: Chatto, 1961).

47. This was also a favorite word of Fannie Lou Hamer's, who would say in many of her speeches that to be born Black in America is to be born in a mess.

48. Garrow, *Bearing the Cross*, 562.

49. On King's support for Carl Stokes's 1967 election campaign for mayor of Cleveland, see ibid., 580.

50. For Huey Newton and Amiri Baraka (LeRoi Jones), see also chap. 5. Baraka passed away on January 9, 2014.

51. Both Walter Sisulu, secretary general of the African National Congress (ANC), 1949–54, and Joe (Yossel Mashel) Slovo, a Lithuanian Jew whose family had emigrated to South Africa when he was eight years old, were members of the South African Communist Party and of the Umkhonto we Sizwe, "Spear of the Nation," the armed wing of the ANC, led by Mandela.

Chapter Four: The Heat of Democratic Existentialism

1. See Barbara Ransby, *Ella Baker and the Black Freedom Movement: A Radical Democratic Vision* (Chapel Hill: University of North Carolina Press, 2003), 170.

2. Ibid., 273.

3. "Receptivity" is a core concept of Romand Coles's theory of radical democracy that proposes the practices of listening and one-on-one relations in grassroots organizing. In an essay on both Cornel West and Ella Baker, Coles submits an extraordinarily perceptive reading of West's work, emphasizing the passages that testify to West's listening rather than his voicing, while at the same time offering a candid critique by juxtaposing West's "incredible passion and charisma" to Ella Baker's "democratic receptivity," because Coles "still think[s] that Cornel West has a great deal to learn from Ella Baker and from Bob Moses" and wants to push him beyond certain limits he discerns in his work. Romand Coles, "'To Make This Tradition Articulate': Practiced Receptivity Matters, Or Heading West of West with Cornel West and Ella Baker," in Stanley Hauerwas and Romand Coles, *Christianity, Democracy, and the Radical Ordinary: Conversations Between a Radical Democrat and a Christian* (Cambridge, UK: Lutterworth Press, 2008), 79, 53, 81.

4. Baker took Robert Parris Moses, a "deeply spiritual young man with a sharp intellect and a perceptive ear" (Ransby, *Ella Baker*, 248), under her wing. For an instructive summary of his educational background, his beginnings as an activist in SNCC, and his excellent rapport with Baker, see ibid., 248–52. Ransby highlights their "similar sensibilities": "Both were intellectuals, thoughtful and analytical, yet at the same time practical and personable. Both were deeply attentive to ideology and the ideological implications of certain tactical decisions, but both were equally willing to do the messy, hands-on work necessary to implement those ideas" (ibid., 251).

5. Baker and Schuyler were close friends in the 1930s; she was a founding member of the Young Negroes' Cooperative League (YNCL), launched by Schuyler in 1930, and became its national director. Among the various factions of anarchism, the economic model of the cooperative as a third way between capitalism and state Marxism was the most prominent concept during the Great Depression. As Schuyler wrote in 1930: "Cooperative democracy means a social order, in which the mills, mines, railroads, farms, markets, houses, shops and all the other necessary means of production, distribution and exchange are owned cooperatively by those who produce, operate and use them. Whereas the Socialists hope to usher in such a Utopia society by the ballot and the Communists hope to turn the trick with the bullet the cooperator (who is really an Anarchist since the triumph of his society will do away with the state in its present form—and I am an Anarchist) is slowly and methodologically doing so through legal, intelligent economic cooperation or mutual aid." *Pittsburgh Courier*, November 15, 1930; quoted in Ransby, *Ella Baker*, 87. Baker considered the cooperative movement as a path toward radical social

change, toward "the day," as Baker wrote in 1935, "when the soil and all of its resources will be reclaimed by its rightful owners—the working masses of the world." "Youthful City Workers Turning to Cooperative Farming," *Amsterdam News*, May 11, 1935; quoted in Ransby, *Ella Baker*, 86. For Du Bois's propagation of cooperative economics in the 1930s, see *Dusk of Dawn*.

6. For Bayard Rustin, see chap. 3, n. 15.

7. Best known as the cofounder of the Catholic Worker Movement and writer for the *Catholic Worker*, Dorothy Day, who converted to Catholicism in 1927, combined her anarchist and socialist convictions with a fervent religious belief. See Cornel West, "On the Legacy of Dorothy Day," *Catholic Agitator* 44, no. 1 (February 2014): 1–3, 6; and Cornel West, "Dorothy Day: Exemplar of Truth and Courage," a lecture given at Maryhouse Catholic Worker, New York City, November 8, 2013, the 114th birthday of Dorothy Day (http://www.youtube.com/watch?v=AcMmXSMqJag). For the anarchist thought of Day, Bayard Rustin, and Henry David Thoreau, see Anthony Terrance Wiley's Princeton PhD dissertation (2011), "Angelic Troublemakers: Religion and Anarchism in Henry David Thoreau, Dorothy Day, and Bayard Rustin."

8. Dutch poet and activist Herman Gorter and Dutch astronomer and theorist of council Communism Anton Pannekoek both criticized Lenin and the party dictatorship of the Bolsheviks. See, for example, Gorter's pamphlet *The World Revolution* (1923) and Pannekoek's *Lenin as Philosopher: A Critical Examination of the Philosophical Basis of Leninism* (1948; rev. ed., edited, annotated and with an introduction by Lance Byron Richey (Milwaukee: Marquette University Press, 2003). There is also a recent English translation of Pannekoek's 1946 *De arbeidersraden*, *Workers' Councils* (Edinburgh: AK, 2003), with an introduction by Noam Chomsky.

9. And yet, Baker's influence on Carmichael is evident in the following remark: "He [the Southern Negro] has been shamed into distrusting his own capacity to grow and lead and articulate. He has been shamed from birth by his skin, his poverty, his ignorance and even his speech. Whom does he see on television? Who gets projected in politics? The Lindsays and the Rockefellers and even the Martin Luther Kings—but not the Fannie Lou Hamers." Stokely Carmichael, "Who Is Qualified?" (1966), in *Stokely Speaks*, 13.

10. Though Baker's focus was the Black freedom struggle, she also dealt with international issues, e.g., the Vietnam War, the Puerto Rican fight for independence, and South African apartheid, as well as national problems of inequity, such as poverty, social injustice, unequal education, and discrimination against women (Ransby, *Ella Baker*, 5).

11. West refers to the following two biographies on Baker: Joanne Grant's *Ella Baker: Freedom Bound* (New York: John Wiley, 1998) and Barbara Ransby's *Ella Baker and the Black Freedom Movement* (cited above, n. 1). For Coles's work, see "'To Make This Tradition Articulate,'" above, n. 3.

12. It would be a mistake to consider Ella Baker as an activist exclusively rooted in practice. In fact, her practice was informed by theoretical reading; for example, according to a friend, "Ella Baker was a student of Marx and we used to debate that often" (Ransby, *Ella Baker*, 68); for further information on Baker's education in Harlem, "a hotbed of radical thinking" (Baker, quoted in ibid., 64), see "Harlem during the 1930s: The Making of a Black Radical Activist and Intellectual" (ibid., 64–104). Ransby summarizes Baker's logic of practice as follows: "Baker's theory of social change and political organizing was inscribed in her practice. Her ideas were written in her work: a coherent body of lived text spanning nearly sixty years" (ibid., 1).

13. Williams, *Long Revolution*.

14. Mary Frances Berry and John Blassingame, *Long Memory: The Black Experience in America* (New York: Oxford University Press, 1982).

15. Saul David Alinsky, a student of sociologist Robert Park at the University of Chicago, was a pioneer of community organizing, and his book *Rules for Radicals: A Pragmatic Primer for Realistic Radicals* (New York: Random House, 1971) has been an influential manual of grassroots organizing. Alinsky established the community organizing network the Industrial Areas Foundation (IAF) in 1940. With his first organizing project, the Back of the Yards Neighborhood Council, located in an industrial area next to the Chicago stockyards, Alinsky joined two basic social forces of the neighborhood: organized religion (the Catholic church) and organized labor. It not only improved the living conditions of the people but also their understanding of the importance of self-organizing: "The organizations and institutions of the people back of the yards feel that the only way that they can get their rights is through a community organization that is built, owned, and operated by themselves rather than by outside interests which in many cases are basically opposed to many of the fundamental objectives which these people want." Alinsky, "Community Organizing and Analysis," *American Journal of Sociology* 46 (May 1941): 807. Ernesto Cortés, trained by the Industrial Areas Foundation in the early 1970s, is now cochair and executive director of the West/Southwest regional network of the IAF.

16. According to West, the best treatment of these issues is Jeffrey Stout's *Blessed Are the Organized: Grassroots Democracy in America* (Princeton, NJ: Princeton University Press, 2010).

17. The FBI considered Baker potentially subversive and observed her for decades, but due to her unconventional behavior and her frequency in changing affiliations with various organizations, the agency, as Ransby puts it, "did not know what to make of this middle-aged hell-raiser who defied categorization" (Ransby, *Ella Baker*, 129).

18. For an extended discussion of the possibilities of Black rebellions and revolutions in the United States, see Harold Cruse's volume of essays *Rebellion or Revolution?* (New York: Morrow, 1968).

19. Among the artists who have inspired West, Chekhov, "the great writer of compassion" ("Chekhov, Coltrane and Democracy," *The Cornel West Reader*, 555), ranks first. In a 1992 interview with the Hungarian philosopher Eva L. Corredor on Georg Lukács's philosophy of history, West accounts for his own "deep Chekhovian strain" by pointing out that though, for Chekhov, love and service are not linked to an optimistic view of life, we are not condemned to cynicism: "What is so great about Chekhov? I think he understood this better than others, that we are able to love, care [*sic*] and serve others—and this is so true of his life and his art—but we are able to do that with there being no deep faith in life or human nature or history or what-have-you. And then it does not mean that we are anti-life, it does not mean that we are cynical toward it, it is simply there" ("The Indispensability Yet Insufficiency of Marxist Theory," *The Cornel West Reader*, 228). See also West's comments on his boundless enthusiasm, especially in the mid-1970s, for Russian literature in general and for his favorite writer, Chekhov, in particular: "Chekhov is the deep blues poet of catastrophe and compassion, whose stories lovingly depict everyday people wrestling with the steady ache of misery and yearning for a better life" (West, *Brother West*, 92–94).

20. In his philosophy of war, Carl von Clausewitz (1780–1831) famously defined war as "an act of violence intended to compel our opponent to fulfil our will." Of the three elements of war that, according to Clausewitz, form "a fascinating trinity" (violence, chance, and reason), West here obviously thinks of the first: "primordial violence, hatred and enmity, which are to be regarded as a blind natural force." Clausewitz, *On War*, ed. Michael Howard and Peter Paret (Princeton, NJ: Princeton University Press, 1984), 89.

21. Singer and songwriter Bernice Johnson Reagon, "one of Ella Baker's political daughters" (Ransby, *Ella Baker*, 12), was active in the civil rights movement, for example, as a member of the Freedom Singers, organized by SNCC. Reagon composed and performed "Ella's Song" for the documentary film *Fundi* (see n. 24 below); reprinted as an epigraph in Grant's biography, *Ella Baker*.

22. This statement should not be misconceived as referring to the individual Ella Baker. In fact, Baker was known for being "a powerful speaker who talked without notes from her heart to the hearts of her audience. Very forceful, with a strong voice that projected even without a microphone. Her speeches [. . .] were to the point [. . .] very human and warm." This observation by one of her female coworkers in the NAACP is quoted in Ransby, *Ella Baker*, 131. Notwithstanding her personal rhetorical power and charismatic gifts, as a woman, Baker would not have been considered suited for the male-denoted model of charismatic leadership. On gender divisions in African American leadership, see Erica E. Edwards, *Charisma and the Fictions of Black Leadership* (Minneapolis: University of Minnesota Press, 2012).

23. For today's legacy of Martin Luther King and Ella Baker, see the movements of the Dream Defenders, led by Philip Harper, and Moral Mondays, led by Rev. Dr. William Barber.

24. The 1981 documentary *Fundi: The Story of Ella Baker* was directed by Joanne Grant, who comments on the film's title as follows: "The designation 'fundi' seemed to characterize her. *Fundi* [. . .] is a Swahili word which denotes the person in a community who passes on the wisdom of the elders, the crafts, the knowledge. This is not done in an institutional way, a way which Baker would have rejected, but as an oral tradition, handed down from one generation to the next" (Grant, *Ella Baker*, 143).

25. For example, Baker maintained in an interview in 1977: "The only society that can serve the needs of large masses of poor people is a socialist society." Wesley Brown and Aeverna Adams, interview with Ella Baker, New York, 1977; quoted in Grant, *Ella Baker*, 218.

26. The radicalism of Ella Baker's political thinking derives from the systemic critique she advocates: "In order for us as poor and oppressed people to become a part of a society that is meaningful, the system under which we now exist has to be radically changed. This means we are going to have to learn to think in *radical* terms. I use the term radical in its original meaning— getting down to and understanding the root cause. It means facing a system that does not lend itself to your needs and devising means by which you change that system." Ella Baker, "The Black Woman in the Civil Rights Struggle," speech given at the Institute for the Black World, Atlanta, 1969, in the possession of Joanne Grant, in Grant, *Ella Baker*, 227–31; see also, Ransby, *Ella Baker*, 1, 377.

27. At the behest of Pedro Albizu Campos, leading activist and president of the Puerto Rican Nationalist Party, Lolita Lebrón, together with three companions, led an attack on the House of Representatives on March 1, 1954,

demanding a free Puerto Rico. For Ella Baker's involvement with the Puerto Rican Solidarity Organization (PRSO), see Ransby, *Ella Baker*, 354–55. The keynote address Baker gave at a Puerto Rican Independence rally in New York's Madison Square Garden took place in 1978. In 1979, after having served twenty-five years in prison, Lebrón and her companions were pardoned by President Jimmy Carter.

Chapter Five: Revolutionary Fire

1. West, *Prophesy Deliverance!*, 143.
2. West, *Race Matters*, 135–36.
3. *The Cornel West Reader*, 7.
4. The Jamaican activist Marcus Garvey was one of the most important and influential Black leaders of the early twentieth century; he succeeded in mobilizing the Black masses with his commitment to Black Nationalism and Afrocentrism, and with his message of Black self-esteem and independence. Like the later Du Bois, Garvey was convinced that organizing a mass movement called for a "cultural nationalism" that offered resplendent parades and pageants endowed with such paraphernalia as gaudy uniforms, banners, and nationalist anthems. Malcolm X's parents were Garveyites. His father, Earl Little, was active in local branches of Garvey's organization, the Universal Negro Improvement Association, and he would often take his favorite son, Malcolm, to UNIA meetings. "The meetings always closed with my father saying several times and the people chanting after him, 'Up, you mighty race, you can accomplish what you will!'" Manning Marable, *Malcolm X: A Life of Reinvention* (New York: Viking, 2011), 27.
5. In 1946, Malcolm X was sentenced to eight to ten years in prison for burglary, for which he served seven years. In 1948, owing to his sister Ella's indefatigable endeavors, he was transferred to Norfolk Prison Colony in Massachusetts, a particularly progressive institution emphasizing rehabilitation. It was at Norfolk that his siblings introduced him to the Nation of Islam and where he subsequently started a rigorous program of self-education that would turn him, paradoxically, into a free man: "From then until I left that prison, in every free moment I had, if I was not reading in the library, I was reading on my bunk. [. . .] [M]onths passed without my even thinking about being imprisoned. In fact, up to then, I had never been so truly free in my life." *The Autobiography of Malcolm X* (1973), with Alex Haley (New York: Ballantine Books, 1992), 188.
6. Elijah Muhammad (born Elijah Robert Poole) led the Nation of Islam from 1934—the year its founder, Wallace D. Fard, disappeared—until his death in 1975. Fard's and Muhammad's religious teachings were not congruent

with orthodox Islam, as Malcolm X realized during his pilgrimage to Mecca. Like Garvey, Elijah Muhammad propagated Black pride and separatism as the only means to gain independence from white domination. The strict dietetic rules and moral laws aimed at the acquisition of a discipline that was to impede whites' control over Blacks. Malcolm X, who "had believed more in Mr. Muhammad than he believed in himself" (ibid., 335), was profoundly shaken when he found out that the adored leader had not adhered to his own moral principles; see also the chapter "Out" in *Autobiography*.

7. Here, as elsewhere in our dialogue, West indirectly hints at remarks by Malcolm X. At the founding rally of the Organization of Afro-American Unity (OAAU), modeled on the Organization of African Unity, Malcolm X praised Patrice Lumumba as "the greatest man who ever walked the African continent. He didn't fear anybody. He had those people so scared they had to kill him. They couldn't buy him, they couldn't frighten him, they couldn't reach him." In his speech in Harlem's Audubon Ballroom on June 28, 1964, Malcolm X quoted from Lumumba's "greatest speech," addressed to the King of Belgium at the ceremony of the proclamation of the Congo's independence (June 30, 1960), advising his Black audience that they "should take that speech and tack it up over [their] door" because, as Malcolm X suggests, Lumumba's message was just as relevant to African Americans as it was to Africans: "This is what Lumumba said: 'You aren't giving us anything. Why, can you take back these scars that you put on our bodies? Can you give us back the limbs that you cut off while you were here?' No, you should never forget what that man did to you. And you bear the scars of the same kind of colonization and oppression not on your body, but in your brain, in your heart, in your soul, right now." Malcolm X, *By Any Means Necessary: Speeches, Interviews, and a Letter by Malcolm X*, ed. George Breitman (New York: Pathfinder, 1970), 64–65.

8. William Faulkner, *Light in August*, opening of chap. 6 (New York: Modern Library, 1012), 110.

9. One instance in which Malcolm X highlighted the importance of history and memory for a people was, again, the speech at the founding rally of the OAAU. In it, he quotes from and expounds upon the propositions in the "Statement of Basic Aims and Objectives of the Organization of Afro-American Unity," written by a committee. The OAAU demands "a cultural revolution to unbrainwash an entire people": "This cultural revolution will be the journey to our rediscovery of ourselves. History is a people's memory, and without a memory man is demoted to the level of the lower animals." "Armed with the knowledge of our past, we can with confidence charter a course for our future. Culture is an indispensible weapon in the freedom struggle. We must take

hold of it and forge the future with the past." Malcolm X, *By Any Means Necessary*, 54–56.

10. This is Malcolm X's answer to Black reporter Claude Lewis's question about how he wanted to be remembered, in an interview that took place in New York in the last months of his life. Peter Goldman, *The Death and Life of Malcolm X* (1973; Urbana: University of Illinois Press, 2013), 238. See also Malcolm X's statement on March 12, 1964: "I am not educated, nor am I an expert in any particular field—but I am sincere, and my sincerity is my credentials" (*Malcolm X Speaks*, 20).

11. Paul Laurence Dunbar, "We Wear the Mask," in *The Collected Poetry*, ed. Joanne M. Braxton (Charlottesville: University Press of Virginia, 1993), 71.

12. On Robert Williams, see chap. 6, n. 19.

13. None of these debates with the long-time leader of the Nation of Islam exists in print. Though West does not ignore "the disagreeable views of Farrakhan," he insists on the minister's "deep love and service for his people. [. . .] He bravely stood up against white supremacy at a time in our history when to do so required courage and character" (West, *Brother West*, 186). "We agree on highlighting black suffering," West wrote in a statement justifying his participation in Farrakhan's Million Man March in 1995 ("Why I Am Marching in Washington," *Million Man March/Day of Absence: A Commemorative Anthology*, ed. Haki R. Madhubuti and Maulana Karenga (Los Angeles: University of Sankore Press, 1996), 37.

14. In three seminal studies James Hal Cone developed a Black theology of liberation that addressed the questions of what it meant to be a Black Christian during the Black Power movement and what the example of the life of Jesus could contribute to the liberation of oppressed Black people suffering from the legacy of white supremacy: *Black Theology and Black Power* (New York: Harper & Row, 1969; Maryknoll, NY: Orbis Books, 1997), followed by *A Black Theology of Liberation* (Philadelphia: J. B. Lippincott, 1970; Maryknoll, NY: Orbis Books, 1990) and *The Spirituals and the Blues* (1972; Maryknoll, NY: Orbis Books, 1991). See also Cornel West's homage to Cone, "Black Theology and Human Identity," in *Black Faith and Public Talk: Critical Essays on James H. Cone's* Black Theology and Black Power, ed. Dwight N. Hopkins (Maryknoll, NY: Orbis Books, 1999), 11–19.

15. "No matter how much respect, no matter how much recognition, whites show towards me, as far as I'm concerned, as long as it is not shown to every one of our people in this country, it doesn't exist for me" (1964), quoted in West, *Race Matters*, 35.

16. See Goldman, *Death and Life of Malcolm X*, 14.

17. For a vivid portrait of his father, see Huey P. Newton's autobiography *Revolutionary Suicide* (1973), especially chap. 4, "Changing," in which he states, for example: "When I say that my father was unusual, I mean that he had a dignity and pride seldom seen in southern Black men. Although many other Black men in the South had a similar strength, they never let it show around whites. To do so was to take your life in your hands. My father never kept his strength from anybody." Huey P. Newton, with J. Herman Blake, *Revolutionary Suicide* (New York: Penguin, 2009), 29.

18. See also chap. 3, n. 30. On the famous murder trial of Bobby Seale and Ericka Huggins, which ended in acquittal on all charges, see the detailed account by Donald Freed, *Agony in New Haven: The Trial of Bobby Seale and Ericka Huggins and the Black Panther Party* (New York: Simon and Schuster, 1973). See also Seale's presentation of the major years of the party's history, *Seize the Time: The Story of the Black Panther Party and Huey P. Newton* (New York: Random House, 1970), as well as his autobiography, *A Lonely Rage: The Autobiography of Bobby Seale* (New York: Times Books, 1978).

19. It is significant that although Ericka Huggins was a high-ranking Black Panther Party leader, at first in the Los Angeles chapter and then as a founder and leader of the New Haven chapter of the BPP, she and so many other female revolutionary activists are far less known than the party's male leaders, just as the party's multifaceted community services have been downplayed. For a long time, scholarship focused almost exclusively on the militant male image of the party, as it had in part been encouraged by male members themselves and certainly enforced by the media. For a revisionist reading of the BPP history, see Ericka Huggins and Angela D. LeBlanc-Ernest, "Revolutionary Women, Revolutionary Education: The Black Panther Party's Oakland Community School," in *Want to Start a Revolution?*, 161–84, with further references to the neglected women's contributions to the revolutionary work of the BPP. For a highly balanced and differentiated assessment of the crucial role of women in the BPP, and the difficulties both male and female members of the party had with gendered power relations, see "A Woman's Party," in Mumia Abu-Jamal, *We Want Freedom: A Life in the Black Panther Party* (Cambridge, MA: South End Press, 2004), 159–84; on Abu-Jamal, see below, n. 26. Interestingly, Abu-Jamal draws attention to Ella Baker's "collectivist model of leadership": "In essence, Baker was arguing against civil rights organizations mirroring the Black church model—a predominantly female membership with a predominantly male clergy—and for the inclusion of women in the leadership of these organizations. Baker was also questioning the hierarchical nature of these groups'

leadership" (ibid., 159). For an emphasis on BPP community services, see *The Black Panther Party: Service to the People Programs*, ed. David Hilliard (Albuquerque: University of New Mexico Press, 2008). In the foreword, West, who as a student participated in the BPP Free Breakfast for Schoolchildren Program, highlights the avant-garde character of the party's political vision: "The Black Panther Party [. . .] was the highest form of deniggerization in niggerized America. The Black Panther Party was the greatest threat to American apartheid because it was indigenous in composition, interracial in strategies and tactics, and international in vision and analysis. It was indigenous in that it spoke to the needs and hopes of the local community. [. . .] It combined bread-and-butter issues of everyday people with deep democratic empowerment in the face of an oppressive status quo. It was interracial in that it remained open to strategic alliances and tactical coalitions with progressive brown, red, yellow, and white activists. And it was international in that it understood American apartheid in light of anti-imperial struggles around the world" (x).

20. For the great impact Malcolm X had on Amiri Baraka (LeRoi Jones), see, for example, "The Legacy of Malcolm X, and the Coming of the Black Nation," in Baraka's collection of "Social Essays" entitled *Home* (1966; New York: Akashi Classics, 2009), 266–79, as well as the new introduction to the reprint, in which he highlights the significance of Malcolm X for the development that Baraka defines as "the open dialectic of the Afro-American national movement, splitting one into two, because my generation—though clearly we had to love and respect Dr. King—rejected that call ['If any blood be shed, let it be ours!'] with our whole-ass selves. Why? Because Malcolm X had begun to appear, and he said, 'Be peaceful, be courteous, obey the law, respect everyone; but if someone puts his hand on you, send him to the cemetery'" (17).

21. In the last months of his life, Malcolm X frequently talked about the necessity of seeking international alliances and of holding the United States responsible for human rights violations. The most extensive passage can be found in one of his most famous speeches, which he entitled "The Ballot or the Bullet," in which, on April 3, 1964, he told his Black audience: "They keep you wrapped up in civil rights. And you spend so much time barking up the civil-rights tree, you don't even know there's a human-rights tree on the same floor. When you expand the civil-rights struggle to the level of human rights, you can then take the case of the black man in this country before the nations in the UN. You can take it before the General Assembly. You can take Uncle Sam before a world court." *Malcolm X Speaks*, 34–35. According to the FBI files on Martin Luther King Jr., two months after this speech, in June 1964, there was a meeting between Malcolm X and representatives of several civil

rights organizations; among others, King's lawyer, advisor, and friend Clarence Jones attended and was authorized to speak for King (who at the time was in jail). As the FBI report maintains, "Jones said that in 'reflecting on today's conference the most important thing discussed was Malcolm X's idea that we internationalize the question of civil rights and bring it before the United Nations.' [. . .] Jones stated that 'we should present the plight of the Negro to the United Nations General Assembly in September of this year.'" Michael Friedly and David Gallen, *Martin Luther King, Jr.: The FBI File* (New York: Carroll & Graf, 1993), 242.

22. James H. Cone, *Martin & Malcolm & America: A Dream or a Nightmare?* (Maryknoll, NY: Orbis Books, 1991; 20th anniversary ed., 2012). See Cone's recapitulatory statement: "We should never pit them against each other. Anyone, therefore, who claims to be for one and not the other does not understand their significance for the black community, for America, or for the world. We need both of them and we need them *together*. Malcolm keeps Martin from being turned into a harmless American hero. Martin keeps Malcolm from being an ostracized black hero" (ibid., 316).

23. "You can't operate a capitalistic system unless you are vulturistic; you have to have someone else's blood to suck to be a capitalist." Speech at the Audubon Ballroom, December 20, 1964, quoted in *Malcolm X Speaks*, 121. For a more elaborate use of the metaphor of the vulture, see the following statement by Malcolm X: "It is impossible for capitalism to survive, primarily because the system of capitalism needs some blood to suck. Capitalism used to be like an eagle, but now it's more like a vulture. It used to be strong enough to go and suck anybody's blood whether they were strong or not. But now it has become more cowardly, like the vulture, and it can only suck the blood of the helpless. As the nations of the world free themselves, then capitalism has less victims, less to suck, and it becomes weaker and weaker. It's only a matter of time in my opinion before it will collapse completely." "The Young Socialist Interview," January 18, 1965, *By Any Means Necessary*, 165–66.

24. In his speeches, Carmichael would highlight the importance of preserving the spirit of the radical Black tradition: "We must listen to Malcolm very closely, because we have to understand our heroes. We cannot let them be used by other people, we cannot let them be interpreted by other people to say other things. We must know what our heroes were saying to us—*our* heroes, not the heroes of the white left or what have you." *Stokely Speaks*, 178; for references to Douglass, Du Bois, and contemporary activists, see also ibid., 62–63, 74–75.

25. The League of Revolutionary Black Workers (LRBW) was a radical organization formed in the aftermath of the Detroit riots in 1969 by auto

industry workers who were frustrated with inhumane working conditions and dissatisfied with the neglect of Black workers' interests in the United Auto Workers union. Kenneth Cockrel and General Gordon Baker Jr. were members of the LRBW's executive committee, and Darryl Mitchell was one of the founding members. For a detailed history, see James A. Geschwender, *Class, Race, and Worker Insurgency: The League of Revolutionary Black Workers* (New York: Cambridge University Press, 1977); it is interesting to note that the classic *Detroit, I Do Mind Dying: A Study in Urban Revolution*, by Dan Georgakas and Marvin Surkin (New York: St. Martin's Press, 1975) was reissued with a foreword by Manning Marable in 2012 by Haymarket Books.

26. Mumia Abu-Jamal, former member of the Black Panther Party and prolific radio journalist and writer, was sentenced to death for allegedly killing a police officer in 1982; the sentence was commuted to life imprisonment in 2012. For the defense's view of the trial, see Abu-Jamal's attorney Leonard I. Weinglass's "The Trial of Mumia Abu-Jamal," in Abu-Jamal's book of autobiographical reflections, *Live From Death Row*, introduction by John Edgar Wideman (Reading, MA: Addison-Wesley, 1995), 195–215. In that book's "Musings on Malcolm" (133–36), Abu-Jamal affirms the significance of Malcolm X for the Black Panthers and stresses the continuity of Malcolm X's fight against systemic racism: "Malcolm, and the man who returned from Mecca, Hajii Malik Shabazz, both were scourges of American racism. [. . .] He stood for— and died for—*human* rights of self-defense and a people's self-determination, not for 'civil rights,' which, as the Supreme Court has indeed shown, changes from day to day, case to case, administration to administration" (136). See also Mumia Abu-Jamal, *Death Blossoms: Reflections from a Prisoner of Conscience*, foreword by Cornel West (Farmington, PA: Plough Publishing House, 1997). West's foreword ends with the urgent question that has motivated the making of *Black Prophetic Fire*: "Will we ever listen to and learn from our bloodstained prophets?" (xii). The Black prophetic fire of Pam Africa and Ramona Africa of the MOVE organization has helped keep the cause of Mumia Abu-Jamal alive—along with the efforts of many others. In his more recent conversations with Marc Lamont Hill, Abu-Jamal also refers to some other great figures of the Black radical tradition; for example, in an extended exchange on Du Bois, he reveals that "my favorite Du Bois book isn't *The Souls of Black Folk*, it's *Darkwater*, which is far rougher and harder and angrier." Mumia Abu-Jamal and Marc Lamont Hill, *The Classroom and The Cell: Conversations on Black Life in America* (Chicago: Third World Press, 2012), 70. See also the excellent documentary film by Stephen Vittoria, *Long-Distance Revolutionary: A Journey with Mumia Abu-Jamal* (Street Legal Cinema, 2013), which clearly situates Abu-Jamal in the Black prophetic tradition, both by references to predecessors

such as Douglass and Malcolm X and by interviews with current intellectuals and activists such as Angela Davis, Alice Walker, and Cornel West.

27. Assata Shakur has been a radical activist since her student days in the mid-sixties; she was a leading member of the Harlem branch of the Black Panther Party but left the BPP for its members' want of an awareness of the Black historical tradition. As she claims in her autobiography, the "basic problem stemmed from the fact that the BPP had no systematic approach to political education. They were reading the *Red Book* [by Mao Tse Tung] but didn't know who Harriet Tubman, Marcus Garvey, and Nat Turner were." Shakur, *Assata: An Autobiography* (1987; Chicago: Lawrence Hill Books, 1999), 221. As to her own steps in self-education, Shakur emphasizes the importance of learning about "Black resistance": "You couldn't catch me without a book in my hand after that [after "i found out about Nat Turner"]. I read everything from [. . .] Sonia Sanchez to Haki Madhubuti (Don L. Lee). I saw plays by Black playwrights like Amiri Baraka and Ed Bullins. [. . .] A whole new world opened up to me" (175). She joined the more radical BPP split-off, the underground Black Liberation Army (BLA). In the so-called New Jersey Turnpike shootout trial, she was found guilty of the murder of a state trooper; she escaped prison in 1979 and eventually fled to Cuba, where she has been granted political asylum since 1984. Classified as a "domestic terrorist" since 2005, the FBI placed her on the Most Wanted Terrorists list in May 2013.

28. As stated in a letter by J. Edgar Hoover in March 1968, the FBI's Counterintelligence Program (COINTELPRO) defined the following five very distinct long-range goals: to prevent "the *coalition* of militant black nationalist groups," to prevent violence on the part of these groups, to prevent them from gaining respectability, and to prevent their growth. In the context of the Black prophetic tradition, the second of these five goals is particularly interesting: "Prevent the *rise of a 'messiah'* who could unify, and electrify, the militant black nationalist movement. Malcolm X might have been such a 'messiah'; he is the martyr of the movement today. Martin Luther King, Stokely Carmichael, and Elijah Muhammed [*sic*] all aspire to this position. Elijah Muhammed is less of a threat because of his age. King could be a very real contender for this position should he abandon his supposed 'obedience' to 'white, liberal doctrines' (nonviolence) and embrace black nationalism. Carmichael has the necessary charisma to be a real threat in this way." This letter and other excerpts from the FBI's BPP files are reprinted in a booklet that speaks to the problem raised by West: Dhoruba Bin Wahad, Mumia Abu-Jamal, and Assata Shakur, *Still Black, Still Strong: Survivors of the U.S. War Against Black Revolutionaries* (New York: Semiotext/e, 1993), 245.

29. Roger Wareham, human rights attorney and long-time political activist, is a member of the New York–based December 12 movement, a nongovernmental organization committed to Malcolm X's legacy of bringing the United States before a world court for its continued violations of Black peoples' human rights.

30. Elombe Brath, graphic artist and long-time activist in the Pan-African movement, was one of the founders of the African Jazz-Arts Society and Studios (AJASS), a collective of Black artists active in the mid-1950s and considered a forerunner of the famous Black Arts Movement (BAM); it was launched by Amiri Baraka after the assassination of Malcolm X. In 1967, H. Rap Brown followed Stokely Carmichael as SNCC chair. While in Attica Prison (1971–1976), Brown converted to orthodox Islam, changed his name to Jamil Abdullah Al-Amin, and became a devout Imam. After a shooting in 2000, he was convicted of murder and sentenced to life in prison without parole. His memoir about growing up Black in America abounds with psychosociological reflections—reminiscent of Fanon's (see chap. 1, n. 23) analysis of the pathology of oppression—such as the following: "When a race of people is oppressed within a system that fosters the idea of competitive individualism, the political polarization around individual interests prevents group interests." H. Rap Brown, *Die Nigger Die! A Political Autobiography*, foreword by Ekwueme Michael Thelwell (1969; Chicago: Lawrence Hill Books, 2002), 16.

31. In the preface to his collection of poems *Don't Cry, Scream* (1969), Haki R. Madhubuti (Don L. Lee) defined his poetics as follows: "Blackpoetry is like a razor; it's sharp & will cut deep, not out to wound but to kill the inactive blackmind." In *Liberation Narratives: New and Collected Poems 1966–2009* (Chicago: Third World Press, 2009), 61. His poetry bears witness to his deep commitment to the Black prophetic tradition. In the collection *Killing Memory, Seeking Ancestors* (1987), Madhubuti pays homage to Malcolm X by asking: "if you lived among the committed / this day how would you lead us?" And he gives the answer: "it was not that you were pure. / the integrity of your vision and pain, / the quality of your heart and decision / confirmed your caring for local people, and your / refusal to assassinate progressive thought / has carved your imprint on the serious." "Possibilities: Remembering Malcolm X," in *Liberation Narratives*, 278.

32. Sonia Sanchez has repeatedly expressed great admiration for and deep gratitude to Malcolm X, most famously in her poem of mourning "Malcolm," from the collection *Home Coming* (Detroit: Broadside Press, 1969), 15–16, and in her play *Malcolm Man/Don't Live Here No Mo'* (1972). In her prose poem "Homegirls on St. Nicholas," Sanchez vividly describes how her life changed radically when she first heard Malcolm X speak, even so "I didn't

want to hear him. His words made my head hurt. [. . .] Why did he bring his hand-grenade words into my space?" But when Malcolm X "demanded, 'Do you know who you are? Who do you really think you are? Have you looked in a mirror recently brother and sister and seen your Blackness for what it is?' [. . .] something began to stir inside me. Something that I had misplaced a long time ago in the classrooms of America. On that cold wet afternoon, I became warm again." *Wounded in the House of a Friend* (Boston: Beacon Press, 1995), 52–53. See also her remarks on Malcolm X in a collection of interviews, especially in the conversation with David Reich (1999), where she states that Malcolm X "became our articulator": "Malcolm articulated all that we thought. For many of us, Baraka and the rest, he gave us his voice." *Conversations with Sonia Sanchez*, ed. Joyce A. Joyce (Jackson: University Press of Mississippi, 2007), 90, 89.

33. "I for one believe that if you give people a thorough understanding of what it is that confronts them and the basic causes that produce it, they'll create their own program. And when the people create a program, you get action." Speech at a meeting of the Organization of Afro-American Unity on the evening of December 20, 1964, *Malcolm X Speaks*, 118–19. As in his famous "Message to the Grass Roots," delivered in November 1963, Malcolm X sets off the people against the leaders by emphasizing the latter's propensity to control rather than ignite the revolutionary fire. Earlier that day, Malcolm X had appeared with grassroots activist Fannie Lou Hamer at the Williams Institutional CME Church in Harlem and had invited her to attend the evening meeting at the Audubon Ballroom; see *Malcolm X Speaks*, 114–15.

34. For West's statements on rising secularism here and below, see statistics on religiously unaffiliated Americans released by the Pew Research Religion and Public Life Project, *Nones on the Rise: One in Five Adults Have No Religious Affiliation* (Washington, DC: Pew Research Center's Forum on Religion & Public Life, October 9, 2012), http://www.pewforum.org/2012/10/09 /nones-on-the-rise-religion/.

35. Ibid.

36. Robert Green Ingersoll was one of the most popular freethinkers of the late nineteenth century and considered one of the best lecturers, if not the best orator, of his time. Though he was best known for his controversial talks on agnosticism (or atheism: in contrast to common understanding, according to which an agnostic claims not to know whether God exists, as opposed to an atheist who denies God's existence, Ingersoll did not think it made sense to distinguish between the two), he delivered speeches on a broad range of topics, and in the name of humanism advocated racial equality, women's rights, and civil liberties. In a speech in honor of Walt Whitman, "Liberty in

Literature," given in the presence of the poet (two years before he delivered a much-praised eulogy at Whitman's funeral), Ingersoll, referring to Shelley, Lord Byron, and Robert Burns, praises the prophetic quality of great poets: "The great poets have been on the side of the oppressed—of the downtrodden. They have suffered with the imprisoned and the enslaved. [. . .] The great poets [. . .] have uttered in all ages the human cry. Unbought by gold, unawed by power, they have lifted high the torch that illuminates the world." *Walt Whitman. An Address. Delivered in Philadelphia, Oct 21, 1890* (New York: Truth Seeker Co., 1890). It does not come as a surprise that Frederick Douglass and Ottilie Assing (see chap. 1, n. 17) were on friendly terms with Ingersoll; see Diedrich, *Love Across the Color Lines*, 358. In a meeting in Washington, DC, to protest the 1883 Supreme Court decision that found sections 1 and 2 of the 1875 Civil Rights Act unconstitutional, Ingersoll—introduced by Douglass—condemned the Court's decision and painted its effects in gruesome colors: "The masked wretches who, in the darkness of night, drag the poor negro from his cabin, and lacerate with whip and thong his quivering flesh, will, with bloody hands, applaud the Supreme Court." Ingersoll, "Address on the Civil Rights Act," *The Works of Robert G. Ingersoll*, vol. XI, *Miscellany* (New York: C. P. Farrell, 1900), 2. See also Susan Jacoby's *The Great Agnostic: Robert Ingersoll and American Freethought* (New Haven, CT: Yale University Press, 2013), 111, and in that book, her "Letter to the 'New' Atheists," who, according to Jacoby, have largely ignored Ingersoll (192–202).

37. Clarence Seward Darrow was a renowned lawyer. Among his famous cases was his defense of John T. Scopes, put to trial for teaching evolution in a classroom in Dayton, Tennessee. In his autobiography, Darrow devotes three chapters to this trial, which he had taken on "solely to induce the public to stop, look, and listen, lest our public schools should be imperiled with a fanaticism founded on ignorance." *The Story of My Life*, with a new introduction by Alan M. Dershowitz (1932; New York: Da Capo Press, 1996), 276. See also the chapter "Questions without Answers," in which Darrow discusses the belief in God (385–95). Together with Wallace Rice, Darrow compiled *Infidels and Heretics: An Agnostic's Anthology* (1928; New York: Gordon Press, 1975). The current revival of atheism mentioned by West is reflected, for example, in the following recent publications: *In the Clutches of the Law: Clarence Darrow's Letters*, ed. and with an introduction by Randall Tietjen (Berkeley: University of California Press, 2013), and *Attorney for the Damned: Clarence Darrow in the Courtroom*, ed. and with notes by Arthur Weinberg; foreword by Justice William O. Douglas (1957; Chicago: University of Chicago Press, 2012).

38. See Baldwin's address to the World Council of Churches, July 7, 1968, "White Racism or World Community," in *Collected Essays* (New York: Library

of America, 1998), 749–56. Referring to his credentials as a speaker, Baldwin says. "I never expected to be standing in such a place, because I left the pulpit twenty-seven years ago. [. . .] And I want to make it clear to you that though I may have to say some rather difficult things here this afternoon, I want to make it understood that in the heart of the absolutely necessary accusation there is contained a plea. The plea was articulated by Jesus Christ himself, who said, 'Insofar as you have done it unto the least of these, you have done it unto me'" (749). In his autobiographical essay "Down at the Cross," originally published in the collection *The Fire Next Time* (1963), Baldwin rejects Christianity's claim of the monopoly on morals: "It is not too much to say that whoever wishes to become a truly moral human being [. . .] must first divorce himself from all the prohibitions, crimes, and hypocrisies of the Christian church" (Baldwin, *Collected Essays*, 314). Yet he also admits that the church service held great attractions for him: "The church was very exciting. It took a long time for me to disengage myself from this excitement, and on the blindest, most visceral level, I never really have, and never will. There is no music like this music, no drama like the drama of the saints rejoicing, the sinners moaning, the tambourines racing, and all those voices coming together crying holy unto the Lord" (306). In a 1965 interview, Baldwin explicates, "I'm not a believer in any sense which would make any sense to any church, and any church would obviously throw me out. I believe—what do I believe? [. . .] I believe in love. [. . .] [By love] I don't mean anything passive. I mean something active, something more like a fire, like the wind, something which can change you. I mean energy. I mean a passionate belief, a passionate knowledge of what a human being can do, and become, what a human being can do to change the world in which he finds himself." James Mossman, "Race, Hate, Sex, and Colour: A Conversation with James Baldwin and Colin MacInnes" (1965), in *Conversations with James Baldwin*, ed. Fred L. Standley and Louis H. Pratt (Jackson: University Press of Mississippi, 1989), 48. It is interesting to note that Sonia Sanchez ends her homage to James Baldwin, written on the occasion of his passing away in 1987, by thanking him "for his legacy of fire. A fine rain of words when we had no tongues. He set fire to our eyes. Made a single look, gesture endure. Made a people meaningful and moral. Responsible finally for all our sweet and terrible lives" ("A Remembrance," *Wounded*, 34).

39. See Malcolm X's speech at the Williams Institutional CME Church in Harlem, December 20, 1964: "I'm not for anybody who tells black people to be nonviolent while nobody is telling white people to be nonviolent. [. . .] Now if you are with us, all I say is, make the same kind of contribution with us in our struggle for freedom that all white people have always made when they were struggling for their own freedom. You were struggling for your

freedom in the Revolutionary War. Your own Patrick Henry said 'liberty or death,' and George Washington got the cannons out, and all the rest of them that you taught me to worship as my heroes, they were fighters, they were warriors" (*Malcolm X Speaks*, 112–13).

40. See Du Bois, "The Propaganda of History," in *Black Reconstruction*, 594.

41. Excerpts from Malcolm X's contribution to the Oxford Union Society debate December 3, 1964, are available in *By Any Means Necessary*, 176–77, 182. The question debated was "Extremism in the defense of liberty is no vice, moderation in the pursuit of justice is no virtue." Almost fifty years later, on November 22, 2012, Cornel West took part in the Oxford Union Society debate on this motion: "This House would occupy Wall Street." Both speeches can be accessed on YouTube.

42. For an in-depth exploration of Black Nationalism, see Michael Lerner and Cornel West, *Jews and Blacks: A Dialogue on Race, Religion, and Culture in America* (New York: Penguin, 1996), 91–114; reprinted as "On Black Nationalism," in West, *The Cornel West Reader*, 521–29.

43. Marable, *Malcolm X*. For an account of the immense difficulties Marable faced in collecting factual evidence on Malcolm X, see his article "Rediscovering Malcolm's Life: A Historian's Adventure in Living History," *Souls* 7, no. 1 (2005): 20–35; reprinted in *The Portable Malcolm X Reader*, ed. Manning Marable and Garrett Felber (New York: Penguin, 2013), 573–600.

44. See the first collection of essays published in reaction to Marable's biography, *By Any Means Necessary: Malcolm X: Real, Not Reinvented; Critical Conversations on Manning Marable's Biography of Malcolm X*, ed. Herb Boyd, Ron Daniels, Maulana Karenga, and Haki R. Madhubuti (Chicago: Third World Press, 2012), which offers a wide range of critical opinions. It opens with Sonia Sanchez's poem "Malcolm" (see above, n. 32) and contains essays by Mumia Abu-Jamal, Amiri Baraka, and many others who, above all, seek to affirm the radical Black tradition. See also *A Lie of Reinvention: Correcting Manning Marable's Malcolm X*, ed. Jared A. Ball and Todd Steven Burroughs (Baltimore: Black Classic Press, 2012), which contains contributions by, among others, Mumia Abu-Jamal, Amiri Baraka, and Herb Boyd. Though most statements criticize Marable's extensive use of conjecture in presenting his arguments, the most severe critique, voiced repeatedly against Marable's portrayal, is that the historian deprived Malcolm X of the political radicalism of his message and turned him into a "mainstream-leaning, liberal Democrat" (6).

45. Harry Haywood, *Black Bolshevik: Autobiography of an Afro-American Communist* (Chicago: Liberator Press, 1978). In the context of the Black

prophetic tradition, it is interesting to note that Haywood praises Du Bois as a pioneer of historical revisionism with his *"tour de force, Black Reconstruction, and the epilogue, 'Propaganda of History,' which contained a bitter indictment of the white historical establishment"* (95).

46. West refers to the 1992 Hollywood film *Malcolm X*, directed and cowritten by Spike Lee, with Denzel Washington in the title role. Given the fierce political struggle over Malcolm X's legacy, it is not surprising to learn that, though the screenplay was largely based on *The Autobiography of Malcolm X*, the film was highly controversial, both during the long history of planning and production, and after its release.

47. On the iconization and commodification of Malcolm X, see Angela Davis's "Meditations on the Legacy of Malcolm X," in *Malcolm X in Our Own Image*, ed. Joe Wood (New York: St. Martin's Press, 1992), 40–41.

48. For the criticism by Baraka and others, see, for example, Evelyn Nieves, "Malcolm X: Firestorm Over a Film Script," movie section of the *New York Times*, August 9, 1991. The new book by activist-scholar Maulana Karenga on Malcolm X as a moral philosopher promises to be a major contribution to our understanding of Malcolm. West wrote the introduction to this text.

49. In 1966, Baldwin accepted the offer by Columbia Pictures to write a screenplay based on *The Autobiography of Malcolm X*, although he had "grave doubts and fears about Hollywood. [. . .] The idea of Hollywood doing a truthful job on Malcolm could not but seem preposterous. And yet—I didn't want to spend the rest of my life thinking: *It could have been done if you hadn't been chicken.* I felt that Malcolm would never have forgiven me for that." Baldwin, "To Be Baptized," from the essay collection *No Name in the Street* (New York: Library of America, 1998), 413. In an interview, Baldwin commented on his disagreements with Hollywood as follows: "To put it brutally, if I had agreed with Hollywood, I would have been allowing myself to create an image of Malcolm that would have satisfied them and infuriated you, broken your hearts. At one point I saw a memo that said, among other things, that the author had to avoid giving any political implications to Malcolm's trip to Mecca. Now, how can you write about Malcolm X without writing about his trip to Mecca and its political implications? It was not surprising. They were doing the Che Guevara movie while I was out there. It had nothing to do with Latin America, the United Fruit Company, Che Guevara, Cuba . . . nothing to do with anything. It was hopeless crap. Hollywood's fantasy is designed to prove to you that this poor, doomed nitwit deserves his fate." Interview with Jewell Handy Grasham (1976), in Standley and Pratt, *Conversations with James Baldwin*, 167. See also Baldwin's screenplay *One Day, When I Was Lost: A Scenario*, based on *The Autobiography of Malcolm X*.

50. *The Black Agenda Report: News, Commentary & Analysis from the Black Left* is a radio and TV program launched in 2006 by long-time radio journalist Glen Ford, life-long activist and community organizer Bruce Dixon, and legendary Harlem activist Nellie Bailey, as well as writer and peace activist Margaret Kimberley and political scientist and activist Leutisha Stills.

51. Carl Dix, self-proclaimed "veteran revolutionary fighter from the '60s," is cofounder of the Revolutionary Communist Party, USA (RCP), established in 1975, and has been a committed activist, for example, on behalf of Mumia Abu-Jamal and as a leading voice in the campaign against New York Police Department's "stop and frisk" practice; see his article "Why I Am Getting Arrested Today" (*Huffington Post*, October 21, 2011), in which he explains the rationale behind the act of civil disobedience, during which he was joined by thirty other activists, including Cornel West. Dix and West have conducted several public dialogues entitled "In the Age of Obama: What Future for Our Youth?" as well as a series of "Mass Incarceration Dialogues." Bob Avakian has been RCP chair since its founding; for his unwavering commitment to radical political activism, see *From Ike to Mao and Beyond: My Journey from Mainstream America to Revolutionary Communist; a Memoir* (Chicago: Insight Press, 2005). Avakian wrote his life story on the suggestion of Cornel West; see preface (ix).

52. Chris Hedges, Pulitzer Prize–winning journalist, best-selling author, and activist, was a foreign correspondent for the *New York Times* (1990–2005) and is now a regular columnist for *Truthdig*. In November 2011, Hedges, West, and others held a mock trial of Goldman Sachs in Zuccotti Park, New York. Glenn Greenwald practiced law as a litigation attorney specializing in constitutional law and civil rights before he became an award-winning journalist and best-selling author; he gained worldwide fame in June 2013 due to his involvement in publishing whistleblower Edward Snowden's documents on US surveillance practices in the *Guardian*. (For Margaret Kimberley, see above, n. 50.) Larry Hamm—a distinguished Princeton University graduate—is the legendary founder and leader of the revolutionary People's Organization for Progress.

53. The best anthology on the Black prophetic tradition remains *African American Religious Thought*, edited by Cornel West and Eddie Glaude Jr. (Louisville, KY: Westminster John Knox Press, 2003).

Chapter Six: Prophetic Fire

1. See Guy Gugliotta, "New Estimate Raises Civil War Death Toll," *New York Times*, April 2, 2012. Gugliotta's report is based on a study by J. David Hacker, a demographic historian from Binghamton University in New York whose recalculation increased the death toll by more than 20 percent.

2. The assassination of Tsar Alexander II, in 1881, which, according to contemporary rumors, was committed by Jews, set off a wave of pogroms that lasted until 1884; this in turn led to considerable Jewish emigration to the United States.

3. In her autobiography, Wells claims that the lynching in Memphis "changed the whole course of my life." *Crusade for Justice: The Autobiography of Ida B. Wells*, ed. Alfreda M. Duster (Chicago: University of Chicago Press, 1970), 47 (hereafter cited as *Crusade*). The three men—Thomas Moss, Calvin McDowell, and Will (Henry) Stewart, whom Wells calls both "Henry" and "Lee"; see *Crusade*, 47, 64—co-owned and ran a cooperative grocery store, the People's Grocery, located opposite a white grocery store that had enjoyed a monopoly in the densely populated suburb of Memphis.

4. Like Wells, T. Thomas Fortune was a pioneering journalist and newspaper editor as well as a staunch activist. Fortune founded the Afro-American League in 1890, a more militant precursor of the NAACP, which faltered for lack of funding. For several years, Wells and Fortune supported each other, but their paths diverged in 1898, when Fortune, due to several personal and financial blows, grew more and more desperate and turned to Booker T. Washington for help. Washington then subsidized the *New York Age* and offered assistance; see Paula J. Giddings, *Ida: A Sword Among Lions; Ida B. Wells and the Campaign Against Lynching* (New York: Harper Collins, 2009), 191.

5. It was the Memphis lynching that opened Wells's eyes: "Like many another person who had read of lynching in the South, I had accepted the idea meant to be conveyed—that although lynching was irregular and contrary to law and order, unreasoning anger over the terrible crime of rape led to the lynching; that perhaps the brute deserved death anyhow and the mob was justified in taking his life" (*Crusade*, 64). But the three men "had committed no crime against white women. This was what opened my eyes to what lynching really was. An excuse to get rid of Negroes who were acquiring wealth and property and thus keep the race terrorized and 'keep the nigger down'" (ibid.).

6. But as her biographer, Paula Giddings, points out, even radically minded Blacks like Ida B. Wells-Barnett and her husband, Ferdinand Barnett, who were highly critical of the imperialist politics of the United States, felt obliged to support Black troops: "Even those like Ida and Ferdinand, who loathed the imperialist impulses that the soldiers carried out in the rebellious Philippines and elsewhere, took pride in their tenacity and courage and supported them with fund-raising parties" (Giddings, *Ida*, 467). Yet, "Ida and Ferdinand helped organize a mass meeting at Chicago's Bethel Church to demand freedom for the Cubans and to deplore the killing of the island's Afro-Cuban military hero, Antonio Maceo y Grajales" (378).

7. The passage referred to builds up toward the experience of violence: "My knowledge of the race problem became more definite. I saw discrimination in ways of which I had never dreamed; the separation of passengers on the railways of the South was just beginning; the separation in living quarters throughout the cities and towns was manifest; the public disdain and even insult in race contact on the street continually took my breath; I came in contact for the first time with a sort of violence that I had never realized in New England; I remember going down and looking wide-eyed at the door of a public building, filled with buck-shot, where the editor of the leading paper had been publicly murdered the day before" (Du Bois, *Dusk of Dawn*, 15). And, in fact, Du Bois recalled that "lynching was a continuing and recurrent horror during my college days," but it was, indeed, more than a decade later when, in the late 1890s, while he was working as a social scientist at Atlanta University, that the case of Sam Hose affected him deeply (34). It is interesting to note that Wells-Barnett published a pamphlet on the Hose case: *Lynch Law in Georgia* (1899).

8. As Wells herself puts it in her diary: "I think of my tempestuous, rebellious, hard headed wilfulness, the trouble I gave, the disposition to question his [W. W. Hooper, president of Rust College (formerly Shaw University)] authority." *The Memphis Diary of Ida B. Wells*, ed. Miriam DeCosta-Willis (Boston: Beacon Press, 1995), 78.

9. "As I witnessed the triumph of the graduates and thought of my lost opportunity a great sob arose in my throat and I yearned with unutterable longing for the 'might have been'" (ibid., 78). Wells had been expelled from Rust College for her insubordination, and once she had to earn a living as a teacher, she was not able to continue her formal education.

10. As Patricia A. Schechter puts it in her highly instructive article "'All the Intensity of My Nature': Ida B. Wells, Anger and Politics," *Radical History Review* 70 (1998): 48–77: "Her 'anomalous' craving for social autonomy or platonic male friends suggests the limited range of social identities available to single middle-class black women. One was either a wife, a former wife, or a wife-to-be—all else was strange or irregular" (52–53).

11. Giddings, *Ida*, 69; see also Wells, *Crusade*, 31. As journalist Lucy Wilmot Smith notes, Wells, who "has been called the Princess of the Press [...] believes there is no agency so potent as the press in reaching and elevating a people" (quoted in *Crusade*, 33). The praise she received by contemporary journalists highlights the fearlessness of her speech. For example, T. Thomas Fortune writes: "She has plenty of nerve and is as sharp as a steel trap" (ibid.).

12. *American Slavery As It Is: Testimony of a Thousand Witnesses* (New York: American Anti-Slavery Society, 1839) was compiled by Theodore Dwight

Weld, one of the founders of the American Anti-Slavery Society; the sisters Sarah Grimké and Angelina Grimké Weld, staunch Abolitionists and early advocates for women's rights, contributed to the volume by bearing witness to the cruelties of slavery they had experienced at their father's plantation in South Carolina.

13. On William Cobbett, see chap. 1, n. 28.

14. On an extended visit to the United States between 1834 and 1836, Harriet Martineau became engaged in the Abolitionists' fight against slavery, closely observed American society (*Society in America*, 1837), and reflected upon the methods of social investigations (*How to Observe Morals and Manners*, 1838). The two books on America established her as a pioneer in sociology *avant la lettre*.

15. Wells, *Crusade*, 65–66.

16. See Giddings, *Ida*, 214. "They had destroyed my paper, in which every dollar I had in the world was invested. They had made me an exile and threatened my life for hinting at the truth. I felt that I owed it to myself and my race to tell the whole truth" (Wells, *Crusade*, 62–63).

17. The Socialist journalist and novelist Upton Sinclair investigated the working conditions in the Chicago meatpacking industry and published his findings at first as a serialized novel in 1905 in the Socialist paper the *Appeal to Reason*. In a review of the 1906 Doubleday edition, Jack London famously called *The Jungle* "the *Uncle Tom's Cabin* of wage slavery"; repr. in *Jack London: American Rebel; a Collection of His Social Writings Together with an Extensive Study of the Man and His Times*, ed. Philip S. Foner (New York: Citadel, 1947), 524.

18. "The lesson this teaches and which every Afro-American should ponder well, is that a Winchester rifle should have a place of honor in every black home, and it should be used for that protection which the law refuses to give. When the white man who is always the aggressor knows he runs as great a risk of biting the dust every time his Afro-American victim does, he will have greater respect for Afro-American life. The more the Afro-American yields and cringes and begs, the more he has to do so, the more he is insulted, outraged and lynched." Ida B. Wells, *Southern Horrors: Lynch Law in All Its Phases* (New York: New York Age Print, 1892), 70.

19. Robert F. Williams recounts the story of how, in 1957, "a Negro community in the South [in Monroe, North Carolina] took up guns in self-defense against racist violence—and used them" in his book *Negroes With Guns* (New York: Marzani and Munsell, 1962), 39, which he wrote in exile in Cuba, from where he broadcast *Radio Free Dixie*. In the prologue, Williams invokes "an accepted right of Americans, as the history of our Western states prove, that where the law is unable, or unwilling, to enforce order, the citizens

can, and must, act in self-defense against lawless violence," and claims that "this right holds for black Americans as well as whites." His example inspired Huey P. Newton and the Black Panther Party; see Timothy B. Tyson, *Radio Free Dixie: Robert F. Williams and the Roots of Black Power* (Chapel Hill: University of North Carolina Press, 1999).

20. "I had bought a pistol the first thing after Tom Moss was lynched, because I expected some cowardly retaliation from the lynchers. I felt that one had better die fighting against injustice than to die like a dog or a rat in a trap. I had already determined to sell my life as dearly as possible if attacked" (Wells, *Crusade*, 62).

21. Like Wells-Barnett, William Monroe Trotter, newspaper editor of the radical *Boston Guardian*, lifelong activist, and cofounder of the Niagara Movement, was known for his fearlessness and militancy. He and Wells-Barnett were often marginalized by more moderate activists. For example, they belonged to the militant faction of the group that prepared the founding of the NAACP, and Du Bois did not think them fit to appear on the list of the Founding Forty.

22. When, in 1909, Wells-Barnett had successfully fought against the reinstatement of a sheriff who had been involved in a lynching in Cairo, Illinois, the *Springfield Forum* praised her as "a lady in whom we are justly proud" and who "towers high above all of her male contemporaries and has more of the aggressive qualities than the average man" (December 11, 1909, quoted in Giddings, *Ida*, 487). Yet the common reaction to female aggression or anger expressed in public was repression or defamation. See Schechter, "'All the Intensity of My Nature,'" which—based on extensive research—highlights the pressure exerted on (Black) female radical activists like Wells, accomplished by an instrumentalization of etiquette that asked women to suppress feelings of rage.

23. In fact, she even published an essay in 1885 on the ideal of "true womanhood," "Woman's Mission," in the *New York Freeman*, edited by T. Thomas Fortune. As Giddings notes in *Ida*, her "well-received essay had made her an authority on the subject," "the nineteenth-century idea of the ideal woman who possessed the Victorian-era virtues of modesty, piety, purity, submission, and domesticity—virtues denied by the conditions that faced black women during slavery and deemed essential to not only their uplift but that of their families, and the community" (12, 86–87).

24. She writes in her diary: "I felt so disappointed for my people generally. I have firmly believed all along that the law was on our side and would, when we appealed to it, give us justice. I feel shorn of that belief and utterly discouraged, and just now, if it were possible, would gather my race in my arms

and fly away with them. O God, is there no redress, no peace, no justice in this land for us?" Entry for April 11, 1887, in the unpublished diary of Ida B. Wells, quoted by her daughter Alfreda M. Duster in the introduction to *Crusade*, xvii.

25. Evelyn Higginbotham, *Righteous Discontent: The Women's Movement in the Black Baptist Church, 1880–1920* (Cambridge, MA: Harvard University Press, 1993); Kevin Gaines, *Uplifting the Race: Black Leadership, Politics, and Culture During the Twentieth Century* (Charlotte: University of North Carolina Press, 1996).

26. See Trudier Harris in her introduction to Wells-Barnett's *Selected Works*: "While she was certainly celebrated by blacks, some of them nevertheless painted her as egotistical or as a crazy woman, a loner who did not represent the sentiments of the majority of forward thinking black intellectuals." *Selected Works of Ida B. Wells-Barnett*, compiled with an introduction by Trudier Harris (New York: Oxford University Press, 1991), 11.

27. In her autobiography, *Crusade for Justice*, Wells expresses her critique by juxtaposing her own "radical" political goals with Washington's policy, a technique that renders the latter downright absurd: "Our policy was to denounce the wrongs and injustices which were heaped upon our people, and to use whatever influence we had to help right them. Especially strong was our condemnation of lynch law and those who practiced it. Mr. Washington's theory had been that we ought not to spend our time agitating for our rights; that we had better give attention to trying to be first-class people in a jim crow car than insisting that the jim crow car should be abolished; that we should spend more time practicing industrial pursuits and getting education to fit us for this work than in going to college and striving for college education. And of course, fighting for political rights had no place whatsoever in his plans" (265). After the publication of Du Bois's *The Souls of Black Folk*, in 1903, when his critique of Washington was ardently debated among whites and Blacks, the "Barnetts stood almost alone in approving them [Du Bois's views] and proceeded to show why. We saw, as perhaps never before, that Mr. Washington's views on industrial education had become an obsession with the white people of this country. We thought it was up to us to show them the sophistry of the reasoning that any one system of education could fit the needs of an entire race; that to sneer at and discourage higher education would mean to rob the race of leaders which it so badly needed; and that all the industrial education in the world could not take the place of manhood" (281).

28. Not only did Wells-Barnett publicly oppose Washington's lenient attitude toward lynching, but she would also repeatedly criticize him sharply for certain political moves, for example, when in 1900 he launched a new

organization, the National Negro Business League, in order to counterbal-
ance the Afro-American Council and its Anti-Lynching Bureau headed by
Wells-Barnett (see Giddings, *Ida*, 423–26). In reaction to Wells-Barnett's
attack in an editorial, Washington's mouthpiece, secretary Emmett J. Scott,
wrote: "Miss Wells is fast making herself so ridiculous that everybody is getting tired of her" (426).

29. Wells-Barnett's great rival, Mary Church Terrell, a highly educated
teacher, journalist, and lifelong activist, also advanced the Black women's club
movement. In fact, according to Angela Davis, "Mary Church Terrell was the
driving force that molded the Black women's club movement into a powerful
political group." Davis, "Black Women and the Club Movement," in Angela
Davis, *Women, Race & Class* (New York: Vintage, 1983), 135. Though Davis
praises Wells and Terrell as "unquestionably the two outstanding Black
women of their era," she also states that regrettably their "personal feud, which
spanned several decades, was a tragic thread within the history of the Black
women's club movement" (136).

30. Mary White Ovington, born to white progressive Unitarians who
were active in the struggle against slavery and for women's rights, was one of
the cofounders of the NAACP and served this organization in various functions for thirty-eight years. It was during the founding phase of the NAACP
that the two women collided, when Du Bois had taken Wells off the list of the
so-called Founding Forty, and Wells felt that Ovington approved of his decision (see Wells, *Crusade*, 325). Wells settled her account with Ovington by
making her responsible for the fact that the NAACP "has fallen short of the
expectations of its founders," because it "has kept Miss Mary White Ovington
as chairman of the executive committee. [. . .] She has basked in the sunlight
of the adoration of the few college-bred Negroes who have surrounded her,
but has made little effort to know the soul of the black woman; and to that
extent she has fallen far short of helping a race which has suffered as no white
woman has ever been called upon to suffer or to understand" (327–28).

31. Wells devotes a whole chapter ("Chapter VIII: Miss Willard's Attitude") of *A Red Record: Tabulated Statistics and Alleged Causes of Lynchings in the
United States, 1892–1893–1894* (Chicago: privately published, 1895), 138–48,
to this battle with the national president of Woman's Christian Temperance
Union, Frances E. Willard; see also "A Regrettable Interview," Wells, *Crusade*,
201–12. Willard's voice was a potent one; after all, she headed the era's largest
and most powerful organization of white women. The more harmful for the
Black community was her claim that Black men were excessively indulging in
both alcohol and sex—and here she "quotes" an anonymous voice from the
South—and consequently became an omnipresent threat to Southern women:

"The colored race multiplies like the locusts of Egypt. The grog-shop is its center of power. 'The safety of woman, of childhood, of the home is menaced at a thousand localities at this moment, so that the men dare not go beyond the sight of their own roof-tree'" (Wells, *Red Record*, 142).

32. According to Wells-Barnett, teaching Sunday school turned her life in Chicago into "one of the most delightful periods. I had a class of young men ranging from eighteen to thirty years of age. [. . .] Every Sunday we discussed the Bible lessons in a plain common-sense way and tried to make application of their truths to our daily lives. I taught this class for ten years" (*Crusade*, 298–99).

33. Jane Addams's famous Chicago settlement project of Hull House was a great model to Wells-Barnett; in fact, she regarded Addams as "the greatest woman in the United States" (*Crusade*, 259) and must have been proud to be called the "Jane Addams among Negroes" by a Danish visitor to the United States (Giddings, *Ida*, 538). However, Wells-Barnett's admiration for the outstanding social reformer did not prevent her from sharply criticizing Addams for failing to question the common charge of rape in an article that condemned lynching on legal grounds. See Jane Addams, "Respect for Law," *New York Independent*, January 3, 1901, and Wells-Barnett's response, "Lynching and the Excuse for It," *Independent*, May 1901. Both articles are reprinted in Bettina Aptheker's unearthing of this dispute, *Lynching and Rape: An Exchange of View*, by Addams and Wells, occasional papers, no. 25 (New York: American Institute for Marxist Studies, 1977). See also Maurice Hamington, "Public Pragmatism: Jane Addams and Ida B. Wells on Lynching," *Journal of Speculative Philosophy* 19, no. 2 (2005): 167–74, which presents this debate as "a wonderful example of public pragmatist philosophy" between the two activists who, despite Wells's critique, would continue to collaborate "on behalf of civil justice despite their public disagreement" (173).

34. See hooks and West, *Breaking Bread*.

35. An early experience of a lack of support in the Black community was when, in 1889, she wrote an article in the Memphis *Free Speech and Headlight* about the poor conditions in Black schools while she was still working as a teacher. As a result of her criticism, the school board did not reelect her. "I had taken a chance in the interest of the children of our race and had lost out. The worst part of the experience was the lack of appreciation shown by the parents. They simply could not understand why one would risk a good job, even for their children. [. . .] But I thought it was right to strike a blow against a glaring evil and I did not regret it. Up to that time I had felt that any fight made in the interest of the race would have its support. I learned then that I could not count on that" (*Crusade*, 37). Wells's belligerent fight

for justice would isolate her throughout her life. As her youngest daughter, Alfreda, remembered: "I've seen my mother shed tears after she'd come home from some organization where she worked so hard to try to get change . . . and had met with just obstinate antagonism" (Giddings, *Ida*, 623). See also Thomas C. Holt, "The Lonely Warrior: Ida B. Wells-Barnett and the Struggle for Black Leadership," in *Black Leaders of the 20th Century*, ed. John Hope Franklin and August Meier (Urbana: University of Illinois Press, 1982), 39–61, especially 58.

36. *Crusade*, 123. As Wells states, the British journalist and reformer William T. Stead "had come late to visit the World's Fair and remained for three months writing his book *If Christ Came to Chicago* and welding the civic and moral forces of the town into a practical working body" (122–23). Stead's book *If Christ Came to Chicago! A Plea for the Union of All Who Love in the Service of All Who Suffer* (1894) became a best seller. See Joseph O. Baylen, "A Victorian's 'Crusade' in Chicago, 1893–1894," *Journal of American History* 51 (December 1964): 418–34.

37. As early as 1891, Wells was aware of the importance of concrete organizational measures for the purpose of unification. Having attended the second national Afro-American League convention, in Knoxville, Tennessee, she complained that the gathering had not addressed the "gravest questions": "How do we do it? What steps should be taken to unite our people into a real working force—a unit, powerful and complete?" (quoted in Giddings, *Ida*, 170).

38. James Melvin Washington, *Frustrated Fellowship: The Baptist Quest for Social Power* (Macon, GA: Mercer, 1986); paperback edition 2004, with a new preface by Quinton H. Dixie, foreword by Cornel West.

39. In May 1910, owing to Wells-Barnett's initiative, the Negro Fellowship League Reading Room and Social Center opened its doors on State Street amid the saloons and gambling houses of Chicago's Black Belt. While Wells-Barnett "was lifted to the seventh heaven and cheerfully went about the work of helping to select the library," there was "great objection among some of our members to going there. Some of them took the ground that State Street was beneath their consideration" (*Crusade*, 304).

40. West alludes to Hazel Carby, *Reconstructing Black Womanhood* (New York: Oxford University Press, 1987), and Angela Y. Davis, *Women, Race & Class* (New York: Vintage, 1983), especially chap. 5, "The Meaning of Emancipation According to Black Women" (87–98).

41. Like Wells, Victoria (Vicki) Garvin (1915–2007) was a long-distance radical, yet, until recently, her lifelong political activism has been unduly neglected (and for this reason is highlighted in this note). Her work focused

on, but was by no means limited to, the struggle for Black workers' rights. In the 1950s, she served as executive secretary in the New York chapter of the National Negro Labor Council (NNLC) and as vice president of the national NNLC, an organization suspected by other unions to be (and in 1951 by the US attorney general officially declared) a Communist front. Garvin belonged to a network of leftist women who had been radicalized in the 1930s and had held on to their radical convictions even when they came under attack during the McCarthy era; see the seminal study by Dayo F. Gore, *Radicalism at the Crossroads: African American Women Activists in the Cold War* (New York: New York University Press, 2011), which unearths the largely neglected history of Black women radicals of the 1950s. See also Gore's article, "From Communist Politics to Black Power: The Visionary Politics and Transnational Solidarities of Victoria (Vicki) Ama Garvin," in the essay collection *Want to Start a Revolution?*, 71–94. In the late 1950s, Garvin moved to Africa and in 1961 settled in Accra, Ghana, where she was a member of the African American community headed by W. E. B. Du Bois and Shirley Graham Du Bois, and where she also met Malcolm X again, with whom she had collaborated closely in Harlem. Encouraged by Du Bois, Garvin accepted an invitation to go to China, where from 1964 to 1971 she taught English at the Shanghai Foreign Language Institute. See the biographical information in the highly instructive article on Black radical activists, e.g. Robert Williams, Huey Newton, and Amiri Baraka, embracing Mao's cultural revolution, in Robin D. G. Kelley and Betsy Esch, "Black Like Mao: Red China and Black Revolution," *Souls* 1, no. 4 (September 1999): 6–41. Back in the United States in the 1970s, Garvin continued her struggle for social justice by working as a community organizer, joining rallies on behalf of political prisoners such as Mumia Abu-Jamal, and through speaking engagements, for example, in March 1981, when she appeared with Harry Haywood in a presentation attended by Cornel West; see West, *Prophesy Deliverance!*, 176. As Gore aptly puts it in *Radical Crossroads*: "Her distinct political legacy rests not in official titles but in revolutionary experience and solidarity efforts that always combined local organizing with a global vision" (73).

42. As to party politics, the Barnetts remained loyal to the party of Lincoln, but Wells-Barnett actively supported unions, for example, in the mid-1920s, she assisted the young Brotherhood of Sleeping Car Porters and Maids (BSCPM), under its new Socialist leader A. Philip Randolph, in its struggle against strong resistance in Chicago, the seat of the Pullman Company (Giddings, *Ida*, 634–41).

43. *Crusade*, 302. Ironically, due to the initiative of the Jewish philanthropist Julius Rosenwald, a successful campaign led to the erection of a YMCA

for African Americans, in 1913. See Giddings: "In the past there would have been more debate among the Chicago black leadership about the propriety of supporting an all-black institution in lieu of demanding that the white-only Y accept African Americans. But by 1912, need, appreciation of the effort by prominent whites, and a growing sense of, and desire for, the black community's emergence as an entity in and of itself resulted in blacks, with few exceptions, supporting the effort" (*Ida*, 506).

44. *Crusade*, 301–2.

45. Wells, *A Red Record*, 75.

46. Wells gives a lively account on her collaboration with Douglass at the 1893 Chicago World's Fair in her autobiography (*Crusade*, 115–20). According to Wells, the pamphlet was turned into "a creditable little book called *The Reason Why the Colored American Is Not in the World's Columbian Exposition*. It was a clear, plain statement of facts concerning the oppression put upon the colored people in this land of the free and home of the brave. We circulated ten thousand copies of this little book during the remaining three months of the fair" (117).

47. Wells-Barnett's relations with Du Bois were strained after Du Bois took her off the list of the NAACP's Founding Forty (see above, n. 30). As Giddings suggests, Wells-Barnett's "ideology and militant views were something that the civil rights organization could, literally, not afford" (*Ida*, 497).

48. On Wells-Barnett's relations with Garvey, see *Crusade*, 380–82. Garvey applauded her by counting her among the "conscientious workers [. . .] whose fight for the uplift of the race is one of life and death" (Giddings, *Ida*, 585). Garvey invited her several times to address his Universal Negro Improvement Association (UNIA) in the fall of 1918, when Wells-Barnett and other radical activists, e.g., William Trotter and A. Philip Randolph, were elected to represent the UNIA at the Versailles Peace Treaty negotiations (but were denied passports by the government). In 1919, Ferdinand Barnett defended Garvey in a libel case; see Giddings, *Ida*, 619.

49. As an exception to the rule, Wells-Barnett recounts her support of Robert T. Motts, who turned his saloon into the Pekin Theater, with its company of Black actors and an African American orchestra. It is typical of Wells's broad-mindedness that, trying to convince other socially active women to collaborate with Motts, she argues "that now [*sic*] Mr. Motts was engaged in a venture of a constructive nature, I thought it our duty to forget the past and help him, that if he was willing to invest his money in something uplifting for the race we all ought to help" and that, furthermore, she "felt that the race owed Mr. Motts a debt of gratitude for giving us a theater in which we could sit anywhere we chose without restrictions" (*Crusade*, 290). In contrast to her

autobiography, the few entries of her short Chicago diary passed down to us clearly manifest her love of music and her regular attendance at concerts, shows, and movies. See *The 1930 Chicago Diary of Ida B. Wells-Barnett*, included in the *Memphis Diary*.

50. Younger than Wells, Mary Jane McLeod Bethune lived to support the election campaign of Franklin D. Roosevelt in 1932 and became a close friend to First Lady Eleanor Roosevelt. Bethune was both a devoted educator (best known for having founded a school for Black girls in Daytona Beach, Florida, in 1904) and an activist focusing on various Black women's associations (she was president of the Florida chapter of the National Association of Colored Women and in 1935 founded the National Council of Negro Women, which united twenty-eight different organizations).

51. In *Prophesy Deliverance!*, West presents Woodbey as a case of an "alliance of black theology and Marxist thought," who "devoted his life to promoting structural social change and creating a counter-hegemonic culture in liberal capitalist America" (126).

Conclusion: Last Words on the Black Prophetic Tradition in the Age of Obama

1. Jason DeParle: "Harder for Americans to Rise from Lower Rungs," *New York Times*, January 4, 2012.

WORKS CITED

Abu-Jamal, Mumia. *Death Blossoms: Reflections from a Prisoner of Conscience.* Farmington, PA: Plough Publishing House, 1997.

———. *Live From Death Row.* Reading, MA: Addison-Wesley, 1995.

———. *We Want Freedom: A Life in the Black Panther Party.* Cambridge, MA: South End Press, 2004.

Abu-Jamal, Mumia, and Marc Lamont Hill. *The Classroom and the Cell: Conversations on Black Life in America.* Chicago: Third World Press, 2012.

Addams, Jane, and Ida B. Wells. *Lynching and Rape: An Exchange of View.* 1901. Occasional papers, no. 25. Edited by Bettina Aptheker. New York: American Institute for Marxist Studies, 1977.

Alexander, Michelle. *The New Jim Crow: Mass Incarceration in the Age of Colorblindness.* New York: New Press, 2010.

Alinsky, Saul D. "Community Organizing and Analysis." *American Journal of Sociology* 46, no. 6 (May 1941): 797–808.

———. *Rules for Radicals: A Pragmatic Primer for Realistic Radicals.* New York: Random House, 1971.

Allen, Gay Wilson. *Waldo Emerson: A Biography.* New York: Viking Press, 1981.

Aptheker, Herbert, ed. *Book Reviews by W. E. B. Du Bois.* Millwood, NY: KTO Press, 1977.

Avakian, Bob. *From Ike to Mao and Beyond: My Journey from Mainstream America to Revolutionary Communist; a Memoir.* Chicago: Insight Press, 2005.

Baldwin, James. *Collected Essays.* New York: Library of America, 1998.

Ball, Jared A., and Todd Steven Burroughs, ed. *A Lie of Reinvention: Correcting Manning Marable's Malcolm X*. Baltimore: Black Classic Press, 2012.

Baraka, Amiri. *Home: Social Essays*. 1966. New York: Akashi Classics, 2009.

Baylen, Joseph O. "A Victorian's 'Crusade' in Chicago, 1893–1894." *Journal of American History* 51 (December 1964): 418–34.

Benjamin, Walter. "Theses on the Philosophy of History." 1940. In *Illuminations*, edited by Hannah Arendt. Translated by Harry Zohn. New York: Harcourt, Brace & World, 1968.

Bercovitch, Sacvan. *The American Jeremiad*. Madison: University of Wisconsin Press, 1978.

Berry, Mary Frances, and John Blassingame. *Long Memory: The Black Experience in America*. New York: Oxford University Press, 1982.

Bin Wahad, Dhoruba, Mumia Abu-Jamal, and Assata Shakur. *Still Black, Still Strong: Survivors of the War Against Black Revolutionaries*. Edited by Jim Fletcher, Tanaquil Jones, and Sylvère Lotringer. New York: Semiotext/e, 1993.

Blackmon, Douglas A. *Slavery by Another Name: The Re-Enslavement of Black Americans from the Civil War to World War II*. New York: Random House, 2008.

Blum, Edward J. *W. E. B. Du Bois: American Prophet*. Philadelphia: University of Philadelphia Press, 2007.

Bontemps, Arna. *Free At Last: The Life of Frederick Douglass*. New York: Dodd, Mead, 1971.

Bourdieu, Pierre. *In Other Words: Essays Towards a Reflexive Sociology*. Translated by Matthew Adamson. Cambridge, UK: Polity, 1994.

———. *Pascalian Meditations*. Translated by Richard Nice. Stanford, CA: Stanford University Press, 2000.

Boyd, Herb, Ron Daniels, Maulana Karenga, and Haki R. Madhubuti, ed. *By Any Means Necessary: Malcolm X: Real, Not Reinvented; Critical Conversations on Manning Marable's Biography of Malcolm X*. Chicago: Third World Press, 2012.

Bradley, Stefan. "The First and Finest: The Founders of Alpha Phi Alpha Fraternity." In *Black Greek-Letter Organizations in the Twenty-First Century*, edited by Gregory S. Parks, 19–39. Lexington: University Press of Kentucky, 2008.

Branch, Taylor. *Parting the Waters: America in the King Years 1954–63*. New York: Simon & Schuster, 1988.

Brown, H. Rap. *Die Nigger Die! A Political Autobiography*. 1969. Chicago: Lawrence Hill Books, 2002.

Brown, Robert McAfee, Abraham J. Heschel, and Michael Novak. *Vietnam: Crisis of Conscience*. New York: Association Press, 1967.

Buell, Lawrence. *Emerson*. Cambridge, MA: Belknap Press of Harvard University Press, 2003.

Buschendorf, Christa. *"The Highpriest of Pessimism": Zur Rezeption Schopenhauers in den USA*. Heidelberg: Winter Verlag, 2008.

———. "'Properly speaking there are in the world no such men as self-made men': Frederick Douglass's Exceptional Position in the Field of Slavery." In *Intellectual Authority and Literary Culture in the US, 1790–1900*, edited by Günter Leypoldt, 159–84. Heidelberg: Winter Verlag, 2013.

———. "The Shaping of We-Group Identities in the African American Community: A Perspective of Figurational Sociology on the Cultural Imaginary." In *The Imaginary and Its Worlds: American Studies after the Transnational Turn*, edited by Laura Bieger, Ramón Saldívar, and Johannes Voelz, 84–106. Hanover, NH: Dartmouth College Press/University Press of New England, 2013.

Byron, George Gordon. *The Works of Lord Byron*. New York: Blake, 1840.

Carby, Hazel. *Reconstructing Black Womanhood*. New York: Oxford University Press, 1987.

Carlyle, Thomas. "Occasional Discourse on the Nigger Question." 1849. In *Collected Works*. Vol. 11, *Critical and Miscellaneous Essays: Collected and Republished in Six Volumes*, vol. VI. London: Chapman and Hall, 1870.

Carmichael, Stokely. *Stokely Speaks: From Black Power to Pan-Africanism*. 1971. Chicago: Chicago Review Press, 2007.

———. "What We Want." *New York Review of Books*, September 1966.

Carmichael, Stokely, and Charles V. Hamilton. *Black Power: The Politics of Liberation in America*. New York: Random House, 1967.

Chester, Michael A. *Divine Pathos and Human Being: The Theology of Abraham Joshua Heschel*. London: Mitchell, 2005.

Clarke, John Henrik, et al., ed. *Black Titan: W. E. B. Du Bois*. Boston: Beacon Press, 1970.

Clausewitz, Carl von. *On War*. Edited by Michael Howard and Peter Peret. Princeton, NJ: Princeton University Press, 1984.

Colbert, Soyica Diggs. *The African American Theatrical Body: Reception, Performance, and the Stage*. New York: Cambridge University Press, 2011.

Coles, Romand. "'To Make This Tradition Articulate': Practiced Receptivity Matters, Or Heading West of West with Cornel West and Ella Baker." In *Christianity, Democracy, and the Radical Ordinary: Conversations Between a Radical Democrat and a Christian*, edited by Stanley Hauerwas and Romand Coles, 45–86. Cambridge, UK: Lutterworth Press, 2008.

Cone, James H. *Black Theology and Black Power.* 1969. Maryknoll, NY: Orbis Books, 1997.

———. *A Black Theology of Liberation.* 1970. Maryknoll, NY: Orbis Books, 1990.

———. "'Let Suffering Speak': The Vocation of a Black Intellectual." In *Cornel West: A Critical Reader*, edited by George Yancy, 105–14. Malden, MA: Blackwell, 2001.

———. *Martin & Malcolm & America: A Dream or a Nightmare?* Maryknoll, NY: Orbis Books, 1991.

———. *The Spirituals and the Blues.* 1972. Maryknoll, NY: Orbis Books, 1991.

Cruse, Harold. *Rebellion or Revolution?* New York: Morrow, 1968.

Darby, Henry E., and Margaret N. Rowley. "King on Vietnam and Beyond." *Phylon* 47, no. 1 (1986): 43–50.

Darrow, Clarence. *Attorney for the Damned: Clarence Darrow in the Courtroom* (1957). Edited and annotated by Arthur Weinberg. Chicago: University of Chicago Press, 2012.

———. *Infidels and Heretics: An Agnostic's Anthology.* With Wallace Rice. 1928. New York: Gordon Press, 1975.

———. *In the Clutches of the Law: Clarence Darrow's Letters.* Edited by Randall Tietjen. Berkeley: University of California Press, 2013.

———. *The Story of My Life.* 1932. New York: Da Capo Press, 1996.

Daughtry, Herbert. *No Monopoly on Suffering.* Trenton, NJ: Africa World Press, 1997.

Davis, Angela Y. *An Autobiography.* New York: Random House, 1974.

———. "Black Women and the Club Movement." In *Women, Race & Class.* New York: Vintage, 1983.

———. *The Meaning of Freedom.* San Francisco: City Lights Books, 2012.

———. "Meditations on the Legacy of Malcolm X." In *Malcolm X in Our Own Image*, edited by Joe Wood, 36–47. New York: St. Martin's Press, 1992.

Davis, Angela Y., et al., ed. *If They Come in the Morning: Voices of Resistance.* New York: Third Press, 1971.

Diedrich, Maria. *Love Across the Color Lines: Ottilie Assing and Frederick Douglass.* New York: Hill and Wang, 1999.

Douglass, Frederick. *Autobiographies.* Edited by Henry Louis Gates Jr. New York: Library of America, 1994.

———. *Frederick Douglass: Selected Speeches and Writings.* Edited by Philip S. Foner. Chicago: Lawrence Hill Books, 1999.

———. *The Frederick Douglass Papers.* Series 1. Edited by John W. Blassingame and John R. McKivigan. New Haven, CT: Yale University Press, 1992.

———. "Lynch Law in the South." *North American Review* (July 1892): 17–24.

Du Bois, Shirley Graham. *His Day Is Marching On: A Memoir of W. E. B. Du Bois.* New York: Lippincott, 1971.

Du Bois, W. E. B. *Autobiography of W. E. B. Du Bois: A Soliloquy on Viewing My Life from the Last Decade of Its First Century.* New York: International Publishers, 1968.

———. *Black Reconstruction in America: An Essay Toward a History of the Part Which Black Folk Played in the Attempt to Reconstruct Democracy in America, 1860–1880.* New York: Harcourt, Brace, 1935.

———. *The Correspondence of W. E. B. Du Bois.* Edited by Herbert Aptheker. Amherst: University of Massachusetts Press, 1954.

———. "Criteria of Negro Art." *Crisis* 32 (October 1926): 290–97.

———. *Darkwater: Voices from Within the Veil.* 1920. New York: Washington Square Press, 2004.

———. *Dusk of Dawn: An Essay Towards an Autobiography of a Race Concept.* 1940. Oxford, UK: Oxford University Press, 2007.

———. *The Negro.* New York: Holt, 1915.

———. *The Oxford W. E. B. Du Bois.* Edited by Henry Louis Gates Jr. Oxford, UK: Oxford University Press, 2007.

———. *The Philadelphia Negro: A Social Study.* Boston: Ginn, 1899.

———. "The Revelation of Saint Orgne, the Damned." Commencement speech, 1938, Fisk University. Reprinted in *W. E. B. Du Bois Speaks: Speeches and Addresses, 1920-1963,* ed. Philip S. Foner, 100–23. New York: Pathfinder, 1970.

———. *The Souls of Black Folk.* 1903. New York: Modern Library, 2003.

———. *W. E. B. Du Bois Speaks: Speeches and Addresses, 1920–1963.* Edited by Philip S. Foner. New York: Pathfinder, 1970.

———. *The World and Africa: An Inquiry into the Part Which Africa Has Played in World History.* 1946. Oxford, UK: Oxford University Press, 2007.

Dunbar, Paul Laurence. *The Collected Poetry.* Edited by Joanne M. Braxton. Charlottesville: University Press of Virginia, 1993.

Edwards, Erica E. *Charisma and the Fictions of Black Leadership.* Minneapolis: University of Minnesota Press, 2012.

Fairclough, Adam. "Was Martin Luther King a Marxist?" *History Workshop Journal* 15 (Spring 1983): 117–25.

Fanon, Frantz. *The Wretched of the Earth*. French original, 1961. Translated by Constance Farrington. Preface by Jean-Paul Sartre. New York: Grove Press, 1963. Richard Philcox translation, New York: Grove Press, 2004.

Feuerbach, Ludwig Andreas. *The Essence of Christianity*. 1841. Translated from the second German edition by Marian Evans. London: Chapman, 1854; New York: Blanchard, 1855.

Fisch, Audrey, ed. *The Cambridge Companion to the African American Slave Narrative*. Cambridge, UK: Cambridge University Press, 2007.

Fleischman, Harry. *Norman Thomas: A Biography: 1884–1968*. New York: W. W. Norton, 1969.

Foner, Philip S. *The Life and Writings of Frederick Douglass*. Vol. 1, *Early Years, 1817–1849*. New York: International Publishers, 1950.

Foner, Philip S., ed. *Jack London: American Rebel: A Collection of His Social Writings Together with an Extensive Study of the Man and His Times*. New York: Citadel, 1947.

Frazier, E. Franklin. *Black Bourgeoisie*. Glencoe, IL: Free Press, 1957.

Freed, Donald. *Agony in New Haven: The Trial of Bobby Seale and Ericka Huggins and the Black Panther Party*. New York: Simon & Schuster, 1973.

Friedly, Michael, and David Gallen. *Martin Luther King, Jr.: The FBI File*. New York: Carroll & Graf, 1993.

Gaines, Kevin. *Uplifting the Race: Black Leadership, Politics, and Culture During the Twentieth Century*. Charlotte: University of North Carolina Press, 1996.

Garrow, David J. *Bearing the Cross: Martin Luther King, Jr., and the Southern Christian Leadership Conference*. New York: Vintage, 1988.

Gates, Henry Louis, Jr., and Cornel West. *The Future of the Race*. New York: Vintage, 1997.

Georgakas, Dan, and Marvin Surkin. *Detroit, I Do Mind Dying: A Study in Urban Revolution*. New York: St. Martin's Press, 1975.

Geschwender, James A. *Class, Race and Worker Insurgency: The League of Revolutionary Black Workers*. New York: Cambridge University Press, 1977.

Giddings, Paula J. *Ida: A Sword Among Lions; Ida B. Wells and the Campaign Against Lynching*. New York: Harper Collins, 2009.

Goldman, Peter. *The Death and Life of Malcolm X*. 1973. Urbana: University of Illinois Press, 2013.

Gore, Dayo F. "From Communist Politics to Black Power: The Visionary Politics and Transnational Solidarities of Victoria (Vicki) Ama Garvin." In *Want to Start a Revolution?*, edited by Dayo F. Gore et al., 71–94.

———. *Radicalism at the Crossroads: African American Women Activists in the Cold War.* New York: New York University Press, 2011.

Gore, Dayo F., Jeanne Theoharis, and Komozi Woodard, ed. *Want to Start a Revolution? Radical Women in the Black Freedom Struggle.* New York: New York University Press, 2009.

Gramsci, Antonio. *Selections from the Prison Notebooks.* Translated and edited by Quintin Hoare and Geoffrey Nowell Smith. New York: International Publishers, 1971.

Grant, Joanne. *Ella Baker: Freedom Bound.* New York: John Wiley, 1998.

Gregory, Raymond F. *Norman Thomas: The Great Dissenter.* New York: Algora, 2008.

Hamer, Fannie Lou. *The Speeches of Fannie Lou Hamer: To Tell It Like It Is.* Edited by Maegan Parker Brooks and Davis W. Houck. Jackson: University Press of Mississippi, 2011.

Hamington, Maurice. "Public Pragmatism: Jane Addams and Ida B. Wells on Lynching." *Journal of Speculative Philosophy* 19, no. 2 (2005): 167–74.

Harding, Vincent. *Martin Luther King: The Inconvenient Hero.* Maryknoll, NY: Orbis Books, 2008.

Haywood, Harry. *Black Bolshevik: Autobiography of an Afro-American Communist.* Chicago: Liberator Press, 1978.

Higginbotham, Evelyn. *Righteous Discontent: The Women's Movement in the Black Baptist Church, 1880–1920.* Cambridge, MA: Harvard University Press, 1993.

Hilliard, David, ed. *The Black Panther Party: Service to the People Programs.* Albuquerque: University of New Mexico Press, 2008.

Hirschfelder, Nicole. "Oppression as Process: A Figurational Analysis of the Case of Bayard Rustin." PhD dissertation, University of Tübingen, 2012.

Holt, Thomas C. "The Lonely Warrior: Ida B. Wells-Barnett and the Struggle for Black Leadership." In *Black Leaders of the 20th Century*, edited by John Hope Franklin and August Meier. Urbana: University of Illinois Press, 1982.

hooks, bell, and Cornel West. *Breaking Bread: Insurgent Black Intellectual Life.* Boston: South End Press, 1991.

Horne, Gerald. *Black and Red: W. E. B. Du Bois and the Afro-American Response to the Cold War, 1944–1963.* Albany: State University of New York Press, 1986.

Horne, Gerald, and Margaret Stevens. "Shirley Graham Du Bois: Portrait of the Black Woman Artist as a Revolutionary." In *Want to Start a Revolution?*, edited by Dayo F. Gore et al., 95–114.

Howard, Michael, and Peter Paret, ed. *On War.* Princeton, NJ: Princeton University Press, 1984.

Huggins, Ericka, and Angela D. LeBlanc-Ernest. "Revolutionary Women, Revolutionary Education: The Black Panther Party's Oakland Community School." In *Want to Start a Revolution?*, edited by Dayo F. Gore et al., 161–84.

Ingersoll, Robert Green. *Walt Whitman. An Address.* New York: The Truth Seeker, 1890.

———. *The Works of Robert G. Ingersoll.* New York: C. P. Farrell, 1900.

Jacoby, Susan. *The Great Agnostic: Robert Ingersoll and American Freethought.* New Haven, CT: Yale University Press, 2013.

Johnson, James Weldon. *Along This Way: The Autobiography of James Weldon Johnson.* New York: Viking, 1933.

———. *The Autobiography of an Ex-Colored Man.* New York: Alfred A. Knopf, 1927.

Kazantzakis, Nikos. *Russia: A Chronicle of Three Journeys in the Aftermath of the Revolution.* Translated by Michael Antonakes and Thanasis Maskaleris. Berkeley, CA: Creative Arts, 1989.

———. *The Selected Letters of Nikos Kazantzakis.* Edited by Peter Bien. Princeton, NJ: Princeton University Press, 2012.

Kelley, Robin D. G., and Betsy Esch. "Black Like Mao: Red China and Black Revolution." *Souls* 1, no. 4 (September 1999): 6–41.

King, Coretta Scott. *My Life with Martin Luther King, Jr.* London: Hodder and Stoughton, 1970.

King, Martin Luther, Jr. *The Autobiography of Martin Luther King, Jr.* Edited by Clayborne Carson. New York: Warner, 1998.

———. *I Have a Dream: Writings and Speeches that Changed the World.* Edited by James M. Washington. New York: Harper, 1992.

———. *A Testament of Hope: The Essential Writings and Speeches of Martin Luther King, Jr.* Edited by James M. Washington. San Francisco: Harper-Collins, 1991.

———. *Where Do We Go From Here: Chaos or Community?* 1967. Boston: Beacon Press, 2010.

Lerner, Michael, and Cornel West. *Jews and Blacks: A Dialogue on Race, Religion, and Culture in America.* New York: Penguin, 1996.

Levine, Robert S. *Dislocating Race and Nation: Episodes in Nineteenth-Century Literary Nationalism.* Chapel Hill: University of North Carolina Press, 2008.

Levine, Robert S., and Samuel Otter, eds. *Frederick Douglass and Herman Melville: Essays in Relation*. Chapel Hill. University of North Carolina Press, 2008.

Lind, Michael. *The Next American Nation: The New Nationalism and the Fourth American Revolution*. New York: Free Press, 1995.

Litwack, Leon F. *Trouble in Mind: Black Southerners in the Age of Jim Crow*. New York: Knopf, 1998.

Lohmann, Christoph, ed. *Radical Passion: Ottilie Assing's Reports from America and Letters to Frederick Douglass*. Translated by Christoph Lohmann. New York: Peter Lang, 1999.

London, Jack. *Jack London: American Rebel; a Collection of His Social Writings Together with an Extensive Study of the Man and His Times*, 517–24. Edited by Philip S. Foner. New York: Citadel, 1947.

Macey, David. *Frantz Fanon: A Biography* (2000). London: Verso, 2012.

Madhubuti, Haki R. *Liberation Narratives: New and Collected Poems, 1966–2009*. Chicago: Third World Press, 2009.

Marable, Manning. *Malcolm X: A Life of Reinvention*. New York: Viking, 2011.

———. "Rediscovering Malcolm's Life: A Historian's Adventure in Living History," *Souls* 7, no. 1 (2005): 20–35.

Marable, Manning, and Garrett Felber, ed. *The Portable Malcolm X Reader*. New York: Penguin, 2013.

McClory, Robert. *Radical Disciple: Father Pfleger, St. Sabina Church, and the Fight for Social Justice*. Chicago: Chicago Review Press, 2010.

Melville, Herman. *Moby-Dick; or The Whale*. 1851. Evanston: Northwestern University Press/Newberry Library, 1988.

Moore, Howard, Jr. "Angela—Symbol in Resistance." In *If They Come in the Morning: Voices of Resistance*, edited by Angela Davis et al., 191–92.

Mossman, James. "Race, Hate, Sex, and Colour: A Conversation with James Baldwin and Colin MacInnes." 1965. In *Conversations with James Baldwin*, edited by Fred L. Standley and Louis H. Pratt, 46–58. Jackson: University Press of Mississippi, 1989.

Newton, Huey P. *Revolutionary Suicide*. With J. Herman Blake. New York: Penguin, 2009.

O'Connor, Emmet. "James Larkin in the United States, 1914–1923." *Journal of Contemporary History* 37, no. 2 (2002): 183–96.

Pannekoek, Anton. *Workers' Councils*. 1946. Edinburgh: AK, 2003.

Petie, William L., and Douglas E. Stover, ed. *Bibliography of the Frederick Douglass Library at Cedar Hill*. Fort Washington, MD: Silesia, 1995.

Rabaka, Reiland. *Against Epistemic Apartheid: W. E. B. Du Bois and the Disciplinary Decadence of Sociology*. Boulder, CO: Lexington Books, 2010.

Rabaka, Reiland, ed. *W. E. B. Du Bois*. Farnham, UK: Ashgate, 2010.

Ransby, Barbara. *Ella Baker and the Black Freedom Movement: A Radical Democratic Vision*. Chapel Hill: University of North Carolina Press, 2003.

Raper, Arthur. *The Tragedy of Lynching*. Chapel Hill: University of North Carolina Press, 1933.

Rowan, Carl T. "Martin Luther King's Tragic Decision." *Reader's Digest*, September 1967.

Ruskin, John. *The Crown of Wild Olive*. New York, n.d. [1866].

Saint-Arnaud, Pierre. *African American Pioneers of Sociology: A Critical History*. French original, 2003. Translated by Peter Feldstein. Toronto: University of Toronto Press, 2009.

Sanchez, Sonia. *Conversations with Sonia Sanchez*. Edited by Joyce A. Joyce. Jackson: University Press of Mississippi, 2007.

———. *Home Coming*. Detroit: Broadside Press, 1969.

———. *Wounded in the House of a Friend*. Boston: Beacon Press, 1995.

Schechter, Patricia A. "'All the Intensity of My Nature': Ida B. Wells, Anger and Politics." *Radical History Review* 70 (1998): 48–77.

Seale, Bobby. *A Lonely Rage: The Autobiography of Bobby Seale*. New York: Times Books, 1978.

———. *Seize the Time: The Story of the Black Panther Party and Huey P. Newton*. New York: Random House, 1970.

Shakur, Assata. *Assata: An Autobiography*. 1987. Chicago: Lawrence Hill Books, 1999.

Sharlet, Jeff. "The Supreme Love and Revolutionary Funk of Dr. Cornel West, Philosopher of the Blues." *Rolling Stone*, May 28, 2009.

Smiley, Tavis, and Cornel West. *The Rich and the Rest of Us: A Poverty Manifesto*. New York: Smiley Books, 2012.

Smith, J. Alfred, Sr. *On the Jericho Road: A Memoir of Racial Justice, Social Action, and Prophetic Ministry*. With Harry Louis Williams II. Downers Grove, IL: InterVarsity Press, 2004.

Spanos, William V. *The Errant Art of Moby-Dick: The Canon, the Cold War, and the Struggle for American Studies*. Durham, NC: Duke University Press, 1995.

———. *The Exceptionalist State and the State of Exception: Herman Melville's Billy Budd, Sailor*. Baltimore: Johns Hopkins University Press, 2011.

———. *Herman Melville and the American Calling: Fiction After Moby-Dick, 1851–1857*. Albany: State University of New York Press, 2008.

Stanfield, John H. "King, Martin Luther (1929–1968)." In *Blackwell Encyclopedia of Sociology*, edited by George Ritzer. Oxford, UK: Blackwell, 2007.

Stauffer, John. "Frederick Douglass's Self-Fashioning and the Making of a Representative American Man." In *The Cambridge Companion to the African American Slave Narrative*, edited by Audrey A. Fisch, 201–17. Cambridge, UK: Cambridge University Press, 2007.

———. *Giants: The Parallel Lives of Frederick Douglass and Abraham Lincoln.* New York: Twelve, 2008.

Stout, Jeffrey. *Blessed Are the Organized: Grassroots Democracy in America.* Princeton, NJ: Princeton University Press, 2010.

Thomas, Norman. *Human Exploitation in the United States.* New York: Frederick A. Stokes, 1934.

Tyson, Timothy B. *Radio Free Dixie: Robert F. Williams and the Roots of Black Power.* Chapel Hill: University of North Carolina Press, 1999.

Wacquant, Loïc. *Punishing the Poor: The Neoliberal Government of Social Insecurity.* Durham, NC: Duke University Press, 2009.

Washington, James Melvin. *Frustrated Fellowship: The Baptist Quest for Social Power.* Macon, GA: Mercer, 1986.

Weld, Theodore Dwight, ed. *American Slavery As It Is: Testimony of a Thousand Witnesses.* New York: American Anti-Slavery Society, 1839.

Wells-Barnett, Ida B. *Crusade for Justice*: *The Autobiography of Ida B. Wells.* Edited by Alfreda M. Duster. Chicago: Chicago University Press, 1970.

———. *The Memphis Diary of Ida B. Wells.* Edited by Miriam DeCosta-Willis. Boston: Beacon Press, 1995.

———. *A Red Record: Tabulated Statistics and Alleged Causes of Lynchings in the United States, 1892–1893–1894.* Chicago: Privately published, 1895. Reprinted in *Selected Works of Ida B. Wells-Barnett*, compiled by Trudier Harris, 138–252. New York: Oxford University Press, 1991.

———. *Selected Works of Ida B. Wells-Barnett.* Compiled by Trudier Harris. New York: Oxford University Press, 1991.

———. *Southern Horrors: Lynch Law in All Its Phases.* New York: New York Age Print, 1892. Reprinted in *Selected Works of Ida B. Wells-Barnett*, compiled by Trudier Harris, 14–45. New York: Oxford University Press, 1991.

West, Cornel. *The American Evasion of Philosophy: A Genealogy of Pragmatism.* Madison: University of Wisconsin Press, 1989.

———. "Black Strivings in a Twilight Civilization." In *The Future of the Race*, edited by Henry Louis Gates Jr. and Cornel West, 53–112, 180–96. New York: Vintage, 1997.

———. "Black Theology and Human Identity." In *Black Faith and Public Talk: Critical Essays on James H. Cone's* Black Theology and Black Power, edited by Dwight N. Hopkins, 11–19. Maryknoll, NY: Orbis Books, 1999.

———. *Brother West: Living and Loving Out Loud.* With David Ritz. Carlsbad, CA: Smiley Books, 2009.

———. *The Cornel West Reader.* New York: Civitas, 1999.

———. *Democracy Matters: Winning the Fight Against Imperialism.* New York: Penguin Press, 2004.

———. *The Ethical Dimensions of Marxist Thought.* New York: Monthly Review, 1991.

———. *Keeping Faith: Philosophy and Race in America.* New York: Routledge, 1993.

———. "On the Legacy of Dorothy Day." *Catholic Agitator* 44, no. 1 (February 2014): 1–3, 6.

———. *Prophesy Deliverance! An Afro-American Revolutionary Christianity.* 1982. Anniversary ed. with a new preface by the author. Louisville, KY: Westminster John Knox Press, 2002.

———. *Prophetic Fragments: Illuminations of the Crisis in American Religion and Culture.* 1988. Grand Rapids, MI: Eerdmans Publishing, 1993.

———. *Prophetic Thought in Postmodern Times.* Vol. 1, *Beyond Eurocentrism and Multiculturalism.* Monroe, ME: Common Courage Press, 1993.

———. *Race Matters.* New York: Vintage, 1994.

———. "Why I Am Marching in Washington." In *Million Man March/Day of Absence: A Commemorative Anthology*, edited by Haki R. Madhubuti and Maulana Karenga, 37–38. Chicago: Third World Press, 1996.

West, Cornel, and Eddie Glaude Jr., ed. *African American Religious Thought.* Louisville, KY: Westminster John Knox Press, 2003.

Wiley, Anthony Terrance. "Angelic Troublemakers: Religion and Anarchism in Henry David Thoreau, Dorothy Day, and Bayard Rustin." PhD dissertation, Princeton University, 2011.

Wilkerson, Isabel. *The Warmth of Other Suns: The Epic Story of America's Great Migration.* New York: Random House, 2010.

Williams, Raymond. *The Long Revolution.* London: Chatto, 1961.

Williams, Robert F. *Negroes With Guns.* New York: Marzani and Munsell, 1962.

Willie, Charles V. "Walter R. Chivers—An Advocate of Situation Sociology." *Phylon* 43, no. 3 (1982): 242–48.

Wolin, Sheldon S. "Fugitive Democracy." *Constellations* 1, no. 1 (1994): 11 25.

Wortham, Robert. "Du Bois and the Sociology of Religion: Rediscovering a Founding Figure." *Sociological Inquiry* 75, no. 4 (2005): 433–52.

———. "W. E. B. Du Bois, the Black Church, and the Sociological Study of Religion." *Sociological Spectrum* 29, no. 2 (2009): 144–72.

Wortham, Robert, ed. *W. E. B. Du Bois and the Sociological Imagination: A Reader, 1897–1914*. Waco, TX: Baylor University Press, 2009.

Wright, Richard. *Black Power: A Record of Reactions in a Land of Pathos*. New York: Harper, 1954.

X, Malcolm. *The Autobiography of Malcolm X*. With the assistance of Alex Haley. New York: Ballantine Books, 1992.

———. *By Any Means Necessary: Speeches, Interviews, and a Letter by Malcolm X*. Edited by George Breitman. New York: Pathfinder, 1970.

———. *Malcolm X Speaks: Selected Speeches and Statements*. Edited by George Breitman. New York: Pathfinder, 1990.

Yancy, George, ed. *Cornel West: A Critical Reader*. Malden, MA: Blackwell, 2001.

Zinn, Howard. *Howard Zinn on Race*. New York: Seven Stories Press, 2011.

Zuckerman, Phil, ed. *The Social Theory of W. E. B. Du Bois*. Thousand Oaks, CA: Sage, 2004.